THE GENOVESE FAMILY

A History of New York's Genovese Mafia Family

ANDY PETEPIECE

Tellwell Talent
www.tellwell.ca

ISBN
978-0-2288-9194-9 (Paperback)
978-0-2288-9195-6 (eBook)

Acknowledgements

To Patti

Always and Forever

To

Digger

To

Beautiful Lena

To

Handsome Leo

To

Janet and Riny, two wonderful friends.

CAUTION

I am not a great writer, and my editing skills are less than perfect. So if these things bother you, please do not buy this book. But, on the other hand, if you are looking for thousands of details on the Genovese Family you are in the right place.

CAUTION TWO

Many decades ago, my belief that everything in an FBI file was honest and accurate was naïve. I had to find at least one more source for the information I pulled from the file. Sadly, this was often not possible due to the nature of the subject. The same was true with court records. Witnesses, police, prosecutors, and FBI Agents would SOMETIMES lie, thankfully rarely. Unfortunately, many Mafia books and newspaper articles repeat errors, sometimes for decades. The best practice is to keep your eyes and mind open to new information contradicting long-held beliefs. For example, for many years, I believed that Anthony Salerno was the Boss of the Genovese Family and said so. As it turns out, I was wrong. It wasn't the first, and it won't be the last time I have made an honest error.

My good friend Jerry Capeci, on February 16, 2023, wrote about an example of what I am discussing. According to lawyers for Capo Teddy Persico of the Colombo Family, an FBI Agent wrongly identified Persico as the Boss of that Family. If I had accessed the documents authorizing three wiretaps in that case, I would have come away with the belief Persico, and not Andy Russo, was the Colombo leader in 2020. That conclusion would have been wrong.
I cannot promise the reader that everything in this book is accurate. This statement is particularly true regarding of history of the Genovese Family's administration. However, I did my best to ensure I based my work on the most accurate information available at the time of writing.

Other Books by Andy Petepiece

The Commission

The Colombo Family

The Bonanno Family

The Lucchese Family

The Gambino Family

I did a tremendous amount of research for the "Complete Idiots Guide to the Mafia" by Jerry Capeci.

Introduction

The Genovese Family has its roots in a small gang formed by Giuseppe Morello around 1902 in New York City's Harlem area. They preyed on vulnerable Italian immigrants by extorting protection payments and operated various forms of gambling. Regrettably for Morello, the Secret Service busted his counterfeiting ring, sending him to prison for a long time.

While Morello was away, some of his followers attempted to carry on with moderate success. Meanwhile, Joe Masseria's gang grew into a Family with the advent of prohibition and its riches. Once Morello gained his freedom in the early 1920s, he amalgamated his group with that of Masseria to gain protection from the powerful D'Aquila (Gambino) Family.

Masseria became Boss of Bosses with the death of D'Aquila but died during the famous Castellammarese War of the early 1930s. Lucky Luciano took his place and helped form the Commission. Unfortunately for Lucky, the government jammed him on a prostitution racket charge and sent him away for a long time. Underboss Vito Genovese ran the Family for a few years but fled to Italy to avoid a pending murder investigation. Capo Frank Costello then took the top seat and quietly led the Family as it increased its activities in gambling, union infiltration, and other rackets.

In 1957 an attempted assassination convinced Costello to step aside for Vito Genovese. Unfortunately for him, the feds convicted Genovese on a narcotics charge, and he spent the rest of his life behind bars while still attempting to run the Family. By this time, the organization was making millions with various rackets associated with controlling crucial locals in many International Unions.

After Genovese died in prison in 1969, the new Boss, Phil Lombardo, instituted a brilliant plan of presenting his Underboss as the "Front" Boss of the Family. In this way, Lombardo avoided pressure from law enforcement but still had control. But, the feds decimated the Family leadership in the 1980s with a series of trials, and their successful attempt to rid powerful unions of mob control seriously cut into the Family income.

From the legal tsunami of the 1980s, a unique Boss emerged. Vince Gigante ran the Family for about twenty-five years while successfully pretending to be mentally incompetent. When the feds finally pulled down the curtain on his act, a series of Acting Bosses attempted to run the Family with varying success. Unfortunately, most of them ended up in the slammer until veteran mobster Liborio "Barney" Bellomo emerged from prison and became the official Boss around 2015.

Best estimates put the strength of the Genovese Family at around 200 soldiers engaged in every kind of racket imaginable. In addition, the old reliables of gambling, loansharking, extortion, and union infiltration continue. Whether Bellomo can stay out of prison remains to be seen. However, the Family has survived over 120 years of violence, changes in leadership, and federal and state crackdowns, so while Bellomo might not continue for long, it's a good bet the Genovese Family will.

Notes

Note One:

The proper name of the American Mafia is Cosa Nostra. I use La Cosa Nostra because that is the practice of the FBI.

Note Two:

I will use the names of the five New York Mafia Families that came into public use in the 1960s to indicate their histories. This decision is not technically correct, but hopefully, it will make following the accounts easier.

Table of Contents

CHAPTER ONE

Giuseppe "Joe, the Clutch Hand, Peter" Morello

Giuseppe Morello is a well-known name to Mafia enthusiasts. However, they also recognize him as "Joe," "Peter," and "The Clutch Hand," the latter label due to him having only one digit on his right hand. Morello was the father of New York City's first Mafia Family, which survived setbacks but expanded by merging with the Masseria Family and eventually became known to the general public in the early 1960s as the Genovese Family.

Below I summarize some of the main points in the early part of this journey. Please keep in mind that hundreds of events are taking place simultaneously. I have isolated the Morello activities to keep the narrative as least confusing as possible.

Note:
The Morello and Terranova names are interchangeable since they were half-brothers. This knowledge might decrease confusion.

DOB
May 2, 1867
Corleone, Sicily

DOD

August 15, 1930

New York

May 2, 1867

Giuseppe Morello was born to Carlo Morello and Rosalie Piazzi in Corleone, Sicily.

1872

Giuseppe Morello's father died.

1873

Giuseppe Morello's mother married Bernardo Terranova.

1877

Ignazio Lupo was born in Palermo

1887

Vincent Terranova was born to Bernardo Terranova and Rosalie Piazzi. This connection made Giuseppe Morello and Terranova half-brothers.

1889

Ciro Terranova was born to Bernard Terranova and Rosalie Piazzi. (Another Morello half-brother.)

December 29, 1889

A shooter gunned down an aspiring Corleone politician, and a passerby claimed Morello was involved. Fortunately for Morello, someone killed the female witness.

1891

Nicholas Terranova was born to Bernard Terranova and Rosalie Piazzi. (Another Morello half-brother.)

1892

Giuseppe Morello illegally entered the United States.

March 8, 1893

The Bernard Terranova family arrived at Ellis Island aboard the Alsatia out of Naples.

LOUISIANA AND TEXAS

1894

The Terranova family moved to Louisiana to join Morello, who had found work there. He and his step-father labored on a plantation growing and harvesting sugar cane.

1894

An Italian Judge sentenced Giuseppe Morello to six years and a fine of 5,000 Lira for counterfeiting. Fortunately for Morello, he was already in the US.

1895-1896

The Terranova and Morello families moved to Texas and made a living growing cotton on rented land.

BACK TO THE BIG APPLE

1897

The Terranova and Morello families moved back to New York. Morello ran a series of saloons over the next two years, but they all failed in succession. So too did a date factory, but he and his step-father Bernard Terranova had more success with a plastering business.

1899

The Secret Service began investigating Morello on suspicion of counterfeiting activities.

1898

Morello's first wife, Maria Marvelesi, died.

1898

Ignazio Lupo killed Salvatore Morello in a business dispute in Italy and fled to England, Montreal, Buffalo, and then New York. Authorities conducted a trial in absentia, the jury found Lupo guilty, and the Judge gave him 18 years.

THE BIRTH OF A MAFIA FAMILY

1900-1903

Morello began forming his Mafia Family, with his top guys being relatives or men he knew from Corleone. The Soldiers came from all over Sicily, but they had to be recommended by a man from Corleone. Dash estimates that the Family had thirty members by 1903.

June 9, 1900

The Secret Service arrested Morello and a group of his men for counterfeiting. Fortunately for Morello, the Judge dismissed his case but sentenced his right-hand man, Calogero Maggiore, to six years.

July 23, 1902

Police found grocer Joe Catania Sr. murdered in a sack on 73rd Street on the river bank in Bay Ridge. Informer Salvatore Clemente told the Secret Service that Morello and another man whacked Catania for talking too much about the counterfeiting racket.

December 1902

Lupo married Morello's stepsister Salvatrice Terranova and Morello wed Nicolina Lima four days later.

December 31, 1902

The Secret Service arrested Giuseppe de Priema, Giuseppe Giallombardo, and Isadore Crocevera for passing counterfeit money in Yonkers. They were Associates of Morello.

March (?) 1903

A jury convicted Giuseppe de Priema of counterfeiting, and a Judge sent him to Sing Sing for four years. Rumors that he was cooperating with authorities were rampant. Moreover, his brother-in-law Benedetto Madonia wasn't happy with the gang's support of de Priema's family.

April 1903

The Secret Service arrested Lupo for counterfeiting, but the Judge discharged him.

December 31, 1902

Banker John Bozzuffi chartered The Ignatz Florio Co-Operative Association with Morello as the treasurer. This association built homes.

THE BARREL MURDER CASE

April 14, 1903

Police found the body of Benedetto Madonia in a barrel on East 11th and Avenue D. He was the brother-in-law of the incarcerated Giuseppe de Priema, a member of the Morello gang.

April 15, 1903

Police held eight Sicilians for the murder of Benedetto Madonia of Buffalo. The Secret Service had been following the gang and saw Madonia with the arrested guys the night before police found his body.

Those arrested were; Lupo, Giuseppe Morello, Vito Laduca, Giovanni Zarcone (killed July 27, 1909), and four others.

April 19, 1903

The first day of the hearings into the Barrel Murder began.

April 21, 1903

A New York Times story said the Morello gang killed Madonia for threatening them because they failed to pay $25,000 owed to Madonia's brother-in-law Giuseppe de Priema who was in prison on a counterfeiting conviction.

April 22, 1903

When Secret Service agents went through papers confiscated from Giuseppe Morello, they found a note from Madonia threatening Morello about the money.

May 1, 1903

The coroner's inquest about Madonia's death began, but Madonia's wife, stepson, and others appeared intimidated by the Sicilians.

May 8, 1903

The coroner ruled that persons unknown killed Madonia. Morello and his friends were free.

August 12, 1904

Angelo Cucozza named the ringleaders of a gang that kidnapped his friend Antonio Mannino the previous Tuesday. The police said it was the same gang that did the barrel murder. By August 15, the police are looking for Vito Laduca as a suspect. They had arrested him in the barrel murder case.

October 24, 1905

Giuseppe de Prima, a brother-in-law of Madonia, traveled to Wilkes-Barrie and killed Thomas "The Bull" Petto. He believed Petto took part in the killing of Madonia because he had a pawn ticket for Madonia's watch.

1906
Police arrested Lupo for the kidnapping of Tony Bozuffi, son of a banker John Bozzuffi who filed the incorporation paper for the Ignatz Florio Co-Operative Association in 1902. Police released Lupo.

OFFICER JOSEPH PETROSINO
AND THE ITALIAN SQUAD

1908
The NYPD appointed Joseph Petrosino to head its new "Italian Squad," whose mandate was to focus on Italian criminal organizations. A powerful tool in their arsenal was a new US law that allowed the deportation of people who had lived in the US for three years or less for crimes committed elsewhere.

Late October 1908
The 1907 recession devastated Morello's attempts at legitimate construction. He then returned to the counterfeiting racket to make up for his losses.

February 5, 1909
L'Avaldo Italiano, a New York newspaper, published a story that included the fact Petrosino would be going to Italy.

February 9, 1909
Petrosino left for Italy.

March 9, 1909
Someone assassinated Petrosino in Palermo.

March 10, 1909
The NYPD Italian Branch received an anonymous letter naming Morello Family members Joe Morello, Vincenzo Terranova, Ciro Terranova, Giuseppe Fontana, Ignazio Milone, and Pietro Inzarillo as being involved in Petrosino's murder. Italian police arrested Vito Cascio Ferro for Petrosino's murder, but

they released him after an Associate provided an alibi. When he lived in New York, Cascio Ferro worked with the Morello men named above.

July 27, 1909

Someone shot and killed Giovanni Zarcone, one of the accused in the barrel murder case, on his porch in Danbury, Connecticut.

NEW ENEMIES: THE GALLUCCIS

September 1909

Police arrested Gennaro Gallucci for carrying a concealed weapon. The jury convicted him of the charge, but the Judge handed out a suspended sentence. Then the Immigration people began proceedings to deport Gennaro to Italy. Police said a recent attempt had been made on Gallucci's life while he sat in his brother's bakery with four shots fired. Gennaro's brother Giosue might have been the intended target, for he was also there.

November 12, 1909

Lupo told a bankruptcy referee that the Black Hand had taken all his money. He filed for bankruptcy a year ago after running a grocery at 210 and 212 Mott Street.

November 14, 1909

Shooters killed Gennaro Gallucci in his brother's bakery/restaurant at 318 East 103rd. Brother Francisco of 146 Hester Street was also there. Police found a revolver with two shots fired in the bakery.

According to the police, a jury convicted Gennaro Gallucci of killing two men in Sicily. The Judge sentenced him to 23 years, but Gennaro escaped and fled to the USA in December of 1908.

THE DOWNFALL

November 15, 1909
The Secret Service arrested Lupo, Giuseppe Morello, and 12 others on counterfeiting charges.

November 22, 1909
Lupo faced charges for extorting $4,000 from grocer Salvatore Manzella of 196 Elizabeth Street. At the time, Lupo's address was 823 Jefferson Street in Hoboken, NJ. However, the accuser didn't appear for the hearing, so the authorities dropped the charges.

January 10, 1910
A Judge arraigned Lupo, Morello, and 14 others on counterfeiting charges.

January 26, 1910
Judge George Ray presided over the trial of eight Morello guys for counterfeiting $2 and $3 notes. The gang took an immigrant to an upstate farm in Highland, New York, to do the counterfeiting.

January 27, 1910
Antonio Comito was the Fed's key witness against the Morello group.

February 16, 1910
In his testimony, Lupo explained how he killed Salvatore Morello in Sicily and fled to England, Montreal, Buffalo, and New York. He ran a wholesale grocery business on Mulberry Street, which went bankrupt. In another court, Lupo's lawyer filed for an extension for Lupo to discharge his bankruptcy.

Giacamo Reina, the father of Tommy Reina, appeared for the defense. He was an olive oil importer and allied to the Morello clan. Tommy Reina's sister, Bernarda, married Vincent Terranova, adding another link to the Reina/Morello/Terranova chain. Later, Tommy Reina would form his own Family from scattered pieces of the Morello Family.

February 19, 1910

The jury found the Lupo gang guilty of counterfeiting. Judge Ray handed out the following sentences:

Giuseppe Chillichio- 15 yrs. and 2 yrs., fine of $600

Giuseppe Morello-15 yrs. and 10 yrs., fine of $1,000

Nicola Sylvestre-15 yrs. and a fine of $1,000

Ignazio Lupo –15 yrs. and 15 yrs. and a fine of $1,000

Antonio Cecala-12 yrs. and 3 yrs., fine of $1,000

Salvatore Cina-15 yrs., $1,000 (he owned the Highland farm)

Vincenzo Giglio-15 yrs., $1,000

Giuseppe Palermo-18 yrs., $1,000

March 7, 1910

Leoluca Vassi, a Morello family member, pled guilty before the Criminal Branch of the US Circuit Court. A grand jury indicted him for having 1,148 counterfeit $2 silver certificates.

April 2, 1910

A New York Times story said the Morello gang was finished.

October 1910

Morello Family member Salvatore Clemente began informing to the Secret Service.

December 10, 1910

A jury convicted Giuseppe Boscarino of counterfeiting. He was part of the Morello gang.

January 17, 1911

A New York Times story said that Morello had been talking to Attorney Walter Dillon, acting on behalf of New York State. Morello claimed to have information on the slaying of Petrosino back on March 12, 1910, in Sicily. However, Morello refused to sign a summary of his statements (disposition).

Rumor was that Morello named Carlo Constanti as the Petrosino shooter. After the killing, Palermo police arrested Constanti and found a telegram to Morello that said, "I am still trying to buy wine from Fontana." New York Police, who went to Sicily to investigate the shooting, also named Constanti, whom the Palermo police held for eight months, then released.

THE LOMONTE BROTHERS TAKE OVER

1911
Morello named the Lomonte brothers, his cousins, as the new leaders of his Family.

April 1912
Someone killed Calogero Morello, the son of Giuseppe Morello. Uncle Nick Terranova vowed revenge, according to informer Salvatore Clemente. The Lomonte brothers lost prestige when they didn't also seek revenge. It turned out that the killers were from a minor gang that had a personal dispute with Calogero.

WAR ON TWO FRONTS

The half-brothers of Giuseppe Morello, the Terranovas, began actions to eliminate the Lomonte brothers to take over complete control of the Morello Family. Unfortunately, this decision put them in conflict with the powerful Harlem gangster Giousue Gallucci who had allied with the Lomontes.

To bolster their strength, the Terranovas formed a loose alliance with two groups of Camorra gangsters from Brooklyn who coveted Gallucci's vast legal and illegal holdings. In addition, Camorra leader Alesandro Vollero was anxious to avenge his friend Nicolo Delguadio whom Gallucci's men shot in 1914. I outline key events in these conflicts below.

June 6, 1912
Morello lost a counterfeit conviction appeal.

December 16, 1912

John Russomanno walked into the coroner's office and admitted to shooting Aniello "Zoppo" Priscio on Sunday in the Gallucci bakery at 318 East 109th because he was protecting his uncle Giosue Gallucci. When Gallucci told the police that Russomano did it in self-defense, they didn't lay any charges. Interestingly, a New York Times account called Priscio an "Italian Blackmailer."

February 18, 1913

Someone wounded John Russomano, a Gallucci nephew, and killed his bodyguard Tony Capilongo. This action was probably retaliation for the Priscio shooting on December 16, 1912.

April 1913

Someone wounded Joseph DiMarco, a former Morello gambling leader, and it is a reasonable guess it was the Morellos.

November 1, 1913

Rosario Cocchiaro murdered Louis Virzi, but a cop then killed him.

November 4, 1913

A gunman killed Joseph Fontana. A source told the Secret Service that Fontana was originally a Morello Family member but defected to the Salvatore D'Aquila group. (Gambino Family). Three weeks later, shooters murdered a second defector Joseph Fanaro.

November 15, 1913

Informer Salvatore Clemente said that killers from the Lomonte (Morello) and Manfredi gangs killed Joseph Fanaro.

Note:

Al Manfredi was the Boss of a Family that later merged with the D'Aquila organization to form what we now know as the Gambino Family.

May 23, 1914

Gunmen killed Fortunato "Charles" Lomonte at 108th and 2nd Ave. He was a cousin of Morello. He had been named leader of the Morello Family by Giuseppe Morello but lost prestige when he didn't avenge the death of Morello's son. The Lomontes had then allied themselves with Giousue Gallucci. According to informer Salvatore Clemente, the Morellos did not know who shot Lomonte.

1915

The NYPD jailed John Russomano for weapon possession.

May 17, 1915

Giosue Gallucci, known as the "King of Little Italy" (Harlem's Little Italy), left his bakery at 318 East 109th and walked with a bodyguard to his son's coffee house at 336 East 109th. Four men entered the coffee house and opened up when the bodyguard left on an errand. There were about fifteen men in the shop, and some returned fire. Gallucci's wounds were in the neck and stomach. His son, Luca, was shot twice in the stomach, then staggered to his father's home, where he collapsed. Ambulances rushed both victims to Bellevue Hospital, but neither would or could identify their attackers before they died. Police described Gallucci as very wealthy.

Informer Leopoldo Lauritano explained that Gallucci's bodyguards, Generoso Nazzaro and Tony Romano, were in on the hit. Nazzaro stood watch at the door while Romano and Camorra member Andrea Ricci did the shooting. Camorra leader Pellegrino Morano blamed Gallucci for the death of a nephew, plus he coveted Gallucci's rackets.

May 18, 1915

The New York Herald wrote that Gallucci "... certainly was the most powerful Italian politically."

October 7, 1915

Shooters killed Ippolito Greco, who was a Morello guy.

October 13, 2015

Shooters killed Tomaso "Joe" Lomonte, the brother of murdered Charles Lomonte, at 116th and 1st Ave. Authorities caught, convicted, and executed shooter Antonio Impoluzzo. However, he did not reveal who hired him to do the hit.

THE MORELLOS/TERRANOVAS BACK IN CHARGE

October 1915

Nick Terranova was now the official Boss of the Morello Family. Fortunately for them, with the killing of Gallucci, the Morello Family retained their control of Italian Harlem.

MORELLO FAMILY vs. NAVY STREET/ CONEY ISLAND GANGS

For a short period, the Brooklyn Camorra gangs allied with the Morellos in their battle with Giosue Gallucci. But, afterward, the riches in Manhattan proved very tempting, and they began plotting to eliminate the Terranova brothers, the Morello Family's leaders. The fighting was over control of artichokes, ice, coal, card games, the Italian lottery, and other rackets.

Coney Island Camorra Gang HQ
Santa Lucia Restaurant
Pellegrino Morano is the superior of Vollero.
Tony "Tony the Shoemaker" Paretti
And others.

Navy Street Camorra Gang HQ
113 Navy Street, Brooklyn
Alesandro Vollero,
Eugene Bizzaro,

Andrea Ricci,

Leopoldo Lauritano.

And others.

July 25, 1916

Shooters killed Giuseppe "Joe" DiMarco and Charles Lombardi in a gambling joint. DiMarco had abandoned the Morellos after authorities jailed Morello and opened an independent gambling saloon. Later, information from informers detailed at least two meetings between the Morellos and Camorra gangs to plot DiMarco's death. Navy Street men, associated with the Morellos, carried out the hit. Then Coney Island boss Morano opened up a gambling operation in Italian Harlem, putting him in conflict with the Morellos.

1916

Police found the body of murdered Salvatore DiMarco, brother of Giuseppe, under the Queensboro Bridge. It was a hit to prevent a revenge attack by Salvatore.

THE CAMORRA ATTACK

Fall 1916

The Navy Street group and those from Coney Island began plotting to eliminate the Morellos. There were some past grievances, but the real reason was a lust for the Morello Family's extensive rackets in Harlem. They decided the best action was to wipe out the Morello Family leaders in one attack.

September 7, 1916

Morano and Vollero (Camorra leaders) invited Nicholas Terranova, and his two brothers, Stefano LaSalle and Charles Ubriaco, to a peace meeting, but it was an ambush. Only Nicholas Terranova and Ubriaco showed up. Two shooters hit Morello six times and luckily killed Ubriaco with a shot from fifty feet away. Unfortunately for the Camorra guys, the entire leadership of the Morello Family didn't show up as they expected. Police speculated the shooting was retaliation for the Galluci shooting of May 17, 1915, but they were wrong.

Later, informer Ralph Daniello named Alesandro Vollero and Antonio Paretti as the organizers of the ambush. He said Alfonso Sgroia, John Esposito, and Mike Notaro were the shooters.

October 6, 1916
Shooters killed Giuseppe Veranzano (Morello guy) in the Occidental Restaurant at 341 Broome Street in Manhattan. Veranzano directed the Morello gambling rackets. It is safe to assume this was a Camorra hit.

January 1917
The Morellos wounded Vollero in an assassination attempt.

THE END OF THE CAMORRISTS

Fall 1917
Navy Street Associate Ralph Daniello, in hiding in Reno, Nevada, decided to turn on his former Boss, Vollero, because of a perceived lack of support. So he contacted New York City detectives and outlined his knowledge of more than twenty murders. Below I have highlighted only the significant trials that resulted from his information.

November 1917
Daniello returned to New York to talk to the police. He revealed information on a long list of murders, and his testimony eventually decimated the Camorra factions. The authorities ran a series of trials, including those of Alesandro Vollero and Pellegrino Morano.

Late 1917
The Navy Street gang killed member Andrea Ricci fearing he might talk.

1918

President Harding commuted Morello's sentence to 15 yrs. (see 1920.)

February 14, 1918

The DA outlined his case in the Alesandro Vollero trial, where he accused Vollero of killing Nick Terranova and Gene Ubriaco.

February 15, 1918

Turncoat Daniello testified in the Vollero trial.

February 18, 1918

Justice Isaac Kapper of New York State's Supreme Court declared a mistrial in the Vollero case.

March 7, 1918

The second murder trial of Alesandro Vollero began in Supreme Court before Judge James C Cropsey. Turncoat Dominic Latteresi testified that Vollero was the chief plotter against the Morellos.

March 9, 1918

Gasparino Vincinanza testified that Vollero planned to murder Nick Terranova.

March 14, 1918

The jury found Vollero guilty of first-degree murder in the Nick Terranova and Gene Ubriaco hits.

March 30, 1918

Judge Cropsey sentenced Vollero to death. However, an appeal court reduced his term to a minimum of 20 years, and the parole board released him in April 1933.

May 14, 1918

Tony Notaro and Ralph Daniello testified against Pellegrino Morano. A jury convicted him of second-degree murder for the killing of Nick Terranova. Judge Van Siclen sentenced Morano to twenty years to life. Defendant Alfonso Sgroia pled guilty to manslaughter, and the Judge gave him a sentence of up to 12 years.

June 6, 1918

A jury found Ciro Terranova not guilty of hiring the killers of Charles Lombardi and Joe DiMarco. (July 25, 1916) The latter deserted the Morello Family and opened a card room.

March 18, 1920

Prison authorities released Giuseppe Morello from his counterfeiting sentence in February 1910.

March 24, 1920

Morello's friends and relatives held a big celebration for the freed Mafia leader. Informer Salvatore Clemente attended and reported on the event.

June 30, 1920

Prison authorities released Ignazio Lupo from his counterfeiting sentence in February 1910.

FOCUS ON D'AQUILA

The General Assembly had elected Salvatore D'Aquila (Gambino Family) as their new Boss of Boss with the incarceration of Giuseppe Morello in 1910. Gradually, the Morello Family came into conflict with D'Aquila, especially after the decimation of the Camorra gangs by the legal system.

Between June-Sept 1921

Salvatore D'Aquila convinced the Mafia General Assembly to condemn Morello, Lupo, Umberto Valenti, and nine others to death.

1921

At various times Giuseppe Morello, Lupo, Umberto Valente, Ciro Terranova, and others fled to Sicily to avoid the General Assembly's death sentences. According to Nicola Gentile, these men approached him in Sicily, hoping he could use his influence to form a commission that would attempt to have the death sentences revoked.

MORELLO ALLIES WITH MASSERIA

1922

At an undetermined date, Giuseppe Morello merged his Family with that of Boss Joe Masseria to protect himself from the D'Aquila death sentence. As a result, Morello became Masseria's Underboss. (We now call this group the Genovese Family.)

January 18, 1922

Saverio Pollaccia and Umberto Valente return to NY from Sicily. Pollaccia later became the Consigliere of the Masseria Family (Genovese Family.)

1922

Jack Lima, a Morello brother-in-law, disappeared in California.

1922

Boss of Bosses Salvatore D'Aquila promised to drop the death sentence on Umberto Valente as long as he killed Boss Joe Masseria, a rising rival of D'Aquila. (See the following chapter for more details.)

May 8, 1922

Umberto Valente and some hoods killed Vincent Morello at 116th and 2nd Ave. Shot from an automobile by the Valente guys, Morello was hit but fired back, then flung his weapon away.

Note:

Please see the next chapter for more details on Umberto Valenti.

May 22, 1922
Lupo returns from Sicily.

June 12, 1922
Immigration authorities released Lupo from Ellis Island, where they held him for three weeks to deport him.

MASSERIA BECOMES THE BOSS OF BOSSES

October 10, 1928
Shooters killed Boss of Bosses Salvatore D'Aquila (Gambino Family.)

The General Assembly immediately elected Joe Masseria (Genovese Family) as the new Boss of Bosses. Giuseppe Morello remains as Masseria's Underboss.

PR MISCUE

December 7, 1929
The Tepecano Democratic Club gave a dinner for Judge Albert Vitale at the Roman Gardens in the Bronx. Seven gunmen arrived at 1:30 AM and robbed everyone, but strangely, Vitale asked a cop in attendance not to say anything. Within hours Vitale had returned all the money and the gun stolen from Detective Arthur Johnson.

January 16, 1930
Police charged Ciro Terranova with the holdup of the Vitale Dinner.

July 16, 1930
A Judge arraigned Terranova for the robbery of the Vital dinner and then freed him on $10,000 bail. Terranova told reporters that he doesn't want

anything to do with artichokes. (Many Mafia battles were over the control of artichokes in NYC.)

GIUSEPPE MORELLO'S END

Note:

Please see the following chapter for an outline of the Castellammarese War that led to Giuseppe Morello's death.

August 15, 1930

Salvatore Maranzano (Bonanno Family) gunman Bastiano "Buster" Domingo and others killed Giuseppe "Peter" Morello at 3:50 PM in an office at 352 East 116th Street. Morello reportedly answered the door and took five shots, one to the forehead killing him. The two shooters then entered and shot Joseph Perrano, who jumped out of the second-story window. Perrano had a ticket for a boat trip to Italy and his passport in his pocket. Gaspar Pollaro was seriously wounded and died shortly after that. The shooters fired fifteen shots; five hit Morello, two Perrano, one Pollaro, and the rest into the walls.

The police investigation showed that Morello's address was 1115 Arcadian Way, West Palisades, NJ, and he had five children. Interestingly his half-brother, Terranova, denied being related to Morello.

October 6, 1930

Shooters killed Carmine Piraino, the 23-year-old son of Giuseppe Morello, in front of the Abyla Court Apartments at 1857 85th Street in the Bath Beach section of Brooklyn.

CONCLUSION

Giuseppe Morello had a thirty-year run in the violent world of La Cosa Nostra. He died amid the Castellammarese War leaving Boss of Bosses Joe

Masseria to fend off their enemies. The next chapter profiles Masseria and his tumultuous life.

Note:

Much of the above is due to the superb research of David Critchley. I also highly recommend Mike Dash's "The First Family." Dash details the milieu in which all the following events took place. It is in sharp and welcome contrast to my dry listing of facts.

CHAPTER TWO

Giuseppe "Joe" Masseria

Joe Masseria was an important Mafioso in the 1920s due to the introduction of prohibition and the amalgamation of his Family with that of the Morellos. With the killing of Boss of Bosses, Salvatore D'Aquila in 1928, Masseria took his place and was the most important Boss until his death in 1931. He had made the mistake of trying to exert influence on other Families in Chicago, Detroit, Cleveland, and New York. When a coalition of forces appeared to be gaining the upper hand, Masseria's top lieutenants killed him in return for peace. It had been quite a run.

DOB
1987
Marsala, Sicily

DOD
April 15, 1931
New York

Description
5' 3"
Stout build
Brown hair
Brown eyes

1887

Joe Masseria

Was born in Marsala, Sicily.

1901

Masseria reportedly moved to the US this year.

1907

A jury convicted Masseria of burglary, but the Judge handed out a suspended sentence.

May 23, 1913

Judge Crain sentenced Masseria to four and a half years for breaking through the roof and robbing Simpson's pawnshop, 164 Bowery Street.

May 26, 1913

Sing Sing Prison admitted Joe Masseria. He gave his address as 217 Forsyth Street in Manhattan, an apartment above a saloon.

June 5, 1917

Masseria registered for the draft and gave his address as 136 E Houston Street, indicating that he worked for the Independent Ice Company of 238 Elizabeth Street. Masseria claimed an exemption from the draft because he had a wife and three children.

1920

NYPD arrested Masseria for the murder of Salvatore Mauro, a hood in the Salvatore D'Aquila orbit, in front of 222 Chrystie Street. The authorities dismissed the charge.

1920

According to the US Census, Masseria and his family lived at 120 East 16th Street in Manhattan. He gave his occupation as the owner of a pool room.

MASSERIA IN CONFLICT WITH THE BOSS OF BOSSES

1920-1930

Joe Bonanno wrote that Masseria grew his Family by absorbing other bootlegging gangs. Unfortunately, this expansion brought Masseria into conflict with Boss of Boss Salvatore D'Aquila (Gambino Family.)

Masseria's bootlegging brought him into association with Vito Genovese and Lucky Luciano, and his territory included areas in Brooklyn, the Bronx, and parts of East Harlem.

May 7, 1922

Shooters firing from a car killed Vincent Terranova on East 116th Street as he headed for his nearby home.

May 8, 1922

Masseria participated in a big shootout on Grand Street. A child, a woman, and four males were wounded. Later, Frederico Petruzziello (35) was brought to the hospital badly injured, as was the dying Silvio Tagliogambe. The cops chased and arrested Joe Masseria as one of the shooters. He had thrown away a .32 automatic, which the police found. Oddly, Masseria had a pistol permit signed by Superior Court Justice Selah Strong. Later a magistrate released Masseria on $15,000 bail. Eventually, a jury found him not guilty.

May 22, 1922

Ignazio Lupo returned from Sicily, where he had been in hiding after Boss of Bosses, Salvatore D'Aquila, convinced the General Assembly to condemn him and others to death.

Someone killed Joseph Peppo, a Morello Associate, at the liquor exchange.

August 8, 1922

Rival hoods ambushed Joe Masseria as he left his home at 80 Second Ave. Two men crossed the Street and tried to kill him. Masseria dodged three shots in front of Helney Brothers, a women's wear store at 82 Second Ave. Two of the bullets hit the window of Helney Brothers. The two gunmen ran to a waiting car and headed up Fifth Street. Some men on strike ran into the Street to stop the shooters, but the shooters opened fire, wounding six, with one dying later in the hospital. The police took Masseria in for questioning but learned nothing.

Note:

According to Nicole Gentile, Umberto Valenti organized the hit to get back into the good graces of Boss of Bosses Salvatore D'Aquila.

August 11, 1922

After Umberto Valenti attended a peace meeting in a spaghetti restaurant at 11:45 AM between 12th Street and 2nd Avenue, hoods killed Valenti. They fired fifteen or twenty shots at Valenti. The New York Times described him as "a notorious gunman and bootlegger." The mutts hit an eight-year-old girl and a street cleaner in their wild attack. Valenti died at St Mark's Hospital at 12:46 PM.

When police picked up Masseria as a suspect, Magistrate Douras held him without bail, claiming it was for his protection. However, Masseria denied having anything to do with the Valenti hit.

October 13, 1927

After a simmering dispute, Cleveland Consigliere Sam Todaro engineered a coup that killed Boss Joe Lonardo and Underboss John Lonardo. He had the backing of Masseria.

MASSERIA IS THE NEW BOSS OF BOSSES

October 10, 1928

Masseria shooters killed Boss of Bosses Salvatore D'Aquila, which led to the General Assembly voting Masseria as the new Boss of Bosses. Al Mineo took over as leader of the combined forces of his and D'Aquila's Families.

June 11, 1929

The son of slain Cleveland Boss Joe Lonardo killed Sam Todaro, but the Porello brothers carried on and were loyal to Masseria.

July 18, 1929

The NYPD picked up Masseria for questioning in the Boston murder of gangster Frank Marlow. They had been looking for "Joe the Boss" Masseria since June 25, 1929. But, nothing came of this inquiry.

1930

According to the US Census, Masseria and his family lived at 6 2nd Ave, and he managed a stable.

February 1930

A shooter shot gunned Boss Tommy Reina (Lucchese Family) outside the apartment of his mistress. Masseria supported Capo Joe Pinzolo as that Family's new leader. However, a small group of Reina loyalists secretly began plotting revenge.

THE CASTELLAMMASE WAR

May 31, 1930

According to Nicolo Gentile and Joe Bonanno, Joe Masseria attempted to gain the support of new Detroit Boss Gaspar Milazzo against Chicago Boss Joe Aiello. Milazzo rejected this alliance which infuriated Masseria. He contacted Milazzo's Detroit rival, Chet LaMare, and urged him to take action.

Gunmen killed Boss Gaspare Milazzo and Sam "Sasha Parino, who were waiting for a peace meeting at a grocery and fish market located at 2739 Vernor Highway. The shooters were Joe Amico and Joe Locano, with Benny "The Ape" Sebastiano driving. These guys were LaMare men.

Note:

A jury acquitted the shooters.

July 5, 1930

Forces loyal to Capo Frank Milano killed Cleveland Boss Joe Porello and a brother. The members elected Milano as their new leader. The loss of Porello damaged Masseria's prestige and his attempt to influence other Families.

August 15, 1930

At 3:50 PM, shooters, including Bastiano "Buster" Domingo, killed Joe "Peter" Morello in an office at 352 East 116th Street. Morello reportedly answered the door and took five shots, one to the forehead killing him. The two shooters entered and shot Joseph Perrano, who jumped out of the second-story window. Perrano had a ticket for a boat trip to Italy and his passport in his pocket. Gaspar Pollaro was seriously wounded and died shortly after that. Morello owned the four-story building. On the ground floor was the Sassone Reality Company. Mrs. Mary Lima lived on the third floor. Buster et al. fired fifteen shots; five hit Morello, two Perrano, one Pollaro, and the rest into the walls.

1928

Joe Masseria made a deal with Al Capone in which he would accept Capone into La Cosa Nostra as a Capo in his Family as long as he wiped out Joe Aiello, the Boss of a Chicago Family. Some accounts state that Masseria first approached Aiello to kill Capone but was rebuffed.

Fall 1930
According to Nicolo Gentile, Masseria successfully arbitrated a dispute between two factions in the Cleveland Family.

October 23, 1930
Capone forces finally killed long-time rival Joey Aiello, Boss of a Chicago Family. Masseria demanded Capone kill Aiello as part of his requirements to enter La Cosa Nostra as a Capo in the Masseria Family. (Genovese Family.)

December 1930
Gaspare Messina, Boss of Boston, became the temporary Boss of Bosses. He called a General Assembly, where the membership appointed a six-man commission to meet with Salvatore Maranzano to achieve peace.

Unfortunately, Maranzano was not interested at the end of the hostilities but used the meeting to rant about all the sinister acts that Masseria caused. Maranzano wanted the General Assembly to condemn Masseria to death.

February 3, 1931
Joseph "Joe the Baker" Catania, a bail bondsman, was shot at about 11:45 AM. He was entering a candy store run by Mrs. Emma Petrella. There is no mention of his wife being with him in the news accounts, but Valachi's version had Catania's wife there. Valachi said Maranzano gunmen Sally Shillanti, Nick Capuzzi, and Buster Domingo did the ambush. Catania was hit six times in front of 647 Crescent Ave in the Bronx.

February 4, 1931
Catania died of his wounds in Fordham Hospital.

February 6, 1931
Detroit Boss Chet LeMare thought he was safe in his home, but his visitors, close Associates, including Joe Amico from the Milazzo hit, killed him. Although charged with murder by the police, a jury refused to convict them.

THE END OF MASSERIA

April 15, 1931

Masseria Capos, including Luciano and Al Capone, decided the best way to end the war with the Maranzano forces was for them to eliminate their Boss. According to Joe Bonanno, Lucky and Maranzano met and agreed on this plan.

Gentile's version said the Masseria Capos were frustrated by his unwillingness to openly battle Maranzano due to his hopes for peace and because the NYPD chief threatened to arrest everyone if the killings didn't stop. So Al Capone and other Capos decided to murder Masseria.

Lucky Luciano lured Boss Joe Masseria to the Nouva Villa Tammara restaurant at 2715 West Fifteenth Street in Coney Island, where Luciano Associates gunned him down. (Three shots in the back, one in the neck, and one just above an eye.) Police found two pistols in the alleyway, three revolvers in a car a few miles away, and four overcoats in the restaurant, one of which belonged to Masseria's Consigliere, Saverio Pollaccia. When the NYPD interviewed Pollaccia, he said he took Masseria to the restaurant to settle a policy (gambling) dispute.

April 20, 1931

The Masseria family held funeral services in their penthouse at 81st Street, followed by burial at Calvary Cemetery in Queens.

1932 approx.

Saverio Pollaccia, Masseria's former Consigliere, turned up missing. Gentile claimed Chicago whacked him out as a favor to Vito Genovese, who lured him to the Windy City.

September 11, 1932

Police found the body of Gerardo Scarpato, owner of the Nouva Villa Tammara, sewn in a sack in the back of a vehicle parked at 216 Windsor

Ave. Earlier Scarpato went to the cops and had them take his fingerprints to help identify his body if Masseria's friends took revenge, figuring Scarpato helped set him up. Nothing came of the investigation.

June 22, 1937

NYPD cops chased a vehicle that contained a man yelling for help. Suddenly, someone tossed a body out, and the culprits escaped. The victim was John Masseria, a brother of the late Boss of Bosses. It remains unclear why they killed him, but one guess would be they feared revenge.

CONCLUSION

Joe Masseria became rich because of prohibition and grew in strength by absorbing other gangs into his Family. Unfortunately historians have only the stories of the "winners" when evaluating Masseria legacy. He must have had a great number of political skills and ruthless determination to head up one Family let alone becoming Boss of Bosses. Masseria was like so many other Mafia leaders in that they never seem to be willing to ride off into the sunset with their millions and more importantly their lives.

CHAPTER THREE

Charles "Lucky" Luciano

Charles "Lucky" Luciano (nee Luciania) is one of America's most famous gangsters. He became prominent during his 1936 trial for organizing prostitution in New York. In the late 1940s, the media again focused on him because New York Governor Dewey commuted his lengthy prison sentence due to his contribution to the war effort.

Lucky remained newsworthy through the 1950s as politicians and the media debated the merits of Dewey's commutation. The Kefauver Hearings labeled him as the sole arbitrator of disputes between what they thought were two major organized crime rings. In addition, the American drug agents named Luciano the king of a worldwide drug conspiracy, which created more headlines. Add to this frenzy was the public's fascination with the 1957 discovery of a mob gathering in Apalachin, NY.

In 1963, famous turncoat Joe Valachi testified about La Cosa Nostra before the McLellan Committee. His story created a sensation worldwide, and Lucky was part of the mix. It wasn't long before writers were describing Luciano as the father of the modern American Mafia. They credited Lucky with creating the structure of La Cosa Nostra with Families and Bosses. In addition, he Americanized the Mafia by focusing on business practices rather than the brute strength model of its era before 1931. Unfortunately, the profile was a myth, but no amount of research based on prime evidence could turn the tide. Lucky Luciano is a legend.

DOB

November 11, 1987

Lercara near Palermo

DOD

January 26, 1962

Naples, Italy

1914-1916

In a 1946 statement at Great Meadows Prison, Lucky said he worked for the Goodman Hat Company during this period.

June 17, 1916

NY Police arrested Luciano for unlawful possession of a narcotic. He served six months of an indefinite term at New York City's prison on Blackwell's Island.

1919-1920

In a 1946 statement at Great Meadows Prison, Lucky said he worked for the Gem Toy Company during this period.

December 15, 1921

Jersey City Police arrested Lucky for carrying a loaded revolver. They later dropped the charge.

June 5, 1923

Police again arrested Lucky for possession of narcotics. However, the drug agents released Lucky after he led them to a truck full of heroin.

June 27, 1926

The police arrested Lucky for driving around in a car with a shotgun, two pistols, and forty-five rounds of ammo. However, a Judge dismissed the case when Lucky proved he had a pistol permit.

December 28, 1926
Police arrested Luciano for felonious assault.

December 29, 1926
Authorities dismissed the felonious assault case against Luciano.

November 17, 1928
The cops arrested Lucky and charged him with assault and armed robbery of a payroll messenger. Authorities dismissed the case.

October 16, 1929
Rival gangsters kidnapped Luciano.

October 17, 1929
Lucky Luciana woke up at 2 AM on Huguenot Beach on Staten Island after being abducted, beaten, and left for dead. He crawled to a nearby police station on Prince's Bay Ave, and officers took him to Richmond Memorial Hospital. Detective Charles Schley of the Tottenville precinct questioned Lucky, who claimed three men abducted him at 6 PM on Wednesday, October 16, 1929. He then clammed up. A Judge held Luciano on $25,000 bail for investigating a robbery but then released him on October 19, 1929.

Note:

Luciano had the nickname Lucky before the above instance.

PROHIBITION

Luciano and Genovese were active in Northern New Jersey, protecting illegal breweries, and Lucky had a hand in distilleries. Unfortunately, we cannot estimate the income Luciano derived from these operations.

May 1929

A meeting of a host of hoods in Atlantic City has become legendary. Many writers claimed this gathering created a nationwide combination of bootleggers and indicated that Luciano was present. Unfortunately, the evidence suggests the scope of the conclave was significantly narrower.

The infamous St. Valentine massacre occurred in Chicago in February. It generated headlines all over the nation, bringing the heat on gangsters of every level. This attention was not good for business; consequently, a prominent peace gathering of gang leaders from Chicago took place in Atlantic City, a neutral ground. Historian David Critchley correctly wrote that contemporary news accounts explained this purpose, plus Al Capone said the same to Philadelphia authorities when they arrested him shortly after the event. Unfortunately, over many decades, authors have turned the Atlantic City pow-wow into the birth of a "National Syndicate" complete with a Commission. The evidence does not support these types of conclusions.

February 27/28, 1930

Florida Dade County detectives raided a gambling operation and arrested 18 men, including Lucky Luciano and Boss Joe Masseria. The big attraction in Miami that night was a heavyweight fight between Jack Sharkey and British champion Phi Scott. Such events often attract serious gamblers; some ended up at the Luciano operation.

March 7, 1930

The Judge fined Lucky $1,000 and Masseria $800 and gave each a 30-day sentence which he suspended as long as the two men left town. A jury had convicted the two men of operating a gambling house.

CASTELLAMMARESE WAR

Note:

I discuss these events in more detail in the Masseria chapter.

The forces of Boss Joe Masseria (Genovese Family) and Boss Salvatore Maranzano (Bonanno Family) were engaged in a violent conflict for power.

Hostilities spread to Detroit and Buffalo, but the primary battle was in New York.

With the murder of Giuseppe Morello in 1930, Lucky became Masseria's right-hand man. He and other Capos, including Al Capone in Chicago, could see that the Masseria forces were losing, and the Boss of Bosses refused to fight, so they decided to take matters into their hands.

Spring 1931

According to Joe Bonanno, Lucky met with Maranzano and agreed that Luciano et al. would kill Masseria to bring the conflict to an end. Nicolo Gentile also wrote that Masseria Capos Luciano and Al Capone had also lost faith in Masseria and planned to kill him.

April 15, 1931

Some of his men, including Luciano, lured Masseria to the Nuova Villa Tammaro in Coney Island, where shooters killed the Boss with five shots to the back. The NYPD found two pistols in the alleyway and three revolvers in a car a few blocks away. Four overcoats were in the restaurant.

Note:

While mobsters killed a handful of Maranzano supporters after his demise, there is no evidence to support the claim of a massive purge of old-line Mafia leaders. Yet, unfortunately, this myth continues to live.

LUCKY IS BOSS

Luciano was now the new Boss of what became known as the Genovese Family. He picked his buddy Vito Genovese as his Underboss, and the members MAY have elected Frank Costello as the Consigliere.

THE RISE AND FALL OF MARANZANO

Late May 1931

Salvatore Maranzano was now the undisputed leader of La Cosa Nostra, and a meeting in Chicago hosted by Al Capone recognized him as the Boss of Bosses. Maranzano blessed both old and new Family leaders, including Luciano. However, it wasn't long before the new peace was in jeopardy.

July 4, 1931

Cleveland police arrested Luciano.

September 10, 1931

Joe Valachi, Joe Bonanno, and Nicole Gentile wrote that Maranzano planned to kill some leading Mafia figures. In a pre-emptive strike, Luciano arranged for some of his Jewish Associates to pose as tax men who killed Maranzano in his office. The era of Boss of Bosses was over. It was time to try a new way of governing.

THE COMMISSION

The most powerful of the La Cosa Nostra Bosses formed a seven-man Commission to set broad policy, arbitrate inter-family disputes, and approve the election and elimination of Bosses. These Commission members would serve a five-year term, at which point a National Convention of the Mafia would authorize a membership for another five years.

The original Commission was composed of Joe Bonanno (Bonanno Family), Lucky Luciano (Genovese Family), Joe Profaci (Colombo Family), Vincent Mangano (Gambino Family), Tommy Gagliano (Lucchese Family), Al Capone (Chicago Family), and Stefano Magaddino (Buffalo Family).

Historians have given Luciano far too much credit for the formation of the Commission. Some have even written that he came up with the idea of Families. It's nonsense. Emerging Families had the same structure as those in

Sicily. There was a Boss, a picked Underboss, an elected Consiglieri, selected Capos, Soldiers, and Associates. Even the Commission idea was not entirely new, for Mafia leaders occasionally appointed temporary "Commissions" to settle problems. For example, they formed a "Commission" to meet with Maranzano to end his war with Masseria. So the Commission formation had to have been a joint proposal by several leading Bosses, not just Lucky.

Note:

Nicolo Gentile, who penned a book on his incredible life in the Mafia, claimed the Commission was his idea.

Note:

My book on the Commission contains a detailed history of this body.

THE GARMENT DISTRICT

Luciano was active in the garment center rackets, often associated with influential Jewish gang leader Lepke Buchalter. Joe Bonanno provided some proof of this statement when he wrote in his autobiography that after the fall of Maranzano, Luciano offered him a piece of the garment district rackets, but he declined.

Like in other industries, the hoods made money in the garment center by controlling unions, including Amalgamated Clothing Workers of America locals. A straightforward example would be the mob-controlled union officials using the threat of a strike to coerce kickbacks from clothing company owners who wanted to pay lower wages. The list of illegal opportunities was endless, creating numerous conflicts among those eager to gain or maintain a piece of the lucrative pie.

Note:

Over time the Genovese, Lucchese, Gambino, and Colombo Families gradually forced the once dominant Jewish gangs of the garment district into inferior positions or eliminated some leaders.

1932
Valachi received permission from Boss Lucky Luciano to operate twenty slot machines. He would have to purchase them but the key permission Luciano gave was the right to have a sticker on each machine which signified to the police that Frank Costello approved them and thus they were not to be touched.

January 5, 1935
Antonio Luciana, the father of Lucky Luciano, died. Joe Valachi attended the wake and spoke to Lucky about his bad luck in the numbers business. Lucky arranged to have Frank Livorsi invest $10,000 in Valachi's operation.

THE WALDORF ASTORIA MYTH

Many books and articles on Luciano describe him residing at the famous Waldorf Astoria, leaving the impression that he was there for a long time. However, his Waldorf residency was for only seven months. (He paid $250/month.)

April 7, 1935
Under the name Ross, Luciano registered for a two-room suite on floor 39 of the Waldorf Towers.

August 28, 1935
In an internal file, the FBI described Luciano as "The leading racketeer along Italian lines. Is very powerful and made considerable money in liquor."

October 29, 1935

Waldorf Towers manager Henry Woelfe evicted Luciano from his suite.

LUCKY'S DOWNFALL

In the early 1930s, vice and political scandals rocked New York City. Judge Seabury investigated the corruption in the magistrate court system, and in 1935 Governor Lehman appointed Thomas Dewey as a special prosecutor. He quickly set his sights on the infamous gangster Dutch Shultz.

October 23, 1935

Gangsters controlled by Lepke Buchalter and Luciano whacked out Dutch Shultz and some of his mutts in Newark, NJ. He had become a liability due to his threats to kill Dewey and his erratic behavior. His control of a vast gambling network was equally important for Lucky, and Lepke coveted it. With Shultz's demise, Dewey shifted his focus to Luciano.

PROSTITUTION

Note:

I highly recommend Ellen Poulsen's terrific book, "The Case against Lucky Luciano." It details this aspect of Luciano's life and provides much background information.

A group of gangsters began consolidating the arms of the mainly independent prostitution rack in the 1930s. It started with them lending money to prostitutes and their bookers (Pimps). They also moved in on the sleazy bail bond agents and lawyers who were very important in the racket, for they helped spring the hookers when the cops arrested them.

Political hack Al Martinelli, propelled into office with Luciano's support, provided political protection to the racketeers. He, using corrupt police officers and court authorities, eliminated competing bookers and their supporters. The main ringleaders of this combination were veteran hoods Dave Betillo and Thomas Pinnochio.

1935
Dewey helped convince Governor Leahman to have the New York State Legislature pass a law that permitted the prosecution of a defendant on many counts under one indictment. (Previously, each charge required one indictment, a complicated and lengthy process.)

February 1936
Dewey's man launched massive raids directed at the prostitution industry. Then they began to pressure some of those arrested to testify against Luciano and his men.

Seeing the coming storm, Luciano hightailed it to Miami, then to the gangster sanctuary of Hot Springs, Arkansas. Finally, Dewey and his men, after a political struggle, managed to return Lucky to New York to face trial on a charge of compulsory prostitution.

April 18, 1936
Luciano arrived at Grand Central Station from Arkansas at 8 AM. At 5 PM, officials arraigned him in Court, and Judge Philip McCook set a $350,000 bond which Lucky could not meet.

April 24, 1936
Judge McCook arraigned the defendants again on a new superseding indictment. It included 90 counts with 30 separate charges.

May 11, 1936
The Luciano trial started before Judge McCook in a New York State Supreme Court. Three defendants, Peter Balitzer, Al Weiner, and David Marcus, pled guilty on the first day.

May 12, 1936

The defense and prosecution agreed on a jury.

June 1, 1936

Another defendant in the Luciano trial pleads out.

June 3, 1936

Luciano testified in his defense then prosecutor Thomas Dewey cross-examined. Lucky admitted to making money from gambling, bootlegging, and narcotics, plus telling the police where he hid a trunk of drugs in 1923. However, he denied making any money off prostitution. A headline read, "LUCIANO CRINGES ON THE STAND." The New York Daily News said, "Luciano, halting and stammering, proved by far his own worst witness."

June 7, 1936

The jury found Luciano and seven others guilty at 5:25 AM.

June 12, 1936

With Luciano's agreement, officials at the Toombs jail took him for a psychological exam.

June 18, 1936

At his sentencing hearing, the Court heard the results of Luciano's psychological exam. The doctors found Luciano of average intelligence with a shallow and parasitic personality.

Judge McCook sentenced Luciano to a term of 30 to 50 years. He warned Lucky that no harm had better come to the witnesses against him.

Then Judge McCook gave key Associate Dave Petillo 25 to 40 years, 25 years to Tommy Pennochio, and lesser sentences to the other five defendants.

Officials took the defendants to the Tombs jail, then hustled Lucky up north to Dannemora to Sing Sing Prison.

1936

Luciano appointed Underboss Vito Genovese as the Acting Boss.

August 24, 1936

A large group of guards brought Luciano from his laundry room job at Dannemora prison to the courthouse in Plattsburgh, New York, for an appeal. Lawyer James W Noonan argued before Judge Thomas Croake that the new 1936 law under which the jury convicted Luciano was not constitutional.

September 14, 1936.

Plattsburgh, NY County Court Judge Thomas Croake rejected a plea of habeas corpus from Luciano's lawyers. They claimed that the law under which Dewey convicted Luciano was unconstitutional. Authorities quickly return Lucky to his cell in Dannemora Prison.

May 7, 1937

State Supreme Court Justice Philip McCook refused to grant Luciano a new trial.

July 16, 1937

The Appellate Division of the New York Supreme Court upheld Luciano's conviction. However, two justices stated that Lucky's sentence was too severe.

April 13, 1938

The Court of Appeals upheld Luciano's conviction and sentence.

June 4, 1938

The New York State Court of Appeals refused to reargue Luciano's case.

October 11, 1938

The US Supreme Court refused to hear Luciano's case

Late 1938

Underboss Vito Genovese fled to Italy, so Luciano appointed Frank Costello as his new Acting Boss.

LUCKY AND THE WAR

Note:

I highly recommend "The Luciano Project" by author Rodney Campbell for an in-depth look at Luciano's activities during World War Two and his subsequent deportation to Italy.

BACKGROUND

Japan attacked Pearl Harbor on December 7, 1941, and the USA formally declared war the following day. Then Germany, Italy, and the other axis powers declared war on the US. Finally, on December 11, Congress retaliated by declaring war on those powers.

The Allies decided to defeat Germany first and then take care of Japan later. Consequently, America needed countless ships to transport food and war supplies to England. Unfortunately, the US Navy ignored the experiences learned by Britain and Canada, who had been at war with Germany since 1939. Wisely, they grouped the cargo vessels in convoys protected by warships. It could have been more foolproof, but it was effective.

Unfortunately, between December 7, 1941, and the end of February 1942, the US and its allies lost seventy-one merchant ships to U-boat attacks. It was a disaster greatly facilitated by the US not using protected convoys plus their lack of blackout of the cities and towns along the east coast. As a result, on the surface, German subs could sit out in the Atlantic and pick off ships perfectly silhouetted against the illuminated coastline. It was a disaster.

Note:

Contrary to many WW2 war movies, subs at the time usually fired their torpedoes while they were on the surface.

February 9, 1941
The French liner S S Normandie caught fire and capsized at a pier in the Hudson River. The US was converting it to a troop ship. The Navy had to contemplate that the disaster was sabotage. (An investigation showed the fire was due to an accident.)

ACTION

A typical submarine could only linger off the US coast for a short period before returning to Europe to refuel and resupply. Since the German U-boats were staying along the east coast, there had to be an explanation. The Navy began to suspect traitor fishermen were providing diesel fuel to the subs, ironically, the allies already knew the real answer from their super-secret intelligence. The Germans had stripped some subs of most armaments, including torpedoes, so that they could transport fuel and supplies to other subs. Unfortunately for the US Navy on the east coast, they were not in the intelligence loop and were off chasing shadows.

Naval intelligence received permission to investigate recruiting gangster James Lanza who controlled the Fulton Fish market. Working with the DA Frank Hogan's office, they established contact with Lanza, who willingly aided the Navy. For example, he eased the Navy's way into the fishing fleet and fish market world. The Navy found this endeavor very helpful.

Afterward, Lanza suggested to Lieutenant Commander Haffenden that he had done as much as possible but that another person might aid the Navy. That individual was the imprisoned Lucky Luciano. Through the DA's office, Haffenden contacted Moses Polakoff, who suggested a vital link would be

Myer Lansky, an old Luciano friend. Lansky agreed to accompany them to visit Luciano.

May 12, 1942

To ease the trip, prison officials agreed to transfer Lucky from isolated Dannemora prison to the state facility at Great Meadows in Comstock, about sixty miles from Albany, NY.

May 14, 1942

Lawyer Morris Polakoff and Myer Lansky held a private meeting with Luciano at Great Meadows. They outlined the Navy's plan and how Lucky could contribute to its success. He was willing to cooperate as long as his name remained out of it, for Lucky feared being labeled a rat in America and Italy.

Luciano had about six more meetings with various characters, including Lansky and Polakoff. In addition, Underboss Frank Costello dropped in once, and Capo Mike Miranda on another occasion. Since Polakoff would seclude himself in a distant corner of the room, one could assume that Mafia business must have been on the table as well as the naval plan.

Now that they had Luciano's blessing, the Navy received excellent cooperation from the dock unions and other entities up and down the east coast. But, of course, the other La Cosa Nostra Bosses were on board. It is impossible to say how much of a role this alliance between the Navy and the Mafia contributed to peace on the waterfront, but sabotage on the docks was a non-factor during World War Two.

THE INVASION OF SICILY

The allies agreed that the best strategy to defeat Hitler was to invade Europe from the south. They had driven the Axis powers out of northern Africa and finally decided that the island of Sicily would be their next target. The major problem was that they needed more intelligence on Sicily's waters, beaches, and terrain. So naval intelligence turned to the Mafia to persuade

Italian Americans to produce maps, pictures, and the like from their former homeland. But, again, the hoods operated with Lucky's blessing.

It is important to note that the Allies couldn't reveal their intended target, so they conducted intelligence gatherings on Greece and other possible invasion possibilities to confuse Hitler. In addition, the British conducted an elaborate deception plan to deceive the dictator and his flunkies into believing the invasion would occur not in Sicily but elsewhere.

My research confirms that Luciano did offer to travel to Sicily to help prepare the way for the invasion, but the Navy wisely turned the idea down.

July 9, 1943
The Allies began their successful invasion of Sicily.

Note:

There are movies, books, and YouTube clips on this famous operation for those interested. Use Google and check out "The Man Who Never Was" and "Operation Mincemeat."

February 1, 1943
Lawyer George Wolf, acting for Luciano, filed a motion in the Supreme Court of New York County to modify Lucky's sentence. However, Luciano insisted that Wolf not mention his aid in the war effort because he feared for his family's safety.

February 8, 1943
In an open hearing before Judge McCook, George Wolf mentioned Lucky's war effort and other reasons for modifying his sentence. Then a letter from the warden at Great Meadows Prison did not say Lucky was aiding the Navy. Additionally, unfortunately for Luciano, the office of DA Frank Hogan insisted that Luciano's conviction and sentence were appropriate. However, Assistant DA Fuld told the Court that Hogan's office was very willing to

cooperate if Judge McCook wanted to delve further into Lucky's application which included a mention of his helping the allies.

February 10, 1943
Judge McCook denied Luciano's application for a sentence reduction but said that if he was assisting the authorities and continued to do so, executive clemency might become appropriate.

HEADLINES

LUCKY WANTS OUT; SAYS HE HAS AIDED US.

New York Daily News, February 8, 1943
Aid to Armed Forces Fails to Help Luciano
New York Daily News, February 11, 1943

ANOTHER ATTEMPT TO GET OUT

May 8, 1945
Lawyer Moses Polakoff swore out a petition for a grant of executive clemency on the same day the Allies declared victory in Europe. He outlined Luciano's model behavior behind bars and his extensive aid to the war effort. Polakoff hoped Governor Dewey would commute Lucky's sentence to time served and supported his petition with a detailed affidavit from Commander Haffenden. Unfortunately for Luciano, the Navy refused clearance from an affidavit from Assistant DA Murray Gurfein. But DA Hogan passed a copy on to Polakoff, in confidence, anyway.

May 23, 1945
The New York Herald Tribune ran a story under the heading, "Luciano Seeks Clemency. Says He Helped Navy."

May 29, 1945

The New York Parole Board began investigating Luciano's petition for parole. The Navy did everything it could to minimize its association with Luciano, for they feared a public and political backlash. But, to the credit of the Division of Parole, they completed an exhaustive investigation despite many obstacles.

December 3, 1945

Chairman Moran of the parole board received the report and discussed it with the other two members. He then passed their recommendation for clemency, but only for deportation, to Governor Dewey.

January 3, 1946

Governor Dewey commuted Luciano's sentence for his valuable services to the country.

January 9, 1946

Prison officials transferred Luciano to Sing Sing Prison at Ossington, New York, from the Great Meadows facility at Comstock. Two of DA Hogan's assistants quizzed Luciano about the Carlo Tresca case. Lucky replied that he knew nothing of the infamous murder of the controversial journalist but would try to find out information from his friends if the government allowed him to remain in the US.

January 16, 1946

After consulting with DA Frank Hogan, his assistant returned to Sing Sing to talk to Luciano again. Assistant DA Pagnucco told Lucky that Hogan decided that if Lucky gave them information on the Tresca hit, he would pass on news of his cooperation to the proper authorities. Luciano rejected the proposal.

February 1, 1946

The New York State Parole Board formally granted Luciano parole for deportation. Prison officials then handed Lucky to the Immigration Service, which quickly transported Luciano to Ellis Island in New York harbor.

February 2, 1946

Lansky, Frank Costello, Morris Polakoff, and Mike Lascari took the 1:15 PM ferry to Ellis Island to visit Luciano. The visitors left on the 3:15 PM ferry.

A later investigation claimed that Polakoff misled authorities by asking for three passes for "relatives" of Luciano.

February 5, 1946

Lansky and Lascari visited Lucky to pick up money he wanted them to convert to traveler's checks. The INS Agents assumed Luciano's two brothers gave Lucky the cash on a previous visit.

February 7, 1946

Lansky and Lascari returned to Ellis Island and gave Lucky $2,500 in traveler's checks. Lucky also had $388 in cash, according to the INS.

February 8, 1946

INS Agents took Luciano on the 1:15 PM ferry from Ellis Island to be placed aboard the Laura Keene at 2:45 PM at Pier 7, Bush Terminal, Brooklyn. The first mate signed the receipt for Luciano.

An INS official phoned various media members at around 7:00 PM and informed them that Luciano was at Pier 7 in Brooklyn and they could meet there at around 10:00 AM on February 9, 1946. The INS official would try to arrange an interview with Luciano.

February 9, 1946

Around 10:00 AM, immigration officials refused entry to Pier 7 for a group of reporters. One of the media called various officials, including an Immigration Assistant Supervisor, and asked for assistance. That ploy didn't work. An INS official visited Luciano, who declined to meet with the press at the gate.

The loading of flour aboard the Laura Keene stopped because of rain.

February 10, 1946

Reporters failed to gain entry to Pier 7 again. Also present was a group of between sixty and eighty stevedores. Accounts of this confrontation vary widely, but it is accurate to say the dock workers intimidated the reporters.

Later in the day, Boss Frank Costello and a few other unidentified men boarded the ship. At supper, Luciano refused to touch the ship's food, so two of the Costello men went to the Fulton Fish Market and returned with lobsters, spaghetti, and several bottles of wine. After eating, Luciano and the others returned to his cabin, where they talked long into the night. Contrary to myth, there wasn't a raucous party with dancing girls on the Laura Keene. Instead, those stories came from someone's fertile imagination, spread, and became part of Mob lore.

The Laura Keene sailed at 8:50 AM. Mayor LaGuardia, on the radio, claimed Costello had been allowed to visit Luciano on Ellis Island and the ship. At some date, a New York paper claimed that Albert Anastasia was also on board the vessel, but the guards say it didn't happen.

Three INS officials were aboard the Laura Keene until about 2:00 PM. when a pilot boat took them back to the harbor.

February 14, 1946

Mayor LaGuardia followed up his rant about the behavior of authorities and gangsters on the Brooklyn dock with a letter to Thomas Clark, Attorney General of the United States. He added a note to J Edgar Hoover, the head of the FBI, and asked him to investigate why authorities permitted Frank Costello access to Ellis Island.

Note:

LaGuardia's letter caused a storm within government circles resulting in a lengthy investigation of the dock incident. But, of course, as could be expected, everyone covered their rear ends.

February 28, 1946

Luciano arrived in Naples. He gave vague answers to most of the reporters' questions but did say his voyage was pleasant. Lucky revealed that his immediate plans were to visit relatives in Naples and then Sicily.

LUCKY IN CUBA

March 6, 1946

Famous columnist Dorothy Kilgallen wrote that Luciano's friends were paving the way for Lucky to travel to Mexico.

March 12, 1946

Noted columnist Walter Winchell wrote that gamblers heard Luciano might pop up in Mexico soon.

March 27, 1946

Kilgallen again wrote about Luciano's flunkies preparing for Lucky to operate from Mexico and Cuba.

May 28, 1946

A report from Naples claimed that Lucky had taken control of the La Marca gang since its leader was in prison. (Nonsense).

September 1, 1946

Reporters saw Luciano dining in a Rome restaurant.

September 2, 1946

An Italian-based New York Daily News reporter wrote that sources told him that Luciano had obtained illegal passage on a freighter for Mexico.

September 3, 1946

A reporter saw Luciano in an expensive Rome restaurant again.

October 29, 1946
Luciano arrived in Cuba by plane with $4,000, according to Cuban police later. He was on a 60-day tourist visa which expired on April 29, 1947.

Fall 1946
La Cosa Nostra held a regularly scheduled National Meeting in Florida.

Christmas Holidays 1946
Despite countless stories, there is no prime evidence to prove Luciano hosted a party for many prominent La Cosa Nostra leaders. For example, in a Gangland News column, I demonstrated that singer Frank Sinatra couldn't have been in attendance as claimed by many. This gathering is a myth.

February 11, 1947
Famous singer Frank Sinatra flew to Havana with Chicago hoods Joe and Rocco Fischetti. A media outlet took a picture of them deplaning, but the photo has disappeared from the internet.

February 16, 1947
Tiempo En Cuba story by Ronald Masferrer revealed that Lucky was in Cuba. New York columnist Robert Ruark of Scripps Howard repeated the story in the US.

February 21, 1947
Colonel Farland Williams, Director of Narcotics Enforcement in the Bureau of Narcotics in New York announced that the US would no longer send legal drugs to Cuba until they expelled Luciano.

February 22, 1947
Police arrested Luciano after he left his home in the Miramar residential area and held him at the Tiscoria Immigration Camp. Secret Police Chief Benito Herrera told the press that they detained Luciano because his presence might cause public disorder.

February 23, 1947

Reporter Francis L McCarthy interviewed Luciano at the Cuban detention center. He found Lucky morose, depressed and complaining bitterly and repeatedly about how the world had treated him.

February 27, 1947

Cuban President Dr. Ramon Grau San Martin signed a decree classifying Lucky as undesirable due to his association with bad guys etc. He ordered officials to deport Luciano.

February 28, 1947

Cuba's Supreme Court rejected a plea from Luciano to be able to remain in Cuba.

March 1, 1947

The Criminal Branch of the Havana Lower Court (Audiencia Court) accepted a petition for a writ of habeas corpus for Luciano. The Court ordered the Immigration Director to produce Lucky on March 3 for a review of his case. Lucky's lawyer, Alfonso Gonzales, charged that Luciano's arrest was due to political pressure from the United States. A second Luciano petition asked for his release so he could depart Cuba, a free man. These Luciano tactics came to nothing.

March 8, 1947

The Criminal Branch of the Havana Lower Court tried for the fifth time to force authorities to bring Luciano before them for a hearing. However, the Minister of the Interior again rejected this move.

March 20, 1947

Twelve detectives armed with rifles escorted Luciano from the Tiscoria Detention Camp to the Dutch ship Dakir. The captain refused to guarantee that he would turn Luciano over to Italian authorities. Instead, he said Luciano was a first-class passenger with all his rights, including departing the ship at its stop at the Canary Islands before arriving in Genoa, Italy.

March 27, 1947

On Cuban radio, Senator Eduardo Chibas charged Senator Francisio Prio Socarras with being closely linked to Luciano when the gangster was in Cuba. The next day, in the Senate chamber, Prio slapped Chibas, saying, "This is from Luciano!" Then, believe it or not, the idiots held a three-round duel with swords. A doctor and aids finally broke up the nonsense because Chibas was bleeding.

BACK TO ITALY

April 11, 1947

Ten Genoa police took a motor launch to the Dakir when it was 12 miles outside Genoa harbor. They awakened a startled Luciano, who protested his arrest for leaving Italy illegally. Police superiors took this tactic to avoid a media circus in the port.

April 12, 1947

Gionavvi (John Michael) Balsamo, a radio operator at the American Embassy in Rome, arrived at the Marassi prison in a black limousine with American diplomatic plates. He told the cops he was a friend of Luciano and was there to pick him up. But, instead, the police told him to get lost.

April 29, 1947

Genoa prison officials gave Lucky a little break by taking him to the port customs office to go through the formalities of retrieving his luggage.

May 1, 1947

Police took Luciano, by train, to Palermo, Sicily. He had three suitcases and his golf clubs. The Genoa police told the press that Lucky had a small personal fortune consisting of; several gold ingots, a belt with his name in diamonds, 100 neckties, several bank books, $1,000 in cash, and a large diamond ring.

May 3, 1947

Luciano signed in with the Palermo police then they escorted him to Lercara to visit his parents.

May 5, 1947

Lucky was back in the Palermo jail.

THE LONG WITCH HUNT

After his return from Cuba, I believe there is no primary evidence linking Luciano to serious crime, especially drug dealing. But, unfortunately for Lucky, his past crimes and media attention turned him into a soft target for ambitious law enforcement officers, politicians, audiences seeking media, and other scrupulous mutts. Below I will outline some of the seemingly endless acts of harassment.

May 15, 1947

A regional commission in Palermo, Sicily, received a petition from Palermo police. They wanted the Commission to declare Luciano a public menace and restrict Lucky to his residence. Instead, the Commission rejected the proposals. Lucky replied to the media, "It's about time I got a break."

June 20, 1947

Partners of Ben "Bugsy" Siegel in the Flamingo Hotel/Casino had the flamboyant mobster whacked out in Los Angeles. The hit made headlines all over the United States.

June 26, 1947

Joseph Bell, chief of the Narcotics Bureau of the Treasury Department, jumped on the Siegel media bandwagon by saying Lucky had the mobster killed for meddling in Lucky's drug enterprise. He ludicrously claimed that Lucky controlled 90% of the vice and gambling in the US.

July 1, 1947

Luciano gave a 20-minute interview to reporters at the Savoia Hotel in Rome, where he was briefly staying. Lucky was irritated by all the reports linking him to crime, including the murder of Bugsy Siegel, so he sarcastically admitted to that hit and for being the king of the underworld.

July 7, 1947

Rome police detained Luciano to question him about a 20-pound seizure of cocaine in the luggage of a passenger about to board a flight for New York.

July 8, 1947

Rome police transported Luciano to prison.

July 18, 1947

Reporter James Welland of the North America Newspaper Alliance claimed that Luciano was behind the criminal activities of the famous Sicilian bandit Salvatore Giuliano. This assertion was groundless.

August 23, 1947

Reporter Robert C Ruark wrote a story about his observations of Luciano while the two men were vacationing at the Hotel Quisiana on the Isle of Capri.

October 28, 1947

Italian film producer Roberto Amoruso told the press that Luciano was considering settling in Naples and perhaps investing in filmmaking.

November 24, 1947

Luciano was staying at the Continental Hotel in Milan when he told reporters about stories connecting him to the infamous bandit Salvatore Giuliano. Not surprisingly, he said, "Their dirty lies will collapse before my statements of fact, and they will have to take them back."

January 7, 1948

The Supervisor of Customs Agents in New York approved a press release, "They had positive proof the Luciano was involved in all illegal transfers of Narcotics from Italy and other Mediterranean countries to the US in recent years." Luciano responded, "This is a big lie. It looks like an old-style frame-up." He was correct. The report was nonsense.

June 13, 1948

To control the media stories about him, Luciano hired a press agent. Lucky explained to the media that he was not involved in nightclubs or rackets as reported in the press. Lucky added that he had a pastry shop in Rome and was considering investing in filmmaking. He concluded by insisting he had no plans to return to the US and wouldn't talk about his 1946 release.

October 2, 1948

When drug agents discovered $200,000 worth of heroin on the ship Vulcania, Harry Durning, collector of customs, said it was an organized mob, and he believed Lucky was behind the operation. Nothing came of his unsupported claim.

July 7, 1949

Rome police questioned Luciano for hours about drug trafficking. They told the media that there was no evidence Lucky was in that racket.

1950

During the race for New York Governor, an opponent of Governor Dewey charged that Dewey acted improperly in the pardoning of Luciano.

February 28, 1951

A Kefauver Crime Hearing report labeled Lucky as the "Czar of the United States Underworld." They believed he arbitrated disputes between the two prominent criminal organizations, one in Chicago headed by Tony Accardo, the Fischetti brothers, and Jake Guzik, and another in New York led by Frank Costello and Joe Adonis.

May 13, 1951
The Kefauver Committee announced that the facts did not justify Luciano's early release from prison.

1952
Author Lawrence D Smith and Will Oursler, in their book, "Narcotics: America's Peril" named Luciano as a dope king.

Author Stern wrote a book claiming Luciano paid Dewey $50,000 for his pardon. Then Stern repeated the charge on a radio show. An incensed Dewey demanded and received a retraction.

November 4, 1952
Earlier, unknown film producer Philip Tucker announced to the press that representatives of Luciano had approached him about doing a picture of Lucky's life as long as it made Luciano look good. Now Tucker told the media that he was bowing out of the proposed project because Lucky insisted that the film showed that the government framed him. However, many wondered if Luciano's people had ever approached Tucker.

November 5, 1952
In a report to the United Nations Narcotics Commission, the Italian Bureau of the International Criminal Police Commission stated that there was no evidence that Luciano was involved in international dope smuggling.

November 14, 1952
In Tangiers, authorities arrested four Brits for boarding a Dutch ship at sea and stealing 2700 cases of cigarettes. One of those captured told the police that Luciano was involved. It was nonsense.

January 26, 1954

The Dewey/Luciano matter became a hot item in the New York State Legislature. One politician rhymed off the names of notorious gangsters; Frank Costello, Myer Lansky, Willie Moretti, Socks Lanza, and Bugsy Siegel, among those who visited Luciano in prison.

January 1954

Governor Dewey commissioned a thorough, private review of all aspects of the Luciano matter by Judge Herlands, who would have the power of subpoena.

January 28, 1954, to September 17, 1954

Judge Herlands completed an exhaustive and definitive review of the Luciano matter.

February 1, 1954

In an interview with a reporter from "Il Messaggero" newspaper, Lucky said he couldn't remember who visited him in prison in the US. Then he lied and said the Americans put him in jail for 50 years for a tax problem. Lucky concluded by adding that the American's accused him of white slavery (Prostitution Racket) but had no proof. That was a lie.

February 7, 1954

The Press and Sun-Bulletin of Binghamton, NY, had a headline that read, "Why Was Vice King Lucky Luciano Freed From Prison?" Reporter Paul Martin wrote the story exploring this issue.

Summer 1954

McKay Publishing released "The Luciano Story" by Sid Feder and Joachim Joesten. The latter was upset because Feder had changed two chapters at the last minute without consulting him. Fortunately, Feder had gained access to the secret Herlands report that absolved Governor Dewey of any wrongdoing in the release of Luciano.

November 19, 1954

The Admonition Board in Naples restricted Luciano's movements from dusk to dawn and limited his travels to within 12 miles of Naples. These orders would stay in place for two years.

January 1955

Reacting to the publicity generated by "The Luciano Story," Judge J Irwin Shapiro, New York's Commissioner of Investigations, declared his intent to look into Governor Dewey's pardon of Luciano in 1946.

January 28, 1956

Assistant US Attorney Paul Windels Jr. said eight ounces of heroin seized in New York came directly from Luciano. Asked to comment on Windels' claim, Lucky told the media, "Tell those fuckers I am fed up. I want to live in peace. And, as far as I am concerned, they can go to hell."

January 17, 1957

When reporters asked Luciano to comment on US reports that he was suffering from ulcers, Lucky replied, "Never felt better."

1958

Siragusa began spreading the story that Lucky and other deportees had muscled in on the rackets of homegrown Italian hoods.

January 24, 1958

US Attorney Paul Williams denied that there was evidence implicating Luciano in a recent big narcotics bust.

April 6, 1959

The head of the Intelligent Unit of the Miami Police Department released a report that claimed Luciano was the President of the International Unione Siciliano in Sicily and Italy. But, of course, this idea was total nonsense.

March or April 1960

Patsy Eboli, brother of Genovese Family Underboss Tom Eboli, visited Luciano. Evidence indicated that he was a frequent visitor to the former Boss.

September 7, 1960

In a brief interview, Luciano told a reporter that Joe Ida (Former Boss of Philadelphia) fled to Italy because he feared prosecution for his attendance at Apalachin in 1957.

November 1960

Underboss Tommy Eboli visited Luciano in Italy.

January 26, 1962

Luciano died in Naples, and his family buried him in St. John's Cemetery in Queen's.

LUCIANO'S FINANCES IN ITALY

1962

An FBI bug hidden in the office of Capo Ray DeCarlo heard a discussion of Luciano's finances. When the feds deported Lucky in 1946, his family's leaders sent over $10,000. After that, they provided $2,000 a month until the last few years of his life, when they upped the pay to $3,000 a month.

At one point, Vito Genovese learned that Lucky owed money for grocery and butcher bills, so he arranged to give Luciano $50,000.

THE LAST TESTAMENT OF LUCKY LUCIANO

December 17, 1974

Nicholas Gage, a respected organized crime writer for the New York Times, cast doubt on the authenticity of "The Last Testament of Lucky Luciano" by Martin Gosch and Richard Hammer.

The publisher, Little, Brown, and Company, said author Gosch taped conversations with Luciano, and then Hammer used them to write the book. However, this advertising was false, for there were no tapes with Lucky. Furthermore, the publisher did not have a signed statement from Luciano authenticating the book. In addition, the text quoted Lucky giving an opinion about an event two years after he died. I recall going through the book back in 1975 and making a long list of factual errors. To me, the book was a joke.

January 1975

Little, Brown, and Company published "The Last Testament of Lucky Luciano," which went like hotcakes. Gage wrote that they sold the paperback rights for $800,000, and Penthouse Magazine purchased the right to serialize the book. I have yet to learn what the gross royalties were/are, but they must be enormous.

March 14, 1975

Nicholas Gage wrote another article that revealed that the FBI sent out warnings to all its organized crime units to discount the information about La Cosa Nostra in the book.

1975

Under significant criticism, author Richard Hammer and the publisher fleshed out the book's background. (Author Martin Gosch died in 1973.)

Gosch claimed to have worked with Lucky on a film proposal, but Mafia superiors nixed the idea. Luciano then agreed to do a book as long as the publisher didn't release it until ten years after his death.

Hammer admitted he did not work from tapes of Luciano's conversations but from Gosch's notes. It remains to be seen whether Gosch taped himself reading some of his notes. The publisher attempted to support the book by revealing that five family and friends signed affidavits that said they knew Gosch was working with Luciano on a project.

BOUGHT OFF?

Lucky's two sisters, a former mistress, his friend Rosario Vitaliti and another person shared 5% of the book royalties and 5% of any future movie. Vitaliti told the press that the book was the real thing.

Note:

A reminder that the FBI canned the work saying, "The passages dealing with Luciano's life and early La Cosa Nostra history appear to have been extracted from street gossip and from previous books and hearing." In other words, it was a complete fraud.

Note:

An FBI file contains a 1962 quote from the Chief of the US Narcotics Bureau in Rome about Gosch. He is "Completely untrustworthy, a liar, and an opportunist who tried to take advantage of his association with Luciano to produce a movie about the dead mobster."

The same file contains another 1962 quote from the FBI's Legal Attache in Madrid. "Gosch said his movie script was largely 'made up out of the whole cloth' and bore little resemblance to reality."

Comment:

I find it difficult to believe that Luciano would agree to a royalty distribution that gave only 5% to his family and friends.

1977

The publishing of "The Luciano Project" by Rodney King finally provided the real story of Luciano's cooperation with the American Navy during World War Two and Governor Dewey's commutation of his long sentence for deportation to Italy.

June 20, 2013

Mike Fleming, writing for Deadline, stated that four producers, including Nicholas Pileggi, optioned "The Last Testament of Lucky Luciano" with the intent of making a movie. He quoted the producers saying, "The book is the only bio the Gotham gangster authorized and collaborated on with the writers." They were aware of the criticism of the work by the FBI and mob historians.

CONCLUSION

The American media turned Lucky into a legendary figure based on little factual evidence. He became Boss of the Genovese Family by betraying Joe Masseria but then only lasted about six years before the government sent him away for a long time on a prostitution rap. We can assume he attempted to retain control from behind bars but there is no primary evidence to support that assumption.

Luciano still had influence as seen by his secret aid to the US Navy during World War Two. Then, when Governor Dewey commuted his sentence in recognition of that assistance, Lucky was in the news again. They lack of clarity about these events left room for all kinds of wild speculation including the ludicrous claim that Lucky accompanied the troops into Sicily. Then, in his abortive attempt to move to Italy, created another wave of Luciano hysteria that the bogeyman was returning to dominate organized crime in America. Add to this the ridiculous claims of the Drug Enforcement officials to lay blame for America's heroin problem at Lucky's feet and the legend is set in stone.

Luciano is an important Mafia figure due to his role in taking over the Family from Masseria during the Castellammarese War plus his contribution to La Cosa Nostra adopting the Commission as their highest authority rather than a Boss of Bosses. There is no evidence that he "Americanized" the Mafia nor that he adopted "business practices" in a modernization move. But Lucky Luciano is an icon and nothing your read here is going to change that now.

CHAPTER FOUR

Frank Costello

Costello was a successful Mafioso who made lots of money with his bootlegging and gambling rackets. But, in looking over his history it is amazing how many legal problems he faced from the 1930s onward. There were political scandals, tax problems, contempt charges and worse yet, the challenge from the ambitious Vito Genovese. However, Costello survived all attacks and lived to die in bed. His story follows.

DOB
January 26, 1881
Lauropoli, Consenza province
Italy

DOD
February 18, 1971
New York

5'7"
170 pounds
Chestnut hair
Dark brown eyes

Descriptions

He was a fine, gentle, decent man, a family man.

Toots Shor (A famous tavern owner in NYC.)

A miserable creature.

Buffalo Boss Stefano Magaddino

Costello was a suave and diplomatic man. His skill at cultivating friendships among politicians and public figures was such that it earned him the nickname "The Prime Minister." He preferred to settle arguments at the conference table rather than in the streets.

Joe Bonanno

Costello is a bum, a tinhorn, and a punk.

NY Mayor LaGuardia, 1934.

Residences

222 East 108th

March 1915

405 Lexington

March 1925

Greystone Hotel

January 1927

585 West End Avenue

1927-1930

241 Central Park West

1931-1937

65 Central Park West

1930-1937

115 Central Park West

Majestic Apartments

April 18, 1895

Costello, his mother, and a brother departed Naples by a ship bound for the USA. The father had immigrated to New York two years previously.

September 22, 1914

Costello obtained a marriage license to wed Lauretta Geigerman.

March 15, 1915

A jury convicted Costello of possessing a concealed weapon, and the Judge sentenced him to a year in jail. (Costello did ten months.) Court evidence showed that two cops became suspicious of Costello, but he ran and threw a pistol in a field. Once caught, the cops said he pleaded for mercy.

April 14, 1915

At Costello's sentencing hearing, the Judge was not impressed by Costello mentioning that cops had arrested him on two previous occasions, although the courts dismissed the charges. Consequently, he felt Costello was an experienced hood and deserved to be in prison for a year. (He served ten months.)

1920s

Costello owned the Horowitz Novelty Company, which sold Kewpie Dolls, razor blades, and punch boards. Unfortunately, this enterprise went bankrupt, sticking several investors with losses. From the ashes rose Dainties Products Company, which sold ice cream bars.

1920-1925

Costello was involved in bootlegging. Some lawmen and politicians claimed he was a significant player.

1922-1925
Costello and others ran the Kolsar Reality Company.

March 26, 1923
Costello filed a Declaration of Intent which was a step on the road to naturalization.

May 1, 1925
Costello filed his naturalization papers.

September 10, 1925
The US government naturalized Costello.

COSTELLO AND PROHIBITION PROBLEMS

December 3, 1925
A grand jury indicted Costello and others for a $25,000,000 liquor smuggling conspiracy. Two of these men acted as witnesses on Costello's naturalization papers.

January 3, 1927
Costello's conspiracy to violate the Volstead Act trial began in New Orleans.

January 20, 1927
Costello's Volstead Act trial ended when Judge J Francis Winslow declared a mistrial for Costello and five co-defendants. The jury acquitted four others.

COSTELLO AND SLOT MACHINES

1928-1931
In later testimony, Costello said he controlled 500 slot machines in New York.

Note:

I have seen a variety of estimates on the number of Costello slot machines ranging from 2,500 to 5,000. Unfortunately, I have been looking for prime evidence for the actual number but have yet to be successful, but I find the above numbers widely out of line.

1928
Costello and Kastel opened the True Mint Novelty Company, which dealt with slot machines.

1931
Costello and Phil Kastel opened the Midtown Novelty Company, which dealt with slot machines.

November 7, 1933
Reform candidate Fiorello La Guardia won the NY mayoral election. However, it was only a short time before he launched a campaign to stamp out slot machines by ordering the police to confiscate them.

January 10, 1934
Brooklyn cops boasted that they had confiscated 1,200 slot machines in their borough.

February 16, 1934
Acting on an injunction request from the Mills Novelty Company of Chicago, makers of slot machines, Federal Judge Grover C Moscowitz ended the NYPD tactic of confiscating slot machines. Unfortunately for the good guys, they had to prove the bad guys were using the devices for gambling. The Second Circuit Court of Appeals upheld Moscowitz's ruling.

May 21, 1934

The US Supreme Court ruled that they needn't bother holding a hearing on the slot machine battle for New York State had passed a law banning the machines.

1934

Costello later testified that Louisiana Senator Huey Long invited him to bring his slot machines to his state. The front plan was that the profits would fund the state's pension fund. But, of course, Long would have to change the gambling laws to permit this.

September 10, 1935

An unstable doctor assassinated Louisiana Senator Huey Long before he was able to legalize slot machines in his state. However, Costello and his partner Phil Kassel made arrangements with Long's successor and continued to operate for a decade or more, although the practice still was illegal.

COSTELLO'S JEWELRY PROBLEM

April 19 to April 30, 1935.

The FBI tapped Costello's telephone concerning a jewelry robbery.

April 30, 1935

The FBI ended their tap on Costello's phone.

May 31, 1935

Police arrested Costello and some others in a jewel robbery operation. Judge J William Bondy set Costello's bail at $75,000. Authorities later dropped Costello as a defendant.

KING'S RANSOM

Britain's William Whitely owned a holding company that owned Whitely Company and the small Edradour Distillery in Scotland, where he produced his flagship product, King's Ransom.

In 1937, a veteran US bootlegger, Irving Haim, purchased Whitley's holding company using bank loans from the New Orleans Whitney Bank backed by Costello, Phil Kastel, and William Hellis. Then Hellis became partners with Heim in the Whitley holding company through a series of transactions. There is no need to labor through those details here. A later belief developed that Hellis was a front for Costello's interest in the holding company due to Costello's poor reputation. If this is true, what percentage each of them held remains unknown.

The new owners hired Costello as the US agent for Whitley products at a yearly salary of $20,000 plus a bonus for each case sold over 50,000.

By 1948 Costello was a household name and considered a public enemy. So the good guys' attacked on every level they could to down the powerful hood. One attempt came from the New York State Liquor Authority. They refused to renew the license for Haim's International Distributors claiming he was associated with racketeers like Costello. Also, Haim had several run-ins with prohibition authorities back in that era. This decision was an atomic bomb for Haim, for his company did between $15,000,000 to $20,000,000 worth of liquor business.

On March 30, 1948, Justice Morris Elder of New York's Supreme Court ruled that the State Liquor Authority had not acted unreasonably. Prosecutors demonstrated that the Haim family members involved with International Distributing had not provided their original names on the liquor license application. Instead, they were trying to hide earlier problems with prohibition laws.

The Appellate Division of New York State's Supreme Court, on September 15, 1948, decided that Haim had no leave to appeal the State Liquor Authorities' denial of a license.

In 1951, Costello, Kastel, Heim, and Hellis faced heavy questioning on this matter before the Kefauver Committee.

COSTELLO'S TAX PROBLEMS

October 9, 1939

Costello was in the Federal Detention Center on a conspiracy to evade taxes charge after being arrested by US Attorney Joseph Cahill.

October 10, 1939

US Commissioner Garrett W Cotter released Costello on $75,000 bail for his conspiracy to evade taxes charge resulting from an indictment in New Orleans.

October 1939

Costello waived extradition to Louisiana, where he faced federal tax charges.

November 6, 1939

The IRS claimed Costello owed about $50,000 in back taxes.

November 8, 1939

A Judge dismissed tax charges against Costello.

May 3, 1940

A Judge ruled that Costello and five others must stand trial for evading $530,000 (approx.) in taxes on slot machines in Louisiana.

May 6, 1940

Costello's tax trial started.

May 15, 1940

Judge J Wayne G Borah granted a defense motion for a directed acquittal in Costello's Louisiana tax trial.

April 27, 1942

Costello registered for the draft.

THE AURELIO AFFAIR

August 23, 1943

The Democratic Judicial Council for the First Judicial District nominated Magistrate Thomas Aurelio for New York State's Supreme Court seat. (Not the highest court level in the state.)

August 24, 1943

The Republicans also nominated Aurelio for the same position.

August 25, 1943

The NYPD recorded Aurelio calling Costello about his nomination win.

Aurelio

Good morning Francesco. How are you? And thanks for everything.

Costello

Congratulations! It went over perfect. When I tell you something is in the bag, you can rest assured.

Aurelio

It was perfect. Right now, I want to assure you of my loyalty for all that you have done. It is undying.

Costello

I know. I will see you soon.

August 28, 1943

DA Hogan charged that Costello helped nominate Magistrate Thomas Aurelio as a candidate for Justice of New York's Supreme Court and released the Costello/Aurelio phone transcripts. The media went nuts.

September 1, 1943

DA Hogan publicized Costello's one-year sentence for gun possession back in 1915.

September 3, 1943

The Democrats dropped Aurelio from their ticket, and the Republicans did as well at some date.

September 18, 1943

Aurelio won a court case putting him back on the Democratic and Republican tickets.

September 27, 1943

The Court of Appeals in Albany supported Aurelio's position

October 13, 1943

Costello appeared before the grand jury investigating the Aurelio affair.

October 25, 1943

Disbarment proceedings against Aurelio began. Costello was a witness.

October 26, 1943

Costello testified in private before the disbarment proceedings.

October 30, 1943

A special disbarment referee declared the allegations against Aurelio were not proven.

November 1, 1943

The Appellate Division upheld the report of the Official Referee Charles Sears, and thus the disbarment attempt was dismissed.

November 2, 1943

In the election, Aurelio came in seventh and claimed the last Supreme Court seat. (The Supreme Court, in this case, is a New York State court level.)

Note:

By all accounts, Aurelio served with honor and distinction while on the bench.

March 23, 1944

Costello bought several properties; 79-89 Wall Street, 148-152 Pearl Street, and 11416 Water Street. The total assessment was $512,000.

April 21, 1944

Costello's lawyer did the paperwork, and 79 Wall Street Corporation became a legal entity. Costello was the President, while his wife was vice-president and secretary.

May 13, 1944

Costello purchased a 12-room, white brick house at 5 Barker's Point Road near Sands Point Road, Sands Point, Long Island. Lawyer George M Levy's firm searched the title for Costello.

June 14, 1944

Costello accidentally left $27,200 (About $450,000 in 2022) in a bag in a cab whose driver turned it into the police.

September 14, 1944

The NYPD Deputy Commissioner started a hearing into the liquor license at the Copacabana nightclub. Some sources claimed that hoods, including Costello, had hidden interests in the place. Costello refused to testify.

September 15, 1944

Costello's presented an affidavit to the police hearing requesting the hearing officer vacate his subpoena. The document also contained a statement in which Costello denied any interest in the Copacabana at any time.

September 24, 1944

At the police hearing, the Copacabana manager testified that in 1941-1942, Costello had a percentage in the gambling activities at the Piping Rock Restaurant in Saratoga Springs. (To this day, the small upstate town of Saratoga Springs holds a popular thoroughbred racing season each August.)

September 25, 1944

Judge Pecora granted the Deputy Police Commissioner the right to file a contempt motion against Costello in the matter of the Copacabana.

October 2, 1944

The Deputy Police Commissioner concluded his hearings in the Copacabana, which meant the court canceled Costello's contempt citation.

October 17, 1945

Judge Jonah Goldstein, the Republican-Liberal-Fusion candidate for mayor, charged that candidate William O'Dwyer had links to Costello and Adonis.

October 18, 1945

Goldstein charged that O'Dwyer visited Costello's home.

DA George Beldock of Brooklyn charged that O'Dwyer was responsible for the 12-month delay in seeking the extradition of Genovese and Miranda. Politics played a role in these charges since the men were in opposing parties, O'Dwyer was running for mayor, and Beldock made the accusations in a political speech.

October 27, 1945

Goldstein repeated charges of an O'Dwyer/Costello link.

Oct 27/44

Supreme Court Justice Carroll Walter ordered the NYPD to hand over Costello's $27,000 to the feds to meet Costello's tax arrears.

November 1945

New York voters elected William O'Dwyer as their new mayor.

March 7, 1946

A lower court upheld New York City's right to Costello's money.

November 19, 1946

A Judge rejected Costello's plea for his lost money.

December 20, 1946

Costello called a press conference and denied he was East Harlem's Boss, the Mafia's leader, or connected to narcotics. He labeled these claims "the worst of lies."

December 21, 1946

Costello failed to regain his money in another hearing.

January 29, 1947

The prosecutor and the defense agreed on a jury for Costello's money trial.

January 30, 1947

Costello admitted bootlegging and lending money to Arnold Rothstein during his money trial.

January 31, 1947

The Costello jury ruled that the money belonged to Costello, who had said the cash was for a real estate transaction and not from gambling. But IRS grabbed the bills to meet some of Costello's back taxes.

February 20, 1947
Costello netted $121.65 from the $27,200 he forgot in a cab.

April 25, 1947
An inquiry into fraud in war work invited Costello to testify about "non-profit" work.

April 30, 1947
The immigration people began checking into Costello's naturalization process.

May 1, 1947
The inquiry into fraud in war work cleared Costello on the ship awards scandal.

March 1948
California Governor Earl Warren's Commission on Organized Crime declared that a nationwide slot machine racket spent $400,000,000 a year on bribes and corruption. It named the leaders as "Murder Inc.," Frank Costello, and the remnants of the Al Capone mob who made an annual profit of $200,000,000.

A year later, Costello penned a letter to Governor Warren denying the Commission's claims as they referred to him. Costello wrote, "I can't fix a traffic ticket."

June 18, 1948
Supreme Court Justice Louis Valente, who was running for Surrogate Judge, denied a political link with Costello.

THE COPACABANA FUND RAISER FIASCO

January 24, 1949

Costello held a fund-raiser for the Salvation Army at the Copacabana nightclub starting at 6:30 pm. Those in attendance included Vito Genovese, five New York Supreme Court Justices, and many other judicial and political powers.

January 25, 1949

Stories about the Costello dinner and the politicians attending dominated the media. Then, the Salvation Army announced that Costello had withdrawn from fundraising for their organization.

THE MAYORAL CAMPAIGN FIASCO

March 9, 1949

Mayoral candidate Clendnin Ryan asked Mayor O'Dwyer if Costello was the real Boss (of New York politics.)

March 11, 1949

The California Commission on Organized Crime said there was a national slot machine enterprise with Costello as its head. Supposedly this enterprise spent $400,000,000 on bribery and political contributions.

March 12, 1949

New York Mayor O'Dwyer disclosed a plot to wiretap himself and other officials.

October 3, 1949

During a radio broadcast Newbold Morris, Republican-Fusion-Liberal candidate for mayor, stated that Costello was the real Boss of New York.

October 13, 1949

Morris said his pressure drove Costello to flee to Hot Springs.

October 22, 1949

Mayoralty candidate Morris said Costello tried to make a deal with him.

October 22, 1949

George Wolf, Costello's lawyer, said Morris asked for help in his campaign.

November 4, 1949

A Morris sound truck in the garment center broadcasted that people had seen Mayor O'Dwyer and Costello talking politics.

November 8, 1949

Incumbent Bill O'Dwyer won re-election as New York's mayor.

November 28, 1949

Time Magazine put Costello on its cover and ran a seven-page article on his life. The cover named him "Gambler Frank Costello" and had a quote, "What do they think I am? Superman?"

April 27, 1950

Costello appeared before a Senate Commerce subcommittee and told the Senators there was no way to wipe out gambling.

July 6, 1950

Virgil Peterson, head of the Chicago Crime Commission, told the Kefauver Committee that Costello and the Chicago Outfit leaders controlled organized crime in the USA.

August 23, 1950

Through his lawyer, Costello announced he had sold properties at 79 Wall Street, 87 Wall Street, and 114 Wall Street for $500,000. Costello later elaborated that he paid $300,000 for the properties and made a profit of $119,756.42 ($2,660,000 in 2022).

August 31, 1950

After a serious police scandal, Mayor Bill O'Dwyer resigned, and President Truman appointed him Ambassador to Mexico.

October 24, 1950

Acting Mayor Impellitteri made a long political speech on radio station WJZ accusing Judge Pecore, a mayoralty candidate, of being in the arms of Costello. In addition, Impellitteri provided a long list of political corruption supposedly spearheaded by Costello.

THE KEFAUVER APPEARANCES

A senate sub-committee, headed by Estes Kefauver, began hearings across the United States to examine whether organized crime was involved with interstate activities. For our purposes, I will focus on Costello's notable appearances before the Committee in New York.

February 13, 1951
Executive session

During a photo op, Costello pointed his finger at Kefauver, which angered Kefauver despite the fact Kefauver had done the same thing to Costello earlier.

February 15, 1951
New York
In a private session of the Kefauver Hearings, Costello admitted meeting Mayor O'Dwyer over war fraud.

Washington
In an interim report, the Kefauver Committee declared that Costello and Joe Adonis were rulers of crime. (Adonis was only a powerful Genovese Capo.)

March 9, 1951

A New York Times story said Costello admitted to some ties to candidates in his executive session (Private session) on February 13, 1951.

March 12, 1951

Lawyer George Levy appeared before the Kefauver Committee in New York and testified to the history of the Nassau County Trotting Association, of which he was President.

Levy testified that after being warned by the Chairman of the NYS Harness Racing Association that Roosevelt Raceway would lose its license if it didn't ensure there was no bookmaking on the premises. So Levy hired Frank Costello to remove the gamblers and paid him $15,000 yearly for 1947, 1948, and 1949.

March 13, 1951, 10 am-5:30 pm

New York

After obtaining an agreement that there would be no filming of his face, Costello testified he did little to drive bookies from Roosevelt Raceway despite being paid to do that. He also admitted to buying and selling liquor smuggled in from Canada in 1927, 1928, and 1929. Costello also said he thought he wasn't in the liquor business when he applied for naturalization and that his witnesses weren't either.

Costello refused to answer questions about his financial situation. However, Costello did describe how in 1935, Louisiana Governor Huey Long invited him to bring his slot machines to Louisiana. Although slot machines were illegal in that state, Long hoped to pass legislation permitting them to help fund old-age pensions. Costello was in business with a group of people there, including Phil Kastel and Costello's brother-in-law.

Costello admitted being in partnership with Carlos Marcello and others in the Beverly Country Club. However, he refused to answer whether gambling was allowed there.

March 14, 1951, 10 am-1:00 pm

New York

Costello at first testified that he had little knowledge about his slot machine business in Louisiana, but the Senators confronted him with wiretap evidence that showed the contrary.

Costello denied hiring a man to check his phone lines for bugs. The man testified to just the opposite.

Kefauver says he might refer Costello's testimony to the Department of Justice to see if perjury charges were warranted.

March 15, 1951

New York

Costello walked out of the hearings after presenting a doctor's certificate.

March 16, 1951

New York

With Costello's doctor on the stand, the Committee ordered Costello to appear at 2 pm. But at that time, Costello's lawyer presented another doctor's certificate, and the Committee excused him but ordered a Senate-approved doctor to examine the gangster.

March 17, 1951

The Kefauver Committee voted to cite Costello, Erickson, and Adonis for contempt. The Committee sent the resolution to the full Senate for a vote.

March 19, 1951, pm

New York

Costello testified that he advised politicians but didn't provide cash. In addition, he denied paying to see if someone tapped his phone. Costello also testified about a visit from Mayor O'Dwyer to his apartment.

Note:

Costello admitted that one of his New Orleans Beverly Club partners was Carlos Marcello. Costello owned 20% of the nightclub and earned $18,000 in 1950.

Former Mayor O'Dwyer testified in the afternoon.

February 1951
Famous Actor and radio commentator Robert Montgomery launched a public campaign urging the US government to deport Costello. Montgomery cited Costello's admission that he was once involved in bootlegging and never paid any federal taxes from 1919 to 1932.

March 29, 1951
The Kefauver passed another resolution asking the full Senate to cite Costello for contempt for refusing to disclose his net worth.

March 31, 1951
The US Senate voted contempt citations against Frank Costello, Joe Adonis, and Frank Erickson for the testimony or lack of it before the Kefauver Committee.

April 12 and April 19
Collier's Magazine, trendy in this era, ran a two-part series on Costello titled America's Number One Mystery Man.

MAFIA MANEUVERING

October 4, 1951
Costello's long-time Underboss was Willie Moretti, a cousin. Moretti began his career in Buffalo but moved to New York, where he became associated with what became the Genovese Family. So when Luciano appointed Costello

as Acting Boss in the late 1930s, Costello selected the loyal Moretti as his Underboss. They made a good team that was both respected and feared.

In 1945, the authorities brought Genovese back from Italy to face murder charges, but a Judge dismissed the case the following year. Costello knew that Genovese had ambitions to be the Boss. At this point, he began political maneuverings to shore up his position.

According to Joe Bonanno, Costello turned to Underboss Albert Anastasia of the Gambino Family for support. This move angered Gambino Boss Vince Mangano, who felt he had been embarrassed. Tensions rose between Mangano and Anastasia and came to a head on April 1, 1951, when Mangano disappeared. It is a reasonable assumption to believe Anastasia was behind the hit and had Costello as an ally.

Costello's closeness to Anastasia angered his Underboss Willie Moretti who felt it was his right to be Costello's "hammer." Now Costello became concerned about Moretti's unhappiness, and there was always the possibility that Moretti would ally with Costello's enemy Vito Genovese.

During this time, Moretti had appeared before the Kefauver Committee, and rather than taking the 5th and saying little; he rambled on entertaining the crowd and media. Costello and Genovese, looking for an excuse to rid themselves of Moretti, began spreading the word that syphilis had damaged Moretti's brain. All the Mafia powers bought into this fraud, thus giving the green light to Costello to whack out his cousin.

Three hoods lured Moretti to a meeting in Joe's Elbow Room restaurant in Cliffside Park, NJ, then filled the old gangster with lead. Joe Valachi said everyone saw it as a mercy killing. The irony was that the coroner discovered that there was no evidence of brain damage from a sexual disease, but at this point, it didn't matter. (Mob historians continue to repeat the myth of Moretti and syphilis to this day.)

The downside for Costello was that he had to appoint his rival, Vito Genovese as the new Underboss. Vito's experience and former position as Underboss in the 1930s made his selection a must. Not surprisingly, Genovese continued his intrigue to gain the throne.

COSTELLO'S FIRST STRIKE ATTEMPT

195?

According to Joe Bonanno, Costello attempted a first strike on his enemies, Boss Tommy Lucchese and Costello's Underboss Vito Genovese, in the early 1950s. Costello laid a charge before the Commission that he had proof that Lucchese was plotting to kill Boss Albert Anastasia.

Two Lucchese men appeared before the Commission and confirmed Costello's charge. Then, after much maneuvering, Lucchese finally admitted the truth and asked for Anastasia's forgiveness. Bonanno claimed to have been behind this strategy which may or may not be valid. In any case, Anastasia forgave Lucchese, and everyone kissed and made up. But, unfortunately for Anastasia and Costello, this peace wouldn't last.

COSTELLO'S CONTEMPT PROBLEMS

July 25, 1951

US Marshalls arrested Frank Costello on contempt charges before the Kefauver Committee. A grand jury also indicted Frank Erickson and Joe Adonis.

January 15, 1952

Judge Sylvester J Ryan declared a mistrial in Costello's contempt trial after the jury could not reach a verdict.

April 4, 1952

A federal jury found Costello guilty of ten counts of contempt before the Kefauver Committee. Judge Ryan dismissed two jurors before the trial was complete. The Judge permitted Costello to remain free on his $5,000 bail while he appealed.

April 7, 1952

Costello's lawyer, Kenneth M Spence, asked Judge Ryan to order a retrial based on the problems with the two removed jurors. Later the Judge rejected the plea.

April 8, 1952

Judge Ryan sentenced Costello to 18 months for contempt before the Kefauver Committee. However, the Circuit Court of Appeals permitted Costello to remain free on $5,000 bail while he continued to appeal.

April 11, 1950

Costello agreed to answer 29 questions about gambling, politics, and nightclubs from a reporter from the NY Herald Tribune. Costello said he was not involved in organized gambling, the liquor trade, or the Black Hand.

August 15, 1952

Costello was in the Federal Detention Center in New York for contempt before the Kefauver Committee.

July 3, 1952

Costello won and lost in his contempt appeal before the Second Circuit Court of Appeals. The net result was that he still had to do 18 months, but the Judge reduced his fine from $5,000 to $2,000.

July 15, 1952

A Judge ordered Costello to prison immediately.

July 18, 1952

Costello appealed for a rehearing in front of the Second Circuit. Consequently, the Judge released him on bond.

August 13, 1952

Supreme Court Justice Jackson refused to continue Costello on bail while he appealed his contempt conviction to the Supreme Court.

COSTELLO TO PRISON

August 15, 1952

Costello surrendered to begin serving his 18-month contempt sentence.

August 16, 1952

Prison officials put Costello in holding cells at the Federal Detention Center and then moved him to Lewisburg prison.

August 22, 1952

Costello arrived at Lewisburg prison.

September 8, 1952

The Department of Justice announced that it would begin denaturalization proceedings against Frank Costello.

October 10, 1952

Costello arrived at Atlanta penitentiary.

October 22, 1953

The federal government asked a Federal Court to revoke Costello's citizenship.

December 26, 1952

Costello arrived at the Milan, Michigan prison.

COSTELLO'S TAX PROBLEMS CONTINUE

1950s Tax Liens
Federal

January 18, 1956,	$10,201.35
February 17, 1956,	$16, 836.73

New York State

December 19, 1955,	$10,806.60
	$83,683.80
	$96,491.84
December 28, 1956,	$2017.89
March 23, 1955,	$2022.69
January 17, 1958,	$3210.76

April 23, 1953

Costello pled not guilty to an indictment that charged him with evading $73000 in income taxes for 1947, 1948, and 1949. Marshalls brought Costello to New York from Milan, Michigan.

May 27, 1953

US Marshalls returned Costello to prison in Milan, Michigan.

October 29, 1953

Officials released Costello from Milan prison, and he eventually took a train to New York.

April 5, 1954

At the income tax trial, Costello was indicted for willfully attempting to evade payment of taxes in the years 1947, 1948, and 1949. The government used a net worth strategy, called 144 witnesses, and used 368 exhibits.

COSTELLO CONVICTED OF TAX FRAUD

May 13, 1954

A federal jury convicted Costello in his income tax trial. Costello's lawyer immediately appealed to Appeal Court Judge Malone for bail, but he refused.

May 17, 1954

A Judge sentenced Costello to five years and fines totaling $30,000 for his income tax conviction. Officials sent Costello to the Federal Detention Center until he paid his fines. The Judge refused to release Costello while he appealed.

June 10, 1954

The Court of Appeals for the Second Circuit refused to let Costello out while he appealed his tax conviction.

July 9, 1954

New York State won a civil tax case against Costello for $292,564.

October 1954

The US Supreme Court rejects a Costello appeal of his tax conviction.

March 23, 1955

New York State Tax Commission filed a judgment against Costello and his wife for $2022.69 in back taxes and penalties for 1953.

April 5, 1955

The 2nd Circuit Court of Appeals removed Costello's conviction for 1947, but he still had five years in jail as he received five years for each of the 1947, 1948, and 1949 concurrent convictions. However, the Judge reduced his fine from $30,000 to $20,000 (Minus $10,000 for 1947).

December 8, 1955

Federal Judge Sidney Sugarman denied Costello's request to be able to travel to Hot Springs, Arkansas, which he did every year. At the time, Costello was free on $50,000 bail while he appealed his tax conviction.

December 18, 1955

The New York State Tax Commission billed Frank Costello $190,982.24 for back taxes and penalties for 1941-1950.

December 27, 1955

Federal Judge Lawrence E Walsh ordered Costello to answer 20 questions previously posed to him at a preliminary hearing for his deportation trial. Costello refused to speak about his bootlegging in the 1920s.

January 11, 1956

Costello failed in his appeal to the Supreme Court to overturn a Tax Commission ruling that they would charge him with contempt for refusing to answer questions on back taxes.

January 18, 1956

The US Supreme Court confirmed Costello's tax conviction.

April 25, 1956

US Attorney Paul Williams rejected Costello's offer of self-deportation as long as the feds stopped trying to revoke his citizenship.

April 25, 1956

The US Supreme Court refused to reconsider its approval of Costello's tax conviction.

April 30, 1956

Judge Ryan ordered Costello to surrender on Monday, May 7, 1956.

May 2, 1956

Federal Judge Ryan ordered a hearing on Costello's motion to cancel his tax conviction or reduce the penalties.

May 5, 1956

US Supreme Court upheld Costello's tax conviction.

May 7, 1956

Federal Judge John F X McGohey ordered Costello to surrender on May 14, 1956. However, the Judge ignored Costello's plea that he had cancer, and no one took Costello up on his offer to self-deport to Italy as long as the US dropped its denaturalization efforts.

The US Court of Appeals denied Costello's plea for rehearing his tax conviction.

May 14, 1956

Costello turned himself into Marshalls at Foley Square, Federal House of Detention on West Street. They took him to the US Public Service Hospital for a complete medical check.

May 15, 1956

Costello filed a motion that claimed his five-year tax sentence should have only been one year according to US law.

May 29, 1956

A Judge ordered Costello to appear in Federal Court on June 11, 1956, for a denaturalization trial.

June 6, 1956

Judge Palmieri granted Costello a delay until September 4, 1956, for his denaturalization trial. Costello claimed he needed the postponement because he was changing lawyers. The Judge also ruled that Costello could stay in the New York House of Detention rather than being shipped off to federal prison, for this would help Costello meet with his lawyer.

August 22, 1956

Costello lost his attempt to have his five-year sentence reduced to one year.

August 23, 1956

Federal Judge John F X McGohey denied a Costello motion to vacate his five-year tax sentence.

August 24, 1956

Judge Palmieri rescheduled Costello's denaturalization trial to September 24, 1956, because Costello had a heart ailment.

September 25, 1956

Costello's new lawyer, Edward Bennett Williams, filed two objections to the US efforts to denaturalize Costello. First, he said the feds used illegal wiretaps, and the government tried to force Costello to testify despite his Fifth Amendment rights.

September 27, 1956

Judge Palmieri reject Costello's plea not to testify due to a heart problem.

September 28, 1956

The US lost its attempt to denaturalize Costello. Fittingly, Judge Palmieri ruled that the Federal Government had used illegal wiretaps and other underhanded means against Costello.

March 11, 1957

Prison officials released Costello after 11 months when the Court of Appeal agreed to hear his tax case.

ASSASSINATION ATTEMPT

May 2, 1957

Costello went to dinner at the upscale Monsignor Restaurant at 61 East 55th Street along with some friends. Afterward, he and promotor Phil Kennedy took a taxi back to Costello's apartment building at 115 Central Park West. Costello exited the cab and walked through the front glass door of the Majestic. He took two steps down and was just about to open the lobby door when a fat man yelled, "This is for you, Frank!" and pegged a shot at Costello just as he turned. The slug went through the side brim of Costello's fedora and glanced off the side of his head. He was not seriously wounded, but that was not immediately apparent. The fat gunman thought Costello was dead, for he quickly fled to a waiting limousine.

The bleeding Costello and his friend Kennedy took a cab to Roosevelt Hospital, where doctors bandaged up his head. Unfortunately for Costello, NYPD detectives found a note in his coat, a financial report on the newly opened Tropicana Hotel/Casino in Las Vegas. An investigation determined that the note was in the handwriting of Lou Lederer, secretary-treasurer of the Tropicana.

Note:

In typical Costello fashion, he paid the $0.45 cab fare with a $5 bill and told the cabbie to keep the change.

Note:

Later information indicated Vincent "Chin" Gigante was the shooter, and hoods Dom Alongi and driver Tommy Eboli were in the get-away vehicle.

Note:

Years later, The FBI taped Buffalo Boss Stefano Magaddino saying that no one told him hoods would kill Costello. When Magaddino contacted that person, he said he didn't tell Magaddino and didn't know himself.

May 7, 1957

General Sessions Judge Jacob Gould Schurman sentenced Costello to 30 days for refusing to answer some questions before a grand jury investigating his shooting. The Judge refused to grant bail, nor would he allow a temporary postponement of the sentence.

May 9, 1957

Supreme Court Justice Edgar J Nathan Jr refused Costello a temporary stay of his contempt sentence. Additionally, officials transferred Costello to Riker's Island on the same day.

June 1957

Federal Judge John F X McGohey began hearings into various dismissal motions by Frank Costello, who hoped to get his tax conviction overturned.

August 19, 1957

Gigante turned himself into the police, who charged the hood with attempted murder. Frank Costello was brought in at 4:45 pm to look at the suspect in his shooting.

August 20, 1957

The Judge arraigned Gigante in Felony Court and set $150,000 bail.

August 22, 1957

A grand jury indicted Gigante for the Costello shooting.

August 23, 1957

A Judge arraigned Gigante in the Costello shooting indictment.

August 29, 1957

Gigante pled not guilty in the Costello shooting.

September 16, 1957

Family and friends of Gigante posted his $100,000 bail (Reduced from $150,000). Rocco Perrotta, who was close to Tommy Eboli, helped bail out Gigante.

September 18, 1957

A Judge released Gigante on bail, but he had to pay a fine for being a scofflaw first.

October 15, 1957

Costello took the stand in the hearings before Federal Judge John F X McGohey. He denied knowing that the feds had obtained the tax returns of 150 potential jurors. Also, he claimed no knowledge that the feds were "watching" (Opening) his incoming mail nor that the IRS had wiretaps on his phones.

ANASTASIA KILLED

October 25, 1957

Hoods associated with Carlo Gambino assassinated Boss Albert Anastasia, an ally of Costello.

November 6, 1957

The US Tax Court in Washington ruled that Costello's Beverley Club in New Orleans owed $175,000 in back taxes.

December 15, 1957

Federal Judge John F X McGohey rejected Costello's motions for a new trial and ordered Costello to surrender on December 23. Costello claimed that the government's use of illegal wiretaps destroyed his chance of a fair trial.

December 23, 1957

Federal Judge John F X McGohey freed Costello on $25,000 bail until January 6, 1958.

April 7, 1958

The Supreme Court threw out Costello's denaturalization proceedings.

May 14, 1958

Phil Kennedy, a Costello friend who accompanied Costello on the night of the shooting, testified he didn't see anyone leave the building after the single shot.

May 15, 1958

The doorman, Norvel Keith, identified Gigante as the shooter.

May 16, 1958

Gigante's defense lawyer very aggressively cross-examined the doorman.

May 20, 1958

From the stand, Costello denied seeing the gunman.

May 20, 1958

The Court of Appeals upheld Judge McGohey's rejection of Costello's appeal for a new trial.

May 21, 1958

Two detectives testified in the Gigante trial.

May 22, 1958

The prosecution rested in the Gigante trial.

May 26, 1958

The defense rested in the Gigante trial.

May 27, 1958

The jury found Gigante not guilty of shooting Costello.

June 17, 1958

The US Court of Appeals freed Costello on bail until the US Supreme Court could hear his tax appeal.

June 30, 1958

The Supreme Court refused to hear Costello's tax appeal. One news reporter claimed that Gigante thanked Costello as he left the courtroom.

July 23, 1958

Federal Judge William B Herlands permitted Costello to remain on bail until July 30, 1958, pending a US Supreme Court ruling on his case.

July 25, 1958

US Supreme Court Justice William Douglas continued Costello on bail until the entire Supreme Court heard his motion for a retrial.

October 13, 1958

Supreme Court turned down Costello's tax case appeal again.

October 20, 1958

US Marshalls took Costello back to prison.

February 20, 1959

US District Judge Archie O Dawson revoked Costello's citizenship. The government alleged Costello misrepresented and concealed information when he got citizenship on September 10, 1925. The government also used Costello's two tax convictions and Kefauver's contempt sentence against him. These charges were yet another round in the government's attempt to deport Costello.

February 17, 1960

The US Court of Appeals rejected Costello's appeal of his loss of citizenship.

February 20, 1961
The US Supreme Court upheld Costello's denaturalization.

March 31, 1961
The feds initiated deportation against Costello by serving him with a show cause order saying why they shouldn't deport him. Additionally, the INS Agents forced Costello to register as an alien. These events took place at Atlanta Penitentiary.

June 20, 1961
Atlanta prison officials released Costello after he finished his tax penalty. However, US Marshalls transferred him to Riker's Island to complete his contempt sentence.

June 28, 1961
Prison officials on Riker's Island freed Costello after he posted a $10,000 bond while he appealed his denaturalization.

October 2, 1961
A special INS hearing officer ordered Costello deported.

January 2, 1962
The Immigration Appeals Court ordered Costello deported.

December 4, 1962
The US Circuit Court of Appeals ruled against Costello in his deportation matter.

April 22, 1963
The Supreme Court agreed to hear Costello's immigration appeal.

DEPORTATION VICTORY AT LAST

February 17, 1964

The Supreme Court ruled that there would be no deportation of Costello. In a brilliant move, Costello's lawyers contended that Costello committed his tax crimes and contempt violation after he became a citizen. Thus, the feds could not use these charges against him in deportation proceedings. As a result, the Supreme Court agreed to end Costello's more than decade-long battle to remain in the United States.

June 3, 1964

While Costello was having lunch in Dinty Moore's tavern, IRS Agents served him with a subpoena to appear before a grand jury investigating gambling. Then the NYPD arrested him for vagrancy. Costello's lawyer Harold Frankel quickly won a dismissal of the ridiculous charge.

As the police escorted Costello out of the tavern, he spoke to a reporter.

"I wasn't doing nothing. I come over to Dinty's for a few drinks and lunch with some guys I know. Next thing, these guys come in and are embarrassing everybody in front of this big crowd. They hustle us out of Dinty's. I don't even get to pay the check. They ask me what I am doing for a living. I say I am retired."

June 5, 1964

Costello appeared for five minutes before a grand jury investigating gambling. They invited him to return at an unspecified date.

May 4, 1970

Joe Coffey, a rising detective in the NYPD, served Frank Costello with a subpoena to appear before a grand jury investigating gambling. At the time, Costello was in the barbershop of the Waldorf-Astoria.

January 28, 1971
Authorities subpoenaed Costello to appear before the New York State Joint Legislative Committee on Crime at their offices a 270 Broadway. They were investigating the relationship between the former Chairman of Schenley Industries (Liquor) and organized crime.

COSTELLO DIES

February 8, 1973
Doctors admitted Frank Costello to Doctor's Hospital.

February 18, 1973
Costello died at Doctors Hospital of an undisclosed illness.

February 21, 1973
Following a short service at the Frank E Campbell Funeral Home, conducted by Reverend Louis Gigante, a few family members and friends led the procession to St Michael's Cemetery in Astoria, Queens, where attendants placed Costello's coffin in the family mausoleum.

COSTELLO'S RETIREMENT ROUTINE

He would visit the barber at the Waldorf-Astoria Hotel daily, followed by a leisurely lunch at some expensive restaurant. After that, Costello might go to a movie or a race track, followed by a visit to the steam baths at the Biltmore Hotel. He occasionally dined out with friends in the evening but often stayed home with his long-time wife, Bobby.

CONCLUSION

Frank Costello was one of America's most powerful Mafia hoods for about twenty years. The imprisoned Charlie Luciano appointed Costello as Acting Boss when Underboss Vito Genovese fled to Italy in 1938 to avoid a murder charge. Costello gradually gained strength, especially when Luciano won his liberty from prison but accepted deportation in 1946.

From then on, everyone accepted that Costello was the official Boss of the Genovese Family. Still, a brief comment overheard on an early 1960s bug in the office of Capo Ray DeCarlo mentioned that Costello's mistake was that he never had himself formally elected as Boss. The implication was that this oversight made Costello vulnerable to the ambitions of Vito Genovese. However, it is most likely that Genovese would have carried out his coup in 1957 even if the Capos had elected Costello.

Costello had an insatiable drive to be recognized as an important, legitimate person. His secret visits to a psychiatrist (Dr. Hoffman) in the late 1940s led to the suggestion that he seek a wider circle of friends. As a result, Costello cultivated politically influential New York personalities in the 1940s and 1950s. His actions led to constant media attention, making him a household name and a target for ambitious prosecutors and law enforcement officers. It is impossible to know whether the political power offset the increased attention. His actions indeed went against the regular La Cosa Nostra habit of remaining in the shadows as much as possible.

CHAPTER FIVE

Vito Genovese

Vito Genovese had little luck during his Mafia career. When it seemed like the Boss position would be open back in 1936 when the government convicted Lucky Luciano, Genovese had to flee to Italy to avoid a murder investigation. When the US Army returned him to New York in 1945 to face a murder indictment, he had some good luck in that Judge dismissed the charges. Then he began a campaign to wrest control of the Family from Frank Costello. When he achieved that Genovese had just a short time to settle in before the Feds nailed him on a narcotics conspiracy and he ended up dying behind bars. Below I summarize Genovese's colorful hard luck life.

DOB
November 27, 1897
Nisigliano, Italy

DOD
February 14, 1969
Springfield Medical Center for Federal Prisoners

May 23, 1913
Genovese arrived in New York aboard the Taormina.

April 15, 1917

A Judge gave Genovese 60 days in jail for illegally possessing a pistol.

VITO AND MARRIAGE

February 2, 1905

Vito's second wife, Anna, was born in New York.

May 25, 1923

Vito's first wife, Donato, gave birth to their daughter Nancy. Years later, Nancy would marry Pasquale Simonetti, and they ran a piano bar at 173 3rd Avenue in Long Branch, NJ.

September 17, 1930

Genovese's wife, Donato, died.

1932

Genovese was living at 43 Fifth Avenue in New York.

March 1932

According to Joe Valachi, Peter Mione and Michael Barrese strangled Gerald Vernotico on Vito Genovese's orders. Police found his body and that of another man on March 16. Vernotico and his wife, Anna, had a daughter named Marie.

March 14, 1932

Genovese married Anna, the widow of Gerard Vernotico. They lived in an apartment at 43 Fifth Ave. in NY. Tony Bender and his wife Edna acted as witnesses. Genovese and his wife did the same for the Benders at the same ceremony.

June 30, 1932

Anna Genovese gave birth to Vito's son Phillip.

July 28, 1932

Genovese attended the wedding reception for Joe Valachi.

July 29, 1932

Three gunmen killed John, James, and Arthur Volpe at 704 Wylie Avenue in Pittsburgh. They shot John in the street while the other two go down in the Roma Coffee Shop. Vito Genovese was outraged, for he was great friends with the three victims. He wanted justice.

According to Nicolo Gentile, Genovese figured that Pittsburgh Boss Joe Bazzano would never have ordered the hits without the support of Albert Anastasia, Boss Vince Mangano (Gambino Family), Capo Joe Biondo, and Gentile. The latter figured Genovese suspected him for the three assassins were in the crew of Gentile when he was a member of the Pittsburgh Family. Gentile denied any involvement in the massacre.

August 6, 1932 (?)

Genovese made plans to kill his four suspects, but Anastasia convinced the powerful Underboss that they were all innocent. Furthermore, Anastasia promised to give Genovese satisfaction. He, Mangano, and Biondo met with Bazzano in New York. Unfortunately for Bazzano, he insisted he had acted properly in the killings, which was not what the others wanted to hear. They quickly killed the Pittsburgh Boss, and some men sewed the body in a bag and dumped it in the street. This revenge appeased Genovese.

August 7, 1932

Then NYPD found the strangled and stabbed body of John Bazzano in a sack in Brooklyn. The cops rushed around and arrested fourteen men, but the DA had to dismiss the charges quickly.

Note:

When three gunmen killed the Volpe brothers, they also wounded a brother of Boss Bazzano.

March 14, 1933

Vito Genovese filed his Declaration of Intent, a step towards naturalization (See Nov 25, 1936). He gave his address as 178 Thompson Street, NY, and his occupation as a contractor.

1934

Joe Valachi and Bobby Doyle Santucci received permission from Vito Genovese to enter the numbers racket.

September 19, 1934

Hoods killed Ferdinand Boccia in his uncle's Circolo Christofolo Club at 533 Metropolitan Ave in Brooklyn. Police did not find his body until May 11, 1937, in the Hudson River. The story was that Boccia had participated in scamming some sucker but was unhappy with his loot cut.

October 3, 1934

Rupolo shot Willie Gallo four times and also stabbed him, but Gallo lived to identify Rupolo. The driver was Ernest Filocomo, who eventually got 4-5 years after pleading to attempted assault.

January 28, 1935

Genovese purchased the Dangler Mansion and its 35 acres at 152 Red Hill Road in Middleton Township, NJ. The Genovese family lived in an apartment in New York and used the mansion occasionally. Genovese had a massive Italian garden constructed that included a functioning replica volcano. The grounds included a tennis court, a three-hole golf course, and a riding stable along with trails.

December 19, 1935

Genovese filed his Petition for Naturalization, giving his address as 43 5th Ave in NY, and also stated he was a contractor.

August 6, 1936

Hoods killed Dominick "Terry Burns" Didato in front of 90 Elizabeth Street. The famous mob veteran Nicolo Gentile claimed Genovese men murdered Didato, who feared Didato was going to make a move for Luciano's throne.

November 25, 1936

The United States naturalized Genovese as a US citizen.

December 14, 1936

The US granted a passport to Genovese Numbered 358060.

1937

The Genovese Dangler Mansion burned to the ground. Several contractors, including Dominic Caruso of Genovese divorce fame, had been working there. Caruso bought the land in 1948 but sold it a few years later. It is now a part of the beautiful Monmouth County Deep Cut Gardens.

December 1937

Genovese traveled to Italy. In the early 1950s, his wife Anna, testified she made three trips to Italy between 1937 and 1939 transporting about $40,000 on each occasion to Vito from his brother Michael.

Note:

Joe Valachi, when he was in the Atlanta Penitentiary with Genovese in 1960, Vito told him he took $750,000 ($15,000,000 in 2022) when he fled to Italy.

Note:

The exact date Genovese left remains to be determined.

May 11, 1937

Police found the body of Ferdinand Boccia in the Hudson River.

1939-1943

Many reports indicated that Genovese ingratiated himself with the Italian fascists, but unfortunately, exaggerated claims have muddied the truth of this cooperation. Whatever the case, Genovese had no trouble switching his support to the victorious allies when they arrived in Italy.

January 1943

Prison authorities released Rupolo, who was serving time on the Gallo murder attempt back in 1934.

September 28, 1943

A Genovese lawyer incorporated the Vito Genovese Trading Company.

July 5, 1944

Authorities took Peter LaTempa into custody as a material witness in the Boccia murder and held him on a $50,000 material witness bond.

August 6, 1944

A grand jury indicted Genovese et al. for the 1934 Boccia murder.

August 15, 1944

Rupolo won an indefinite postponement in his sentencing for his first-degree assault charge because he was cooperating with the good guys.

August 27, 1944

Provost Marshall Constance Dickey arrested Genovese in Italy for black market activities. Fortunately, his investigation revealed the Genovese murder indictment, so Dickey began a frustrating journey to get authorities interested in bringing Genovese back to the US to face trial.

November 3, 1944

A Genovese lawyer dissolved the Vito Genovese Trading Company and renamed it the Colonial Trading Company with an office at 270 6th Ave, NY.

November 24, 1944

Acting DA Thomas Hughes announced the apprehension of Genovese by the army in Italy.

December 6, 1944

Peter LaTempa attempted suicide by hanging in Brooklyn Civil Prison, where he was a material witness in the Boccia murder from 1934.

January 15, 1945

Correctional officers took LaTempa out for a walk, and he visited a drug store. Later that day, his brother Sylvester saw him in prison.

January 16, 1945

Guards found Peter LaTempa (35) dead in his cell at 8 AM in Brooklyn Civil Prison. He had been held there since July 5, 1944.

February 9, 1945

Assistant DA Edward Hefferman announced he received an official report from the city toxicologist, Dr. Alexander Gettler, stating that LaTempa died of an overdose of sleeping pills. Hefferman also said his investigation showed that no one could have murdered LaTempa in the civil prison.

May 17, 1945

Genovese and Army Provost Marshall Constance Dickey boarded the SS James Lykes at Bari, Italy.

June 1, 1945

Genovese arrived back in the USA aboard the ship James Lykes in the custody of Dickey.

June 2, 1945

A Judge arraigned Genovese in Kings County Court, where the gangster denied his guilt in the Boccia killing.

October 18, 1945

On radio station, WOR DA George J Beldock of Brooklyn charged that O'Dwyer was responsible for a 12-month delay in seeking the extradition of Genovese and Mike Miranda from Italy.

November 19, 1945

Judge Samuel Leibowitz disclosed that an informant had told him of a plan to poison Rupolo in the old Bronx County Jail six months ago.

June 7, 1946

Genovese's defense filed a motion to have the case dismissed.

June 10, 1946

Judge Leibowitz dismissed the case but told Genovese, "...if there were even a shred of corroborating evidence, you would have been condemned to the electric chair."

June 11, 1946

Officials released Genovese.

1946

Genovese purchased his Atlantic Highlands home at 130 Ocean Blvd.

June 15, 1946

As a reward for his cooperation in the Genovese case, the Judge gave Ernie Rupolo a suspended sentence in the Boccia killing.

June 18, 1946

Genovese registered for the draft. He gave his address as 29 Washington Street W NY.

September 16, 1946

Mike Miranda surrendered in the Boccia case after Judge Leibowitz dismissed the charge against Genovese. Authorities held Miranda without bail.

June 9, 1947

Judge Leibowitz freed defendants Smurra, DeFeo, and Frasca in the Boccia case.

THE GENOVESE DIVORCE SAGA

March 1950

Anna Genovese left the family home.

1951

The Vito Genovese-owned Atlantic Highlands Wharf burned to the ground, and Genovese dissolved the company.

September 8, 1951

Philip Genovese married Rose Marie Calandriello.

January 10, 1952

Superior Court Judge Donald McLean ordered Vito Genovese to pay his wife $300 weekly in temporary support.

September 19, 1952

According to Joe Valachi's testimony in 1963, Lucky Luciano passed word from Italy that Soldier Eugene Giannini was an informer. Capo Tony Bender gave this information to Valachi and explained that they had difficulty finding the rat. However, everyone knew Giannini owed Valachi money, so he became fearful that his leaders would think he was hiding Giannini so he would get paid. To counter this possibility, Valachi offered to take care of Giannini.

Valachi recruited Joe and Pasquale, the Pagano brothers, and his nephew Fiori Siano, all Associates anxious to earn their buttons in the Genovese Family. They arranged to walk Giannini to a gambling den, but one of them put two .38 slugs in his head. Ironically, other gangsters threw the body in a car and dropped it off several blocks away to avoid responding police discovering the gambling joint.

November 21, 1952

Feds start denaturalization proceedings against Genovese in Newark.

December 22, 1952

Caruso Construction filed a $32,724 suit against Genovese for non-payment of construction work on his home. This claim was a Genovese ploy in his support battle with his wife.

1953

Genovese began living in a rented modest bungalow in Atlantic Highlands, NJ., at 68 West Highland Ave.

December 9, 1952

Before Judge McLean, Anna Genovese sued for separate maintenance. Genovese sued for divorce, claiming Anna abandoned him.

1953

Joe Valachi later claimed that Genovese ordered the murder of Dom "The Gap" Petrilli for being an informer. Valachi testified that Ettore Cocco was the driver and that Anthony Lo Pinto was involved. He also believed that Joseph Bendinelli and Anthony Castaldi were in on it.

January 3, 1953

A New York Journal American story said Anna Genovese said that Vito wanted to marry the wife of Thomas Calandriello, the father-in-law of Genovese's son Philip. Calandriello ran SeaCoast Liquor Distributor for Genovese.

January 30, 1953

Judge McLean again ordered Genovese to start paying his wife $300/month in temporary support plus $1500 for her lawyer. He doesn't.

February 10, 1953

Anna Genovese petitioned Judge McLean to imprison Vito Genovese for his failure to pay support. The Judge reserved a decision but also denied Vito a stay in making payments.

March 2, 1953

Anna Genovese testified that one racket brought Vito a net of $20,000 to $30,000 per week. Anna also described a meeting with Nazi power Herman Goring and Mussolini's relative Count Ciano in Italy before the war. Judge McLean was also hearing Vito's divorce petition.

March 5, 1953

Anna Genovese claimed she received threats.

March 10, 1953

Judge McLean held Vito in contempt for failing to pay his wife temporary support. However, he withheld issuing a warrant to give Vito time to appeal.

March 12, 1953

Genovese's lawyer said Vito couldn't pay the $32,999 judgment against him from Caruso Construction. Vito's wife wouldn't sign papers so he could mortgage their home to get the money.

March 19, 1953

Anna Genovese testified for 2 hours before a Hudson County Grand Jury.

March 23, 1953

The Appellate Division of the NJ Supreme Court upheld Judge McLean's January 30, 1953, ruling that Genovese had to start making support payments and cough up $5,700 in missed alimony or risk going to prison.

March 25, 1953

Mrs. Genovese appeared before the New York State Law Enforcement Council and testified that Vito had no interest in Club 82 or the Moroccan

Club. The Council attempted to learn whether gangsters had hidden interests in these joints.

April 6, 1953

The Sheriff was to sell Genovese's home to meet a $32,000 judgment against Vito by the Caruso Construction Company, which worked on the residence in 1948 and 1949. Caruso had testified for Vito in his divorce trial. He said the home was worth $55,000, while Mrs. Genovese said it was worth $250,000.

Judge McLean gave Vito a delay so Vito could have a fair chance to show why he should be allowed to sell the family home to meet his financial responsibilities.

April 10, 1953

One of the witnesses in Anna's maintenance suit was a doctor. He testified that contrary to Anna's testimony earlier in the year, he never treated her for injuries suffered at the hand of Vito.

April 11, 1953

Judge McLean heard testimony from the lawyers for Vito and Anna that there were plans to sell the family home to meet Vito's financial obligations. Accordingly, he provided a two-week delay in Vito's contempt situation.

April 17, 1953

In testimony before the New York State Liquor Authority, Anna Genovese denied Vito held any interest in licensed premises in New York State. This account contradicted her statements in divorce court.

April 24, 1953

Judge McLean gave Vito two more weeks to ante up in arrears support payments, or he would send Genovese to prison.

May 7 and 8, 1953

O'Reilly's Plaza Art Galleries auctioned some of Genovese's furniture to meet his back support payments. They netted $7,200.

May 9, 1953

Anna Genovese complained to Judge McLean that Vito still needed to meet his financial obligations to her. As a result, the Judge held Vito in contempt but withheld issuing an arrest warrant until Vito's appeal took place.

May 11, 1953

Genovese appealed to the NJ Superior Court Appellate Division. He wanted to avoid paying the $300/month Judge McLean ordered. Mrs. Genovese's lawyer said Vito was trying to avoid tax problems.

June 12, 1953

In an affidavit, Vito told Judge McLean that he was so broke he had to sell his car. Genovese also denied making rackets money as his wife claimed. As a result, Judge McLean delayed a decision.

June 18, 1953

Joe Valachi later testified that Genovese had Steve Franse killed. He was a partner with Anna in a nightclub, and according to Valachi, Genovese had ordered Franse to keep an eye on his wife while he was in Italy. Genovese was not pleased with Franse's work.

August 19, 1953

Judge McLean dismissed Mrs. Genovese's temporary support payments and Vito's divorce petition.

August 25, 1953

The Sheriff was to sell the Genovese home to meet a $32,000 construction bill Genovese still needed to pay.

September 11, 1953

Judge McLean dismissed Anna Genovese's maintenance suit plus Vito's plea for a divorce. Judge McLean commented that Anna "...ought to go back and live with Vito." Earlier, on the stand, both said that they were willing to reconcile. The Judge said Vito should give Anna $9,000 in back alimony plus $6,000 for her lawyer fees.

December 21, 1953

Mrs. Genovese asked the NJ Superior Court Appellate Division to reinstate her temporary $300-month support. The court reserved its decision.

January 27, 1954

The Superior Court Appellate Division upheld Judge McLean's dismissal of a separate maintenance suit by Anna Genovese.

May 18, 1955

Anna Genovese testified before the Waterfront Commission, investigating whether the ILA should fire five hiring officials at the Leonardo New Jersey Naval Pier. The Commission accused the men of insisting on pay from those they hired.

Mrs. Genovese said Thomas Callandriello visited their home nearly daily and gave Vito money. In addition, Anna testified the men talked about hiring, bookmaking, and loansharking. She also said she reneged on reconciliation with Vito because she feared him.

Note:

While Vito was in Italy, his wife made a living by managing nightclubs in New York. For example, she ran the Club Caravan at 578 Broadway and worked as the manager of Club 82 at 82 East Fourth Street. Both these venues featured gay performers, which attracted a sizeable gay clientele. In addition, she and Steve Franse opened the 181 Club in Manhattan, which continually faced police pressure due to its openly gay theme. Eventually, the NY State Liquor Authority pulled their license.

At some point, Vito testified that Anna drew $300 a month from the Vito Trading Company from 1939-1946.

In later life, Anna worked in public relations for the prestigious Warwick Hotel and was openly gay, at least to her close friends. She died in January 1982. Former mob Boss Joe Bonanno wrote that no one ever mentioned Anna in Vito's presence.

Note:

An Apple podcast called "Mob Queens" delves into Anna's colorful life. It has at least 12 chapters, and although I have never listened to it, a friend claimed it was fascinating.

August 16, 1955
US District Court Judge Philip Forman stripped Genovese of his citizenship.

August 22, 1956
The Third Circuit Court of Appeals upheld Judge Forman's ruling on Genovese's citizenship.

December 17, 1956
The US Supreme Court refused to review the revoking of Genovese's citizenship.

May 2, 1957
As I outlined in the Costello chapter, Soldier Vince Gigante, a Genovese man, wounded Boss Frank Costello leading to his resignation as leader of the Family. Vito took over.

November 14, 1957

New York State troopers disrupted a National Meeting of La Cosa Nostra at Boss Joe Barbara's estate near Apalachin, NY. They identified Vito Genovese as he departed the scene in a 1957 Chrysler Imperial. Underboss Russ Bufalino drove the vehicle, and his other passengers were Genovese Family Underboss Jerry Catena, Philadelphia Boss Joseph Ida, and Dom Olivetta.

December 11, 1957

Genovese appeared before a Special GJ of the SDNY investigating the Apalachin meeting.

July 2, 1956

Before the Senate Rackets Committee, Genovese took the 5th 150 times to various questions.

July 7, 1958

Federal narcotics agents arrested Genovese, Gigante, and others in a narcotics conspiracy. US Attorney Paul Williams described Genovese as "The hub around which the entire conspiracy revolved."

July 8, 1958

Authorities arraigned Genovese, Gigante, and others before Federal Judge Williams Herlands. He released Genovese on $50,000 bail.

1958

The Journal American interviewed Genovese in his modest home. The gangster told a tale of innocence and bewilderment about why he was a target.

January 5, 1959

The Genovese drug trial began.

April 3, 1959

A federal grand jury convicted the following people of a drug conspiracy: Federal Judge Alexander Bicks made the subsequent rulings:

Genovese-no bail

Gigante-cont'd on bail

Natale Evola-cont'd on bail of $35,000

Salvatore Santora-remanded

Charles DiPalermo-remanded, later released on $15,000 bail

Joseph DiPalermo-remanded

Charles Barcelona-remanded

Jean Capece-cont'd on bail of $5,000

Daniel Lessa-remanded

Nicholas Lessa-remanded

Rocco Mazzie-remanded

Carmine Polizzano-cont'd on bail

Ralph Polizzano-remanded

Benjamen Rodgriquez-remanded

Alfredo Aviles-remanded

April 17, 1959

Federal Judge Alexander Bicks handed out the following sentences:

Genovese - 15 yrs. and no bail

Gigante-seven yrs.

Natale Evola-10 yrs., $20,000, bail raised to $50,000

Salvatore Santora-20 yrs.

Charles DiPalermo-12 yrs. bail raised to $25,000

Joseph DiPalermo—15yrs, $20,000, no bail

Charles Barcelona—5yrs

Jean Capece—5yrs, bail increased to $12,000

Daniel Lessa—14yrs

Nicholas Lessa—12yrs

Rocco Mazzie—12yrs

Carmine Polizzano-8yrs

Ralph Polizzano-7yrs

Benjamen Rodgriquez-10yrs

Alfredo Aviles-10yrs

May 1959

A grand jury indicted Valachi in a narcotic conspiracy, but he fled.

June 5, 1959

The Second Circuit Court of Appeals released Genovese on $150,000 bail.

June 11, 1959

In testimony before the NJ State Investigation Committee, Genovese said he naively went to Apalachin at the request of friend Joseph Ida (Then Boss of Philadelphia). Genovese, Ida, Jerry Catena, and Dom Olivetto flew from Newark to Binghamton together. Also on the same plane were Jerry Catena and Mike Miranda. Genovese stated that he didn't know host Joe Barbara and that this incident made him a target of law enforcement officers and the media, leading to his unfair conviction in his drug trial.

1959

Genovese transferred his shares of Erb Strapping to his brother Michael.

July 1, 1959

New York Governor Nelson Rockefeller rewarded Cantellops for his Genovese testimony by reducing his prison sentence from 3 1/2 years to two years and eight days. The parole board would release Cantellops when they met on July 16.

September 25, 1959

Shooters killed Capo Augie Pisano and Janice Drake as they sat in Pisano's Caddy. They had been dining with two other couples and Tony Strollo at Marino's Restaurant when Pisano received a call from Frank "Frank Cassina" Cucola to arrange a meeting. (Apparently, Bonanno Associate Anthony Mirra was also in the restaurant.) So Pisano and Drake drove off in the gangster's Caddy. A witness saw two men fleeing from Pisano's vehicle parked in front of 24-50 94th Street in Jackson Heights, Queens. The cops came and discovered the two bodies.

An autopsy revealed that Pisano had a shot to the left temple and one to the left neck. Another killer fired one shot into Janice Drake's head from behind. The hoods used .32 and .38 pistols. At least one must have been a semi-automatic, for cops found one spent shell in the back seat.

Police never charged anyone with the murders, but everyone understood that Vito Genovese was involved.

September 28, 1959
Pisano's family held a wake for the murdered Capo.

November 19, 1959
Narcotics agents arrested Valachi then the Judge released him on $25,000 bail.

January 12, 1960
The Second Court of Appeal rejected the appeal of Genovese and nine other defendants. A quote from their decision, "There is sufficient proof against those planning and strategizing of the conspiracy and expansion of business... such a Vito Genovese."

February 8, 1960
The Judge refused to permit Genovese to remain free while he appealed to the US Supreme Court.

February 11, 1960
Genovese surrendered to Federal Judge Sidney Sugarman.

February 1960
Valachi fled New York and hid with Buffalo Soldier Albert Agueci in Toronto.

February 26, 1960
Prison officials sent Genovese to Atlanta.

March 28, 1960

Valachi pled guilty to narcotics conspiracy in NYC and later admitted to talking with narcotics agents.

April 5, 1960

Michael Genovese visited Vito in Atlanta.

April 26, 1960

Solicitor General J Lee Rankin asked the US Supreme Court to refuse to review Genovese's drug conviction because a grand jury was investigating a bribe involving the chief prosecution witness Nelson Cantellops.

May 1, 1960

Judge Bricks denied a new trial for Genovese and other defendants.

CANTELLOPS RECANTATION SUMMARY

Starting in January of 1960, Cantellops began receiving a series of calls asking him to change his trial testimony. Finally, on January 24, he signed a recantation statement in a lawyer's office. Three days later, the lawyer, accompanied by others, taped Cantellops' recantation. The following day in lawyer Siegel's office, defendant John Ormento gave Cantellops $3000 and promised $30,000 more if the plan worked.

On February 2, 1960, Cantellops got cold feet and rushed to the FBI and explained about the recantation plot. He claimed that it was fear and bribery that caused him to participate. The following day the DA hauled him in front of a grand jury to repeat his tale.

Surprisingly the hoods did not give up on Cantellops. Instead, at the request of Ormento, the witness went to lawyer Siegel's office twice more, and a hidden recording device captured his disjointed and muffled statements on June 20 and June 22, 1960. Cantellops later told the court that he was acting under suggestion and duress. Various Judges accepted this explanation and rejected his statements as grounds for a new trial.

May 16, 1960

The US Supreme Court refused to hear the appeals of Genovese and other defendants.

June 3, 1960

A Judge sentenced Valachi to 15 yrs. and a $10,000 fine after a jury convicted him of a narcotics conspiracy.

June 12, 1960

The Second Circuit Court of Appeals refused a new trial for Genovese and the other defendants.

June 17, 1960

Valachi was in Atlanta.

Note:

Valachi said Genovese was very sentimental about his former wife Anna and claimed he saw tears in Vito's eyes on one occasion when her name came up.

July 28, 1960

Michael Genovese visited his brother Vito for about twenty minutes in Atlanta.

October 1960

Man's Magazine featured a story under the byline Nelson Cantellops with Don Frasca entitled "I Squealed on the Mafia." It was a highly fictionalized account of the Nelson Cantellops affair. Genovese vainly tried to use the article in a more significant attempt for a new trial.

August ??, 1961

Prison officials returned Valachi to New York for a second drug trial. Again, authorities held him in the Federal Detention Center with Buffalo Solder Albert Agueci.

August 25, 1960
Michael Genovese visited Vito for about an hour in Atlanta.

September 15, 1960
The INS made out a deportation warrant against Genovese.

February 13, 1960
A Judge sentenced Valachi to twenty years for a narcotics conspiracy.

April 8, 1962
Former Genovese favorite Capo Tony Bender disappeared from his Fort Lee, NJ home. On a secret FBI tape, Capo Ray DeCarlo was recorded saying he told Chicago Boss Sam Giancanna that Genovese Soldier Little Pussy Russo hit Bender. Turncoat Joe Valachi told the FBI that Bender angered Genovese, who responded with a hit order.

April 12, 1962
Edna Strollo reported her husband missing to Fort Lee, NJ cops.

April 14, 1962
Three FBI Agents visited Edna Strollo at her home. They didn't learn much. Later reporters talked to Mrs. Strollo, who said she was surprised Strollo was missing, for the FBI had been following him for years.

April 5, 1963
Hudson County Prosecutor James A Tumultoy ordered a search of an abandoned quarry in North Bergen, NJ, but there was no sign of Strollo's body.

June 26, 1963
The FBI taped Acting Underboss Tom Eboli talking to Mike Genovese, brother of Vito. Eboli explained that Genovese had repeatedly warned Capo Augi Pisano about infractions by Vito Genovese. When Pisano continued to disobey Vito's orders, Vito had him killed.

October 16, 1963

Under heavy guard, Valachi testified before a grand jury investigating mob murders.

1963

The Second Circuit Court of Appeals rejected a new trial for Genovese, Gigante, and others.

October 21, 1963

The US Supreme Court ordered a review of Genovese's conviction by the Second Court of Appeals. They had rejected the defenses' contention that the good guys violated the defendants' rights when they didn't turn over the interview notes of witness Nelson Cantellops. At this point, Vito was in Leavenworth prison in Kansas.

October 16, 1964

The Second Court of Appeals rejected a new trial for Genovese, Gigante, et al.

March 1, 1965

The US Supreme Court upheld a Second Court of Appeals ruling that dismissed appeals by Genovese and nine other defendants.

April 6, 1965

A recording device in the office of Michael Genovese captured Eboli telling Genovese that Acting Boss Jerry Catena wanted to step down and that Eboli wanted Capo Phil Lombardo as the new Boss. Eboli claimed to have several capos supporting his view. Apparently, Lombardo was very cautious and wanted to talk to Catena personally. Eboli said he would act as Lombardo's Underboss.

June 15, 1965

Turncoat Harold "Kayo" Konigsburg, a Bonanno Associate, told the FBI about the Bender murder. He believed Tommy Eboli was the main instigator because Bender was dealing junk. Eboli got Acting Boss Jerry Catena onside, and then they received Genovese's approval. Associate Pepe Sabato called Bender and took him to the parking lot of the Milestone Restaurant in Fort Lee, NJ. Eboli and Dom DeQuatro killed Bender and buried him on an upstate NJ farm. Konigsberg also said that the Genovese leadership demoted Bender before his hit and that Dom DeQuatro was appointed Acting Capo.

COMMENT

It seems unlikely that Genovese et al. would put Bender on his guard with this demotion.

July 15, 1965

Nelson Cantellops, the Genovese witness, died in a barroom brawl when a mutt knifed him. There is no evidence of this being a revenge hit for the Genovese case.

July 22, 1966

District Court Judge Weinfeld rejected Genovese's drug appeal stating there was conclusive evidence that he was involved in the drug conspiracy. He said, "There is no substance to Genovese's contention that evidence was lacking to support knowledge of the illegal importation of drugs."

March 28, 1967

Informant NKT-2 told the FBI that Genovese had made Capo Phil Lombardo the new Family Boss.

1968

The Waterfront Commission was investigating the Erb Strapping Company, so Michael Genovese sold his shares back to the entity for $60,000 plus interest.

Note:

Arthur Erb founded the company and died in 1945. His son Arthur Jr took over but was an alcoholic forcing his sister to take the reins. Genovese reportedly bought 49% of Erb for $450. The company expanded into Philly and the Miami docks. The company's 1955 gross was $100,000, while 1970 was $1.5 million.

December 25, 1968

A New York Times story reported that Genovese still ran the crime Family from prison.

February 14, 1969

Genovese died of a heart attack in the Medical Center for federal prisoners in Springfield, Missouri. The family had his body transported to the modest Andersons Funeral Home in Red Bank, NJ.

February 18, 1969

Genovese's family held a funeral in St Agnes Church in Atlanta Highlands with about 150 mourners present. They interred his body in the family mausoleum at St John's Cemetery in Middle Village Queens.

June 24, 1969

Lawyers released Genovese's September 5, 1950 will, but it did not include a total of his worth. He gave his daughter Nancy 90% while his son Philip got 10% of an unknown amount.

CONCLUSION

Vito Genovese was the epitome of an Italian American gangster. He was cunning and vicious and never hesitated to use murder as a weapon to gain or hold on to his position. Sadly for him, he only had a few years on the street as Boss. The rest of the time he was locked away trying to maintain control from behind bars. His only real legacy was having his criminal organization named after him more than fifty years after his passing.

CHAPTER SIX

Jerry Catena

Catena was a well-known name in the 1960s. Vito Genovese had appointed him as Acting Boss supported by Acting Underboss Tommy Eboli and Consigliere Mike Miranda. Since he was located in New Jersey, Miranda delegated Eboli as the man to see in New York. However wiretaps and informers made it clear Miranda had the top spot. Miranda's power began to wane when he refused to testify before the New Jersey Investigation Committee. Except for some furloughs and medical visits, Miranda spent five years behind bars. On his release in 1975 Miranda retreated to Florida and was a non-factor afterwards. His story follows.

DOB
January 9, 1902
South Orange, NJ

DOD
April 23, 2000
Florida

Wife
Catherine McNally
Five kids
Brother Eugene Catena
Two sisters.

1930

The US Census found Catena living at his father's home at 176 Oliver Street in Newark.

September 19, 1930

During a raid on the Rising Sun Brewery, someone shot and killed Prohibition Agent John G Finiello. Future Decavalcante Boss Nick Delmore quickly became a suspect. Later a jury found him not guilty of the killing, but the feds laid an obstruction of justice charge against Delmore in 1933.

Catena comes into the story at this point as explained below.

May 26, 1933

Superior Court Judge Joseph B Perskie of New Jersey announced he would investigate firearm licenses after the press revealed that many hoods were walking around with legal guns.

June 9, 1933

Common Pleas Judge Harry Truax conducted four days of hearings into gun permits in Monmouth County in New Jersey. When Catena appeared, he voluntarily gave up his gun license.

January 20, 1934

Catena, a Toms River cop, and two other men visited juror Alonzo C Applegate at his home and offered him $100 if he helped acquit Delmore of his obstruction of justice charge. In addition, they promised him another $400 to help acquit other defendants. Applegate revealed the bribe event to federal agents who set up a sting.

January 23, 1934

Applegate agreed to meet Catena et al. at the home of the Toms River cop. After Applegate entered the house and exited with the $100 bribe, officers raided the residence and arrested the four men.

January 24, 1934
US Commissioner Marvin A Spaulda arraigned Catena and the three other men and set bail at $10,000 each. He put another hearing for January 31.

February 1, 1934
A jury found Nick Delmore not guilty of obstructing justice with a firearm.

March 13, 1934
Rather than testifying at the trial of former Toms River Police Chief John Costa, Catena pled guilty to the bribery charge. Federal Judge Phillip Foreman sentenced him to three months in jail and a $500 fine.

1937
Abner Zwillman and Associate Mike Lascari purchased the Public Service Tobacco Company from Catena.

December 12, 1950
The Kefauver Hearings were supposed to examine Catena, but an alleged heart ailment confined him to bed. Nevertheless, gambling and racketeering in New York City and New Jersey were the focus of the Committee at this time.

February 14, 1951
Catena refused to talk about his income in his testimony before the Kefauver Committee. Probably, he was concerned about a possible tax probe.

March 26, 1951
At the Kefauver Hearings, Abner Zwillman revealed his 1937 purchase of a vending machine business from Catena. He also testified that he had known Catena for a long time and was aware that Catena regularly golfed with Frank Costello (Boss of the Genovese Family).

October 4, 1951

Shooters killed Genovese Family Underboss Willie Moretti. Police held Catena as a material witness, but nothing came of this line of investigation.

November 14, 1957

New York State Troopers discovered a National Meeting of La Cosa Nostra near Appalachia, NY. Among the gangsters, they identified were Genovese Boss Vito Genovese, Underboss Jerry Catena, and Consigliere Mike Miranda.

November 19, 1957

In response to the Appalachia affair, the Newark Police questioned attendees Tony Riela (Bonanno Family) and Frank Majuri (Decavalcante Family) because they were residents of New Jersey. They were unable to find Catena.

December 1957

A Mercer County grand jury questioned Vito Genovese, Catena, Philly Boss Joe Ida, and Dom Olivetto.

November 13, 1958

When a new owner took over a Newark tavern, she bought a new vending machine from a non-union company. Unfortunately, Catena's Runyon Vending refused to remove their device, and Teamster Local 575 quickly began picketing the joint unless the new provider joined the union. These tactics forced the police and politicians to look into the vending business and its connection to organized crime.

November 1958

The New York State Commission of Investigation began an inquiry into the jukebox industry.

1959

Boss Vito Genovese, jammed up on a narcotics charge, and elevated Underboss Jerry Catena to Acting Boss.

Capo Tom Eboli became the Acting Underboss. Mike Miranda continued as the Family's Consigliere.

February 10, 1959

Catena appeared before the Senate Rackets Committee but took the 5th to most questions. The Committee focused on the link between labor unions and the vending machine business. At this time, Catena's Runyon Vending Sales owned about 800 jukeboxes, about 200 cigarette machines, and a similar number of pinball games.

March 13, 1959

Two FBI Agents interviewed Catena at his Runyon Sales Company in New Jersey.

October 10, 1960

Catena was at the Arlington Hotel in Hot Springs, Arkansas.

November 2, 1960

FBI informant LR T-6 told his handler that he saw Catena in Hot Springs, Arkansas, at the Arlington Hotel.

November 7, 1960

Informant LR T-6 saw Catena talking with notorious gangster Owney Madden in Hot Springs.

Informant PH T-9 told the FBI that a dispute between Genovese Capo Ray DeCarlo and Philadelphia Soldier Caponigro required a sit down with Genovese Acting Boss Catena and Philly Boss Bruno. The argument was over who would be in charge of controlling police protection for gambling in Newark.

January 1, 1963

Soldier Dom La Placa died. Catena arranged to have money passed to his widow.

January 1963

FBI informer NK T-33 said that Catena, Abe Green, and two other men applied for $100,000 life insurance whose beneficiary would be the NJ Tobacco Company.

February 23, 1963

An FBI bug overheard a mobster claiming that Jerry Catena supported Angelo Bruno as the new Boss of Philadelphia because Bruno bought all his cigarette vending machines from Catena.

March 12, 1963

FBI informant NK T-34 said that Catena was back from Florida.

March 1963

Capo Richie Boiardo met with Catena in Florida to discuss the recent murder of James Del Grosso at the Essex County Fishing Club in Newark. Later information revealed that the killing had nothing to do with the mob but sparked a series of gambling investigations.

March 1963

Genovese Soldiers Peter De Feo and Lorenzo Bresica had the right to transport bananas from the New York docks. However, the banana boats had been unloading at Port Newark, so the two mobsters met with Capo Eugene Catena to ensure they would continue to hold the rights of banana transportation at that location.

April 25, 1963

Catena returned from a trip to Florida.

May 1963

An FBI bug in the office of Boss Sam Decavalcante overhead Sam explained that Las Vegas skim money traveled to Catena with Capos Richie Boiardo and Angelo DeCarlo receiving a cut.

FBI informant NK T-13 said that Catena received $150,000 yearly from the Las Vegas skim.

May 5, 1963
Philadelphia Boss Angelo Bruno told Buffalo Boss Stefano Magaddino that he had advised Genovese Acting Boss Catena to flee to Italy to avoid increased police surveillance.

June 1963
Catena threw his support behind Teddy Gleason in his run for president of the International Longshoremen. (Gleason won the election and held the post until his retirement in 1987.)

1964
Catena settled a dispute with the Gambino Family by returning the rights to collect garbage at the Copacabana to the Gambinos. However, Acting Underboss Tommy Eboli was not happy with this decision.

January 25, 1964
An FBI bug heard Capo Angelo DeCarlo criticize Acting Boss Catena because he rarely met with DeCarlo.

March 1964
Eugene Catena, Jerry's brother, sent word that Genovese Soldier and union power George Barone should stay out of the Newark docks.

March 1964
A secret FBI bug overheard Boss Sam Decavalcante telling some of his men that Underboss Jerry Catena ran New Jersey for the Genovese Family. At the same time, Capo Tom Eboli controlled New York.

November 1964
An FBI bug in the office of Buffalo Boss Stefano Magaddino overheard him say that Catena "Is another disgrace." Magaddino was not pleased with the

lack of support from Catena in Magaddino's efforts to expel Bonanno Boss Joe Bonanno.

December 9, 1964

An informant told the FBI that Catena ordered all members of the Teamsters to cooperate with Tony Provenzano in New Jersey.

January 19, 1965

A federal grand jury in New York questioned Catena and Eboli about the whereabouts of Joe Bonanno. The two gangsters knew nothing.

January 27, 1965

Catena told Tony Provenzano that Port Newark was for the International Longshoremen, not the Teamsters. Provenzano was a Genovese Family member and a Teamster power.

April 29, 1965

An Essex County grand jury disclosed that the PR Director of the Newark Police also was a part-time employee of Catena's Automatic Merchants Inc. (A vending company.) The grand jury was investigating police protection of gamblers.

May 6, 1965

The Newark Mayor Hugh Addonizio fired the PR Director of the Newark Police.

Note:

Addonizio was crooked and later went to prison.

August 1965

Violent Bonanno Associate Harold Konigsberg told the FBI that Genovese Acting Boss Jerry Catena disliked Genovese Acting Underboss Tommy Eboli.

August 4, 1967
Capo Gene Catena died of heart failure.

CATENA VS A&P

In 1964 Nathan Sobol, President of the North American Chemical Company, wished to increase the sales of his new cleaning product. Through a long-time friend, Frank Palmieri, he met and discussed the matter with Gene Catena, owner of the Best Sales Company. Sobol signed a ten-year contract after Best Sales promised the moon.

Sobol then presented his product to the A&P, but, unfortunately, the company found "Poly-Clean" inferior to its competitors. Then in 1965, shooters killed A&P manager James Walsh on January 23 and John Mossler on February 5. In addition, 15 A&P warehouses or stores suffered arson attacks. Fortunately, A&P did not fold under pressure.

In 1968 the Waterfront Commission held a hearing at which Nathan Sobol testified about his relationship with Best Sales and Gene Catena. Sobol said he bought back his contract with Best Sales after Catena said he was sick and wanted to retire. (Sobol paid $28,800 yearly for 13 years.) No one paid much attention to this story until Queen's DA Thomas J Mackell announced the indictment of an A&P warehouse employee for arson. Mackell linked that fire to 15 other arsons or attempted arsons against A&P and the murder of two A&P managers.

Then someone leaked the Waterfront Commission report to the New York Times, which featured an account of the extortion on June 27, 1969. This report caught everyone's attention. A year later, Reader's Digest carried the story, "Mafia War on the A&P."

In October 1971, the Congressional Commerce Committee held hearings on the matter. Officials from A&P explained that Irving Kaplan, secretary-treasurer of Local 863 of the Meat Cutters Union, and Joe Pecora, from Local

464 of the Teamsters, pressured them to accept the product. NY Detectives identified Jerry Catena as the Boss of the Genovese Family and his brother Gene, the sole owner of Best Sales, as a Capo.

November 18, 1969

Catena appeared in a private session with the McClellan Rackets Committee.

THE DECARLO TAPES

January 6, 1970

During an extortion trial of Capo Angelo DeCarlo and two other men, a defense lawyer demanded any government records of his client. To his shock, Judge J Robert Shaw agreed and ordered the prosecution to turn over those materials. Consequently, the FBI produced 1200 pages of transcripts from a bug in DeCarlo's office from 1961 to 1965, and the Judge gave access to the press. It was a bombshell, and Jerry Catena's name stood out. For example, when a mutt asked DeCarlo about his influence in NJ unions, DeCarlo replied, "Gene Catena has it all tied up with Jerry (Catena). They make $100,000 or $200,000 a year with the unions.

Note:

"The Jersey Mob" by Henry Ziegler contains a summary of the DeCarlo tapes.

February 17, 1970

Catena appeared in a private session with the McClellan Rackets Committee. He refused to testify even when granted immunity. Officials then hauled him to Superior Court.

CATENA'S CONTEMPT

March 4, 1970

A Judge in Superior Court ordered Catena to jail until he agreed to talk. Consequently, officials sent him to Yardville Prison.

September 2, 1971

A federal court ruled that the NJ witness immunity law was unconstitutional and ordered authorities to free Catena. The State appealed.

May 30, 1972

The US Supreme Court reversed a lower court ruling that the NJ witness immunity law was unconstitutional. However, it remanded Catena's case to the Third Circuit Court of Appeals to decide whether the NY Commission of Investigation was legal.

August 8, 1972

The Third Circuit Court of Appeals ruled that the NJ State Commission of Investigation was legal. Catena remained in jail.

December 1973

Catena claimed his incarceration was no longer coercive but punitive. Fortunately for him, a trial court agreed that he had proven he would not talk. The State appealed.

November 6, 1974

The Supreme Court of New Jersey ruled that Catena was still in contempt, but he had the option of testifying to support his claims.

August 19, 1975

A Superior Court Judge ordered the release of Catena from his contempt sentence. From his initial jailing on March 4, 1970, until his freedom, Catena enjoyed 100 days on "leave" or for medical reasons.

CASINO PROBLEMS IN NEW JERSEY

In the mid-1960s, Catena held a secret interest in Chicago's powerful Bally Corporation, a maker of slot machines. By the late seventies, Bally had a considerable investment in an Atlantic City casino and was subject to scrutiny from the New Jersey Casino Control Commission. Their Division of Gaming enforcement carried out the background checks.

Among the discoveries was the relationship between Bally's CEO and Catena going back to the early 1960s and continuing until 1974. This revelation caused a media storm, and the Casino Control Commission would only give Bally a temporary license once Bally CEO William T O'Donnell stepped down. He did so, but Bally still had to apply for a permanent permit.

December 23, 1980
The Casino Control Commission denied Bally a permanent license, but the legal fight continued.

December 29, 1980
After much negotiation, the Casino Control Commission granted Bally a permanent license. O'Donnell agreed to put his considerable holdings in Bally into escrow, pending his appeals for the Commission's decision that he had to step down.

July 1982
The Appellate Division of New Jersey's Superior Court ruled that the Casino Control Commission had the right to exclude O'Donnell from Bally as a condition of that company obtaining a casino license. O'Donnell appealed.

December 8, 1982
The New Jersey Supreme Court refused to hear O'Donnell's appeal of the Casino Control Commission's ruling that he had to step down.

1975

Catena moved permanently to 2100 Crescent Road in Boca Raton, Florida. He was never again a power in the Genovese Family.

1976

A Florida grand jury had Catena testify in their probe of gambling.

October 22, 1986

Fortune Magazine placed Catena at position four in its list of the wealthiest mobsters. (Opinion: This list was nonsense.)

April 23, 2000

Catena died in Florida.

CONCLUSION

Jerry Catena was a powerful figure in the 1960s. Standing in for Genovese he took part in the Commission discussions to oust Bonanno Boss Joe Bonanno and helped arbitrate the war between the Joey Gallo faction and Boss Joe Profaci. In addition Catena participated in the vote to deny new Colombo Boss Joe Magliocco his seat because he plotted to kill Bosses Carlo Gambino and Tommy Lucchese. However, Catena was voting as the imprisoned Vito Genovese wanted and everyone knew it. Nevertheless, Catena ran the Family for about ten years and thus was a major Mafioso.

CHAPTER SEVEN

Tommy "Tommy Ryan" Eboli

Eboli was a colorful, volatile character all his life. Genovese appointed him as the Acting Underboss when he went to prison and this position gave Eboli a lot of clout. From illegal FBI bugs the feds learned that Eboli didn't hesitate to criticize other mob leaders including Commission member Carlo Gambino. He didn't have political skills and once his mentor, Genovese died behind bars it was just a matter of time before the new leaders whacked Eboli. His story follows.

DOB
June 13, 1911
Scisciano, Italy

DOD
July 16, 1972
NYC

Father
Luigi Eboli
Mother
Madalena Eboli
Brothers
Patsy Eboli

John Eboli
Louie Eboli
Ralph Eboli

Description
5' 11"
185 pounds
Black balding hair
Brown eyes

Residences
42 King Street
NYC

992 Phelps Road
Teaneck, NJ.
June 3, 1949-May 16, 1961

379 Forest Road
Englewood Cliffs, NJ
May 16, 1961-1972

923 Elaine Terrace
Fair Lawn, NJ.
1972

Legitimate Businesses
E&D Trucking Company
1946-1952

Tryan Cigarette Service
April 1952-April 1958
Partners with Mike Genovese (Vito's brother)

Burger Village Restaurant
September 1956-1958

Promo Records
Patterson, NJ
1969-1972
Partners with Morris Levy
Bought 50% in 1969 and received
$1,000 a week in salary

Descriptions of Eboli

Recording star Tommy James
(Tommy James and the Shondells had 1960s hits like Hanky Panky,
Mony, Mony, and Crimson and Clover.)
He was actually pretty friendly. I never had any problem with him. I didn't
realize who he was.

March 1912
Arrived in the United States.

1930s
NY police arrested Eboli six times in the 1930s on minor charges, most of
which the court dismissed.

October 26, 1931
Married Anna Arioli.

They had two sons.

September 18, 1932
Eboli and a bunch of other Mafiosi attended the wedding of Joe Valachi.

193?

Capo Tony Bender ordered Soldier Joe Valachi to have two men in the Lucchese Family beaten. Valachi recruits Tommy Eboli, and another mutt pounded one of the men viciously with baseball bats, and only Valachi's intervention saved his life. (This is an example of Eboli's temper.)

September 3, 1937

Eboli divorced Anna Arioli using a questionable mail-order Mexican method.

1937

Eboli married Mary Porcello.

They had three children.

January 11, 1952

Eboli was the manager of boxer Rocky Castellani, whom Ernie Durando beat Castellani in the 7th round at Madison Square Gardens. Eboli was incensed at a technical knockout ruling and pounded referee Ray Miller in the ring. Then, Eboli and others hammered boxing promoter Al Weill in the dressing room.

NY State Athletic Commissioner Bob Christenberry suspended Eboli's boxing license indefinitely.

January 18, 1952

NY State Athletic Commissioner Bob Christenberry revoked Eboli's boxing license for life. He also fined Eboli $3,000 and banned him from any arena holding a sanctioned boxing match.

January 22, 1952

NY Police arrested Tommy Eboli and his brother Patsy after a grand jury indicted them for assault on January 11, 1952. The indictment charged Eboli with assaulting referee Ray Miller and both brothers for attacking boxing promotor Al Weil. Justice Doris I Bryne arraigned the two men and set Tommy's bond at $1,000.

February 6, 1952

Eboli petitioned for a jury trial before Special Sessions Justice Joseph V LoScalzo, but the Justice rejected Eboli's motion.

March 24, 1952

Supreme Court Justice Morris Eder rejected an Eboli petition requesting the dismissal of charges.

May 26, 1952

Eboli pled guilty to assaulting referee Ray Miller and boxing promotor Al Weill on January 11.

June 20, 1952

In Special Sessions court, the Justice gave Eboli a $500 fine and a six-month suspended sentence for his assault on the referee and boxing promoter on January 11, 1952.

July 21, 1958

FBI Agents interviewed Eboli.

GENOVESE JAILED

February 1960

In 1959 the federal government convicted Boss Vito Genovese and others of a narcotics conspiracy. The judge freed Genovese while he appealed his case, but in February 1960, the feds sent him off to Atlanta Penitentiary.

1960

The imprisoned Boss, Vito Genovese, appointed Underboss Jerry Catena as Acting Boss and elevated Capo Tommy Eboli to Acting Underboss.

August 22, 1960

Naturalized in NYC. Eboli gave his address as 177 Thompson Street, NYC.

November 15, 1960

He obtained his American passport # 2485114. Eboli indicated he intended to fly to Europe on TWA with an organized tour with the plan to visit relatives.

February 6, 1961

Eboli arrived in New York City aboard the Leonardo Da Vinci, which sailed from Gibraltar. This event must have been the end of the European tour mentioned above.

December 21, 1961

FBI informer NY T-3 stated that Jerry Catena, Tom Eboli, Phil Lombardo, and Mike Miranda were running the Genovese Family because Boss Vito Genovese was in prison.

January 5, 1962

FBI HQ sent Eboli's tax returns to its New York office. Below are Eboli's declared incomes gleaned from these papers.

1955 $12,099.71
1956 $10,592.72
1957 $ 8,375.26
1958 $29927.93
1959
1960 $18742.04

1962

Eboli attended a Commission meeting in Miami as the representative of Acting Boss Jerry Catena. Relatively inexperienced at this level, Eboli brought veteran Miami-based Capo Mike Coppola to better deal with the veteran Commission members whom Eboli referred to as "The Tigers."

September 4, 1962

Informant NK T-1 told the FBI that Tommy Eboli controlled gambling in Greenwich Village. This racket used to belong to the late Anthony Bender Strollo.

1963

FBI information indicated that Eboli and Mike Genovese controlled a waste paper association. In addition, the report claimed Eboli dominated Local 958 of the Water Matter Sorters, Trimmers, and Handlers.

February 7, 1963

The FBI overheard Eboli's brother, Patsy, claiming that Tom Eboli was the Acting Boss (This was incorrect.)

July 20, 1963

Eboli ordered that no one in the Genovese Family should deal with narcotics. The decision must have included the other Family leaders if this report is accurate.

September 1963

Famous turncoat Joe Valachi testified before a Senate Committee. Among the many, he identified as Mafiosi was Tommy Eboli. Reporters from The Record in Hackensack, NJ, questioned Eboli about Valachi's claims. Eboli replied, "I don't know these people."

October 20, 1963

Informant NK T-1 told the FBI that Eboli, Peppe Sabato, and Tony Provenzano played cards at the Englewood Country Club.

November 5, 1963

Informant NK T-1 told the FBI that Eboli met with Genovese Capo Tony Provenzano at the Englewood Country Club. The two hoods got into an argument over some union.

1964

FBI secret recordings captured Eboli explaining a conflict with Boss Carlo Gambino. The latter wanted the Copacabana garbage stop to revert to the Gambino Family. Eboli refused to give up the $2,000 a month pick-up; however, Acting Boss Jerry Catena overruled Eboli but with much flattery. Catena didn't want to anger the powerful Gambino for a mere $2,000 a month, but he also needed to keep Eboli loyal.

Note:

Former Genovese Boss Frank Costello reportedly had "control" of the Copacabana during his reign. So a reasonable guess would be that this was when the Genovese Family picked up the lucrative garbage stop. The Gambinos must have had it earlier and thus wanted it back.

February 14, 1964

An FBI report contained information from an informer in November of 1963 that Eboli, Peppe Sabato, Tommy Eboli, and Patsy Eboli controlled a big crap game in New Jersey.

October 9, 1964

An FBI report corrected an earlier conclusion that Eboli was the Acting Boss of the Genovese Family while Jerry Catena was the Underboss.

The new information correctly placed Catena as Acting Boss.

JOE BONANNO

1962-1965

According to his own words, secretly taped by the FBI, Eboli was involved in the Joe Bonanno overthrow by the Commission. A rough summary follows.

Eboli attended several Commission meetings about Bonanno. Unfortunately, FBI bugs of Eboli and Mike Genovese provided a one-sided version of the Commission debates and actions. In summary, Bosses Carlo Gambino and Tommy Lucchese accused Boss Joe Magliocco of plotting to kill them. Magliocco appeared before the Commission in the fall of 1964 and admitted to the conspiracy.

However, Magliocco Capo Joe Colombo, who revealed the plot, also mentioned that Bill Bonanno, son of Joe Bonanno, was present with Magliocco during this period. So naturally, Gambino et al. suspected Magliocco was working in concert with Bonanno. Magliocco denied this and said that Bill Bonanno was in his home due to a marital dispute with a Magliocco niece. The Commission fined Magliocco and ordered him to step down, which he did.

Suspicious of Bonanno, the Commission ordered him to appear before them. Bonanno, not being stupid, weaved and dodged, claiming he never got the messages but that he would show up if he first had a meeting with Commission members Angelo Bruno and Joe Zerilli.

The FBI recorded Eboli explaining that at a Commission meeting held at Runyon Sales, Boss Tommy Lucchese outlined a plan to try to set Joe Bonanno up for a hit.

Later, Eboli's version of events got interesting. He described a Commission meeting at which he told the Commission he understood Bonanno's wish to have Bruno and Zerilli meet with him. Furthermore, Eboli claims he challenged Boss Carlo Gambino to show proof that Bonanno plotted against him. However, according to Eboli, Gambino could not provide critical evidence.

Eboli said that Boss Tommy Lucchese accused him of attempting to overturn the Commission's decision to ban Bonanno. He added that Boss Carlo Gambino claimed that Eboli did not have all the facts the Commission had. It would be interesting to find proof of the truth of Eboli's claims to have stood up to powerful Bosses like Gambino and Lucchese. In any case, the Commission did expel Bonanno whether or not Eboli voiced any objections.

The tape recordings of Eboli contained the statement that when Commission representatives consulted Chicago Boss Sam Giancanna on the Bonanno problem, Giancanna told them to kill Bonanno and end the dispute.

The tape recordings showed that Eboli understood the importance of Bonanno's defiance of the Commission order. He said that if one member can dispute a Commission order, you can say goodbye to La Cosa Nostra, for the Commission is the organization's backbone.

January 14, 1966
Criminal Court Judge Ruben Levy dismissed charges against Eboli and four others because the state did not have enough proof to prove a consorting charge.

August 11, 1966
A news story out of Washington stated that the Justice Department had proof that Mafia hoods held hidden interests in Las Vegas casino. Those named included Boss Vito Genovese, Mike Genovese, Acting Underboss Tommy Eboli, Capo Angelo DeCarlo, and Soldier Anthony Boiardo.

August 13, 1966 - August 28, 1966
An FBI report stated that Eboli was at the Naples Hotel in San Germano on these dates (San Germano is near Turin in the Piedmont province of Italy.)

LA STELLA MEETING

September 22, 1966, 4 PM
New York Police discovered Eboli and other Mafia leaders having lunch in the basement of the La Stella Restaurant in Queens. They arrested the 13 hoods. Please see the chapter on "La Stella" for complete details.

December 30, 1966

Police arrested Eboli and four other men in a Greenwich Village establishment at 177 Thompson Street. They detained Eboli, Joseph Sabato, Dom Cirillo, Sebastian Ofria, and Edward Cohen for consorting with known criminals.

September 26, 1968

An FBI report stated that Jerry Catena was the Acting Boss of the Genovese Family while Eboli was the Acting Underboss.

VITO GENOVESE DIES

February 14, 1969

Boss Vito Genovese died in prison. Capo Phil Lombardo became the new Boss. Acting Underboss Tommy Eboli became the official Underboss and Acting Boss of the Family.

February 16, 1969

The Record newspaper of Hackensack, NJ, carried a major story identifying Tommy Eboli and Jerry Catena as the new leaders of the Genovese Family.

February 27, 1969

Eboli appeared before the NJ State Investigations Committee and took the 5th to a series of questions. He then collapsed and was rushed to University Hospital.

March 4, 1969

Eboli avoided appearing before the La Stella grand jury because he was in University Hospital complaining of a heart attack.

March 8, 1969

University Hospital doctors released Eboli after a series of tests on his heart.

July 8, 1969

In the lobby outside the hearing room for the New Jersey State Investigations Committee, reporters observed Eboli taking pills, presumably for his heart problem. Eboli avoided testifying by going to the hospital complaining of a heart attack.

1969

Eboli paid $100,000 for a 50% interest in Morris Levy's Promo Records based in Patterson, NJ. This company mainly dealt with records returned to stores by customers or promotional copies. (Cut-outs) Promo employees would mark the merchandise, indicating they weren't new, then sell the records to wholesalers at a deep discount.

COMMEDIAN PHIL FOSTER

In the 1960-1970 era, Foster was a well-known comic with screen credits on his resume. In the mid-sixties, he lived in a ground-floor apartment in the upscale Horizon House complex in Fort Lee, NJ. Gangster Tommy Eboli resided on the 14 floor in a luxurious setup. The two men played cards at the Englewood Golf Club.

1965

Eboli was moving out of his residence, and Foster was to take over the apartment. Foster purchased some of the furniture for $1,100 with cash and a check.

May 21, 1970

Two FBI Agents interviewed Phil Foster after finding his check among Tommy Eboli's papers. Foster told them he purchased some furniture for a total of $1,100.

June 25, 1970

Phil Foster appeared before a federal grand jury investigating Eboli's tax returns. He testified that he paid $3,800 to Eboli for the furnishings.

September 17, 1970

A grand jury indicted well-known comedian Phil Foster for his alleged involvement in an Eboli tax scheme. Foster told the IRS that he paid $1,100 for some Eboli furniture which Eboli did not have to declare on his return. Later, Foster claimed he gave Eboli $3,800 and that the $1,100 was merely a down payment.

September 25, 1970

In District Court in Newark, Foster pled not guilty to the perjury charges. Judge Anthony T Augelli released the comedian on a $2,500 personal recognizance bond.

June 9, 1971

After the prosecution presented its argument in Phil Foster's five perjury charges, Judge Anthony T Augelli threw out the case.

May 10, 1971

The evening before his scheduled appearance before the Waterfront Commission, Eboli went to Holy Name Hospital in Teaneck, NJ, complaining of a heart attack.

EBOLI'S MURDER

July 16, 1972, at about 1:00 AM

A hood, firing from a truck, gunned down Eboli. An autopsy found five bullets hitting him on the left side of the head and neck. There were powder burns and glass fragments on the right front seat. Nearby the police found a stolen Plymouth, a red and yellow truck, a .32 pistol, and a silenced machine gun. The thinking with the bullet in the front seat was that one shot was fired at the driver breaking the driver's window of the 72 Caddy. Eboli was visiting lady friend Mrs. Elvira "Dolly" Lenzo, who lived at 388 Lefferts Avenue in

Crown Heights. Eboli was wearing a blue jumpsuit, a diamond ring, and a solid gold crucifix and had $2077.60 on him.

July 17, 1972

Joseph Sternfeld, Tommy Eboli's driver, turned himself in to the NYPD at their Canarsie, Brooklyn station house. He admitted he drove Eboli to his girlfriend's apartment and was opening the passenger door of Eboli's blue, 1972 Cadillac Fleetwood caddy when a man, firing from a red and yellow truck, killed Eboli at about 12:50 AM. Sternfeld also told the police that he parked Eboli's vehicle in the garage at Eboli's new home at 923 Elaine Terrance in Fair Lawn, NJ.

The police took Sternfeld to Brooklyn Supreme Court, where Justice Michael Kern set bond at $250,000. Unfortunately, Sternfeld could not meet the bond, and the authorities locked him up on Riker's Island. Police questioned Sternfeld over three days, but he stuck to his story that he did not recognize the shooter.

July 19, 1972

Eboli's Family held his sparsely attended wake at the Romanelli Funeral Home in Ozone Park, where about 100 people were in attendance, including his wife Mary and ex-wife Anne but not Eboli's brothers or any Mafia mutts. Next, St. Anthony's Church in Greenwich Village was the location of his thirty-minute funeral mass; then, the entourage, with four flower cars, drove to George Washington Memorial Cemetery in Paramus, NJ, for the burial.

October 6, 1972

Eboli's driver appeared before a special grand jury.

October 10, 1972

Eboli's driver appeared before a special grand jury.

October 19, 1972

A special grand jury indicted Eboli's chauffeur, Joseph Sternfeld, on one count of perjury. DA Eugene Gold said that Sternfeld had not been truthful about the events surrounding the murder of Eboli. Supreme Court Justice Vincent D Damiani set bail at $75,000.

Note:

The police never charged anyone for the Eboli hit.

CONCLUSION

While there is no concrete proof, it is reasonable to conclude that the leadership of the Genovese Family organized and approved the Eboli hit. He had risen through the ranks as a Vito Genovese protégé and owed his Acting Underboss position to the imprisoned Boss.

Acting Boss Jerry Catena gave Eboli a lot of freedom to handle the Family's day-to-day activities and worked to keep Eboli happy. A key factor was that Catena was fully aware that Genovese still had power behind bars, and Catena didn't need any problem from that direction.

Eboli was a volatile character, evidenced by his explosion in the boxing ring in 1952. That personality trait also jumped out in some of the secret FBI tapes of Eboli. An example is his arguments with powers Carlo Gambino and Tommy Lucchese over the handling of the Bonanno affair. His rivals put up with his ego while Genovese was alive, but after his death, all bets were off.

The leaders of the Genovese Family, including rising Capo Phil Lombardo and others, had Eboli killed, for they did not want him to retain power, let alone win the throne of the Family. But, like so many others, Eboli never saw it coming.

CHAPTER EIGHT

Michael Miranda

Miranda survived about fifty years in La Cosa Nostra with hardly a scratch and rose to the powerful position of Consigliere in the administrations of Bosses Frank Costello, Vito Genovese, and Phil Lombardo. But, unfortunately, there is little information on his life, for the lawmen never jammed him up on serious charges. What follows is a summary of some details of his life.

DOB
July 26, 1896
San Giuseppe Vesuviano, Italy

DOD
September 16, 1973
Boca Raton, Florida

March 29, 1912
Miranda arrived in the United States aboard the ship Canada. Records suggest he had been here previously, but this is the date Miranda provided on his citizenship papers.

1915
Miranda received a thirty-day sentence for pickpocketing.

November 29, 1926

Miranda obtained a license to marry Lucia DiLauenzio.

April 26, 1929

Miranda filed his Naturalization Petition.

January 21, 1932

The US granted Miranda his citizenship. He gave his address as 1002 5th Street in Forrest Hills, Long Island.

September 19, 1934

Shooters killed small-time hood Ferdinand "The Shadow" Boccia in the Circolo Christofolo Club and Café at 633 Metropolitan Ave in Brooklyn. A decade later, a grand jury indicted Vito Genovese, Mike Miranda, Gus Frasca, Pete DeFeo, and George Smurra for the hit.

December 2, 1937

The US issued Miranda with a passport numbered 249124.

March 31, 1938

Miranda returned to the United States from Naples aboard the Conte Di Savoia.

December 6, 1939

Miranda returned to the United States from Naples aboard the Vulcania.

1940

The US Census found Miranda, his wife, and his son living at 110-02 68th Drive in Queens. Miranda indicated he ran a restaurant.

1942

Miranda registered for the draft and named his wife Lucy as his next of kin, and gave 110-02 68th Drive in Forrest Hills as his residence.

August 7, 1944

The Kings County DA issued arrest warrants for Vito Genovese, Mike Miranda, Gus Frasca, Pete DeFeo, George Smurra, and John Doe regarding the 1934 murder of Ferdinand Boccia.

June 1946

At the Genovese murder trial, turncoat Ernie "The Hawk Rupolo" gave this version of the Boccia murder conspiracy:

In 1934, Rupolo met with Mike Miranda, who said, "Frasca tells me that you are a good boy, that you could do a good job. The Shadow (Boccia) and (William) Gallo are no good. I want you to put Gallo and the Shadow on the spot so they can be killed."

Rupolo testified that he told Miranda he would rather shoot the men than set them up. Miranda then had Rupolo come to a meeting the next day, where he met Genovese. The Underboss agreed to let Rupolo shoot Gallo while three other mutts would take care of Boccia. Miranda then gave Rupolo $175 and told him to meet with Pete DeFeo.

Unfortunately for Rupolo, he only wounded Gallo, who told the police who attacked him. The other guys successfully killed Boccia. A jury convicted Rupolo, but he did not talk. Later, when jammed up in another shooting, Rupolo told his version of the Boccia conspiracy, which led to the indictment of Miranda, Genovese, and others.

June 10, 1946

Judge Samuel Leibowitz dismissed the Boccia murder charge against Vito Genovese.

September 16, 1946

Miranda surrendered to the NYPD to face an indictment charging him with participating in the murder of Boccia in 1934. Miranda knew Judge Leibowitz acquitted Genovese of the same charge, so he must have felt confident turning himself in.

February 13, 1947
At the prosecutor's recommendation, Judge Sam Leibowitz dismissed Miranda's Boccia murder charge.

1950
The US Census found Miranda living at 156 Greenway W in Queens with his wife Lucy and son Anthony. Miranda claimed to be a car dealer.

May 2, 1957
Under orders from Underboss Vito Genovese, Vince Gigante attempted to assassinate Boss Frank Costello but only wounded him. Nevertheless, Costello stepped down, and Genovese took his place.

THE APALACHIN FIASCO

The Commission called for a National Meeting of La Cosa Nostra at the estate of Boss Joe Barbara near Apalachin, NY. A year earlier, a regularly scheduled National Meeting occurred at the Barbara estate. However, the next one was not supposed to be until 1961.

The primary purpose of the meeting was to introduce Vito Genovese as the Genovese Family leader and Carlo Gambino as his Family's new Boss. Gambino, Genovese, and their supporters hoped that receiving the blessings of the nation's Mafia Bosses would thwart any dissidents' attempts to overthrow them.

Note:

Below I focus on Miranda's situation concerning Apalachin.

November 14, 1957
Genovese, Joe Ida, Mike Miranda, Dom Olivetto and Jerry Catena arrive in Binghamton by plane. Someone drives them to Barbara's.

New York State Troopers accidentally discovered the gathering, and the hoods fled by vehicle and on foot. But unfortunately, a few smart ones stayed in Barbara's home, and the Trooper never identified them.

Trooper Frederick Allen Tiffany picked up Trafficante, Lombardozzi, and Mike Miranda on McFadden Road. Miranda said he came to Binghamton by train with Gambino, Castellano, and Rava, then took a cab to Barbara's.

November 24, 1957
The NYPD brought Miranda in for questioning about Apalachin.

Watchdog Committee

At a subcommittee hearing, Miranda took the 5th, as did others.

February 4, 1958
Tioga County grand jury.

Mike Miranda appeared along with others.

August 15, 1958
NY State Investigation Committee.

Miranda refused to testify, and a Judge jailed him for contempt after he granted Miranda immunity, and he still refused to testify.

September 3, 1958
Washington: Supreme Court Justice Harlan refused to release the five men who had appealed their jail sentences. (Mancuso, Riccobono, Castellano, F Valenti, Miranda).

March 13, 1959

The New York Court of Appeals rejected the release of Miranda and six other men and ruled the government could keep them indefinitely if they refused to talk.

May 21, 1959

A grand jury indicted Miranda and 26 other men for their refusal to cooperate in the Apalachin investigation.

Indicted:

Bonanno

Bufalino

Cannone

Castellano

Civello

Cucchiara

DeMarco

Desimone

Evola

Falcone

Ida

LaDuca

Larasso

Lombardozzi

Magaddino, Antonio

Magliocco

Majuri

Miranda

Montana

Ormento

Osticco

Profaci

Riela

Scalish

Sciandra, Angelo

Scozzari

Turrigiano

August 12, 1959

Miranda testified before the New York State Investigations Committee and admitted that Joe Barbara invited him to the gathering.

September 30, 1959

Judge Kaufman upheld the indictment of Miranda and 22 other men. He also denied a change of venue and separate trials.

Conspiracy Trial

October 26, 1959

Jury selection began in the trial of the 22 for conspiracy to obstruct justice. Judge Kaufman severed Joe Bonanno due to a heart problem and did the same with James DeLuca a few days later.

Conspiracy Trial:

December 2, 1959

Judge Kaufman ruled the raid was legal.

Conspiracy Trial:

December 18, 1959

Conspiracy Trial:

The jury convicted Miranda and nineteen other men of conspiracy to obstruct justice.

Bufalino

Ignatius Cannone

Castellano

Civello

Desimone

Evola

Larasso

Lombardozzi

Magliocco

Majuri

Miranda

Montana

Ormento

Osticco

Profaci

Riela

Scalish

Anthony Sciandra

Scozzari

Turrigiano

Conspiracy Trial:

January 13, 1960

Judge Kaufman sentenced Miranda and nineteen other men for conspiracy to obstruct justice before various committees, grand juries, and Government Agencies investigating Apalachin. The twenty were:

Bufalino-5 yrs. and $10,000

Cannone-3 yrs.

Castellano-5 yrs. and

Civello-5 yrs.

Desimone-4 yrs.

Evola-5 yrs. and $10,000

Larasso-4 yrs.

Lombardozzi-5 yrs. and $10,000

Magliocco-5 yrs. and $10,000

Majuri-5 yrs.

Miranda-5 yrs. and $10,000

Montana-4 yrs. and $10,000

Ormento-5 yrs. and $10,000

Osticco-5 yrs. and $10,000

Profaci-5 yrs. and $10,000

Riela-4 yrs. and $10,000

Scalish-5 yrs. and $10,000

Sciandra-5 yrs. and $10,000

Scozzari-5 yrs. and $10,000

Turrigiano-5 yrs.

January 13, 1960

NY State Investigation Committee

Authorities arraigned Miranda, but another guy testified.

January 19, 1960

NY State Investigation Committee

A Judge charged Miranda with perjury committed before the committee.

Conspiracy Trial:

November 28, 1960

US Court of Appeals Second District ruled there was insufficient evidence to prove a crime and threw out the twenty convictions.

Conspiracy Trial:

December 27, 1960

The Feds decided not to appeal the Apalachin trial reversal.

March 15, 1963

Members of the Queen's DA's office observed Miranda, Tommy Lucchese, and four other guys meeting at 95-25 Queen Blvd between 1 and 3 PM.

VALACHI HEARINGS

October 1, 1963

Turncoat Genovese Soldier Joe Valachi named Mike Miranda as the Family Consigliere.

October 7, 1963

At the Valachi Hearings, NYPD Inspector John F Shanley said, "I think Mike Miranda will be the power if Vito (Genovese) stays in prison."

July 20, 1964

The Nassau County DA questioned 25 men, including Miranda, about the extortion of a Long Island vending machine company owner.

May 21, 1965

Turncoat Bonanno Associate Harold Konigsberg told the FBI that Tommy Eboli relied on Miranda. He added that Anthony Carillo performed many Miranda tasks when the latter was ill.

1965

An FBI file stated that Miranda was associated with the Bricklayers Helpers Union on Long Island. Phil Lombardo assisted him.

October 29, 1965

NYPD detectives arrested seven men at Lombardi's Restaurant at 53 Spring Street in Manhattan. They charged Miranda, Tommy Eboli, Barney Miranda, Anthony Carillo, Peter DeFeo, James Napoli, and Phil Kovolick with consorting for unlawful purposes. The magistrate released all of them on recognizance.

November 3, 1965

Judge Frank Composto dismissed the charges against Miranda and the other six men.

LA STELLA

The meeting of a group of gangsters at the La Stella restaurant caused a media sensation. To this day, it is unclear if the gathering followed a Commission meeting or if it was a stand-alone sit-down. Ambitious politicians and law enforcement officials milked the event for all the publicity they could. Unfortunately for them and us, the reason for the gathering still needs to be discovered. What follows is a summary of the pertinent events.

??, 1966

New Orleans Boss Carlos Marcello informed Immigration USA that he would travel to New York City.

September 22, 1966

Around 2:30 PM, detectives from the 112 precinct arrested 13 men having lunch in the basement dining room of La Stella in Forrest Hills, Queens.

Arrested were: Santos Trafficante, Carlos Marcello, John Marcello, Anthony Gagliano, Anthony Corolla, Anthony Carillo, Mike Miranda, Joe Colombo, Carlo Gambino, Joe N Gallo, Tom Eboli, Dom Alongi, and Aniello Dellacroce. Police took the men to the 112 precinct, strip-searched them, and correctly identified the hoods. They were then held in a civil jail awaiting arraignment and bail.

Note:

At some point, Philadelphia Boss Angelo Bruno told an informant that he was supposed to be at that meeting but wasn't able to for some reason.

September 23, 1966
A justice released all thirteen men on $100,000 bail each.

September 26, 1966
A grand jury began hearings in the Criminal Courts Building at Kew Gardens.

September 30, 1966
Anthony Carillo appeared before the grand jury for 50 minutes. Next was Mike Miranda (30 min) and then Santos Trafficante (8 min).

At lunchtime, the following hoods went to La Stella for lunch accompanied by lawyers Jack Wasserman and Ragano: Carlos Marcello, John Marcello, Santos Trafficante, Anthony Carolla, and Anthony Gagliano.

After lunch, the following four hoods were called before the GJ: Gagliano, Carlos Marcello, John Marcello, and Anthony Corolla.

October 3, 1966
Authorities called Eboli, Dom Alongi, Joe Colombo, Joe N Gallo, and Dellacroce before the grand jury.

May 18, 1967
Police arrested Miranda, Carillo, Gallo, and Dellacroce for criminal contempt before the grand jury investigating the gathering.

September 20, 1967
Officials dismissed indictments against Alongi, Eboli, Carillo, and Miranda. Later, they dismissed charges against Colombo, Dellacroce, and Joe Gallo.

January 1967
The Appellate Division overruled the dismissal of indictments against Miranda, Eboli, Alongi, and Carillo. In addition, the good guys also appealed the dismissal of charges against Colombo, Dellacroce, and Gallo. In any case, nothing came of these highly publicized arrests.

September 14, 1969

Vito Genovese died in prison. He appointed Capo Phil Lombardo as his replacement before his death; the exact date remains unclear. However, Miranda continued as the Consigliere for Lombardo until he retired in 1972.

September 16, 1973

Miranda died in Boca Raton, Florida.

September 21, 1973

The Miranda Family held a service at the Most Holy Crucifix Church at Broome and Mulberry Street in New York, followed by burial at Woodlawn Cemetery. They had the wake at 2nd Street and 2nd Ave at the Provenzano-Lanza Funeral Home.

CONCLUSION

Miranda led a charmed life in La Cosa Nostra. He did a bit for shoplifting in the 1920s and dodged a big bullet when the Ferdinand Boccia murder charge fell apart in 1946. The murder of Underboss Willie Moretti didn't touch him, but the 1957 Apalachin fiasco cost Miranda two years in the slammer for contempt, let alone many thousands in lawyer fees. Another blip was the 1967 La Stella meeting, but the only penalty was more bad publicity. Fortunately for him, Miranda was a level-headed survivor and died in bed, unlike many of his fellow Mafiosi.

CHAPTER NINE

Frank "Funzi" Tieri

Tieri was a long-time La Cosa Nostra member who rose to the Underboss position in 1974. Part of the Genovese Family Underboss's responsibility was acting as the Boss to protect the leader, Phil Lombardo. Unfortunately, the feds believed Tieri was the Boss and launched a RICO suit against him in 1980. This legal action made Tieri a household name, especially when a jury convicted him of being the Boss. In truth, he had retired due to illness in 1978, and at the time of his trial ordeal, he was an old, very sick non-entity. His story follows.

DOB
February 22, 1904
Castel Gondolfo, Italy

DOD
March 29, 1981
NYC

Description
5'7"
170 lbs.
Brown eyes

March 18, 1911

Tieri entered the USA after traveling on the SS Archambault.

1922

A jury convicted Tieri of armed robbery.

October 27, 1957

NYPD detectives questioned Tieri about the recent murder of Gambino Family Boss Albert Anastasia. They learned little except that Tieri was a Hoboken, NJ, clothing manufacturer.

1961-1966

The US Immigration Department began the process of deporting Tieri but gave up in 1966. He lived as a resident alien.

January 7, 1963

FBI informant NY T-8 said that Boss Vito Genovese elevated Tieri to Capo. He had been a Soldier under Consigliere Mike Miranda.

TIERI DODGES A KNOCKOUT

Background

Ernie Terrell was a six-foot-six heavyweight boxer from Chicago who was the Champion of the World Boxing Association from 1965 until 1967. When authorities dethroned champ Muhammed Ali because of his anti-war stance, Terrell won the vacant title in a runoff match.

February 11, 1965

NYPD detectives and FBI agents observed a sit-down of some significant Mafia figures in a W 55th Street restaurant. At the table were: Tieri, Tommy Eboli, Bonanno Boss Gaspar DiGregorio, Lucchese Family power Carmine Tramunti, and Associate Julie Isaacson from Local 118 of the Fur, Leather, Plastic, and Novelty Workers. He also owned a piece of heavyweight boxing contender Ernie Terrell.

December 6, 1965

Julie Isaacson denied public reports that someone had pushed him out as Terrell's manager. He said union matters took up too much of his time to be involved in boxing and claimed he sold his "piece" to Terrell, not Glickman.

Comment:

Mob powers probably ordered Isaacson to give up his piece of Terrell because the good guys now knew Isaacson was associating with mobsters. The denial that he sold to Glickman would be for the same reason due to Glickman's connection to the Chicago Outfit. The Mafia wanted to cash in on a Terrell/Ali fight and knew Terrell had to look clean.

One of Terrell's weaknesses was that his agent, Bernie Glickman, was associated with Chicago Outfit power Tony Accardo. This fact came into play after Terrell signed a lucrative contract to fight Ali in New York in March 1966. To their credit, the World Boxing Council did not dethrone Ali, so this was going to be a "Unification Fight" so that the world would have one heavyweight champion instead of two (WBA and WBC.)

January 28, 1966

The New York Athletic Commission refused to grant Terrell a license due to his connection to Bernie Glickman. Terrell was incensed and claimed Glickman was just the agent for his rock group, "The Heavyweights." Then the promotors tried to stage the battle in Chicago, but politicians there nixed that idea due to anti-war comments by Ali.

Meanwhile, Glickman was in a match of his own. He was upset by interference by New York mobsters and foolishly appealed to his "friend" Chicago's Tony Accardo for help. Accardo assigned Capo Phil Alderisio to represent Glickman in New York against Frank Tieri, but things went south. Alderisio returned to Chicago and gave Glickman $30,000 for his piece of Terrell on a take-it-or-leave-it basis. When Glickman got mouthy, Alderisio beat him in Glickman's apartment.

Fearing for his life, Glickman made a deal with the FBI, who were incredibly anxious to be able to charge Tony Accardo. But, unfortunately, in his grand jury testimony, Glickman denied that Accardo played any role in his boxing problems. This testimony was perjury, and the Feds could no longer use Glickman as a witness. Among others, Frank Tieri dodged a knockout with this decision.

Note:

Terrell finally met Ali in Houston on February 5, 1967. Before the battle, Terrell incensed Ali by refusing to call him by his Muslim name. All through the fight, as Ali hammered Terrell, he kept saying, "What my name! What's my name?"

Note:

When Diana Ross went solo in 1970, Terrell's sister Jean replaced her in the Supremes. She performed with the revamped group for about three years.

July 5, 1968

An examiner for the US Immigration Department recommended that they deny Tieri citizenship due to his bad character. Police arrested him six times between 1922 and 1959 with a conviction for a robbery (1922) and bookmaking (1946).

December 22, 1968

An informant told the FBI that Tieri, Tony Peroz, Leo Carlino, and Paddy Macchirole owned Frigid Express Inc.

GENOVESE DIES

February 14, 1969

Boss Vito Genovese died in prison.

March 18, 1969

The Plainfield New Jersey Courier News carried the headline;

"Darkhorse Frank Tieri Seen as Genovese Heir." Other reports said Tieri lived at 68 28th Street in Bay Ridge, Brooklyn, but he had another home for his second family plus an apartment for a mistress.

July 22, 1969
A District Court denied Tieri citizenship and the Second Court of Appeals confirmed that decision.

February 22, 1973
A Newark grand jury indicted nine men, including Tieri, for a series of offenses involving extorting Herbert Gross, a lowlife gambler and drug dealer. A Judge would later dismiss the charges against Tieri due to his alleged illness.

March 1977
Police found the body of one-time Genovese power Patrick Macchirole.

June 28 and 29, 1980
FBI Agents witnessed Tieri at the Club Napoli and two successive nights.

At his arraignment a day later, his lawyers claimed Tieri was too ill to proceed.

TIERI AND THE ANGELO BRUNO HIT

March 21, 1980
Consigliere Anthony Caponigro shot gunned Philly Boss Angelo Bruno to death while he sat in a vehicle outside his home. Many Mafia historians believe that Caponigro thought he had the Commission's permission to whack Bruno because Tieri conned him into that belief. But then, when the Genovese administration hauled Caponigro onto the carpet, Tieri claimed he had only told Caponigro to fix things up with Bruno, not kill him.

March 22, 1980
Around 1 PM, Philly Consigliere Nicky Scarfo met with Genovese Consigliere Bobby Manna in Newark about the Bruno hit. Later that evening, Scarfo,

Soldier Phil Leonetti, Capo Sal Merlino, Capo Lawrence Merlino, Soldier Sal Testa, and Underboss Phil Testa met at Scannicchio's restaurant in Atlantic City. Scarfo told them the Bruno hit came from Caponigro.

March 22, 1980

Philly police observed Capos Frank Sindone and John Simone visiting Soldier John Stanfa in the hospital. They were whispering. Stanfa drove Bruno on the night Caponigro killed him and slightly wounded Stanfa.

March 23, 1980

Philly police observed a meeting of Caponigro, Sindone, Alfred Salerno, and a few others at Capo John Simone's home in Yardley. These were the guys who plotted Bruno's death.

March 24, 1980

Police observed Caponigro talking to Underboss Phil Testa on a South Philadelphia street.

March 25, 1980

The Bruno family held a wake at the Pennsylvania Burial Company.

March 26, 1980

The Bruno family held a private funeral.

GEORGE FRESOLONE'S BRUNO AFTERMATH STORY

Philadelphia Associate George Fresolone became an FBI informer and taped his induction into La Cosa Nostra. He also gave the FBI his version of the Angelo Bruno hit aftermath.

March 27, 1980

Stanfa went to New York with Capos Frank Sindone, Pasquale Martirano, and Soldier Alfred Simone. They were to meet Caponigro and hook up with

Genovese guys at the Skyline Motel on 49th Street in Manhattan. They were in NY to explain the Bruno hit to the Commission.

March 31, 1980
A grand jury investigating Bruno's death called Soldier John Stanfa as a witness because he drove the Philly Boss on the night Caponigro killed him.

April 17 or 18, 1980
Fresolone said he drove Caponigro to the Newark train for a New York trip where he expected the Commission to anoint him as the new Philly Boss. Instead, later that day, Fresolone learned that Salerno and Caponigro were dead.

VINCENT "FISH" CAFARO'S BRUNO AFTERMATH STORY

Vincent Cafaro was a long-time Genovese Soldier best known for being the right-hand man of Underboss/Front Boss Tony Salerno. After a dispute with Salerno, Cafaro rolled over and started talking.

Shortly after the Bruno killing, Underboss Phil Testa met with Gambino Boss Paul Castellano, Lucchese Underboss Sal Santora, Lucchese Boss Anthony Corallo, and Genovese Underboss/Front Boss Anthony Salerno. A few hours later, Anthony Caponigro met with the same group.

Philly Underboss Sal Testa returned to New York a week later and met with Salerno. Cafaro testified that it was then that he met Testa.

A week later, Caponigro met with Salerno, who said he didn't want to be involved and that Caponigro should go and see Gigante.

Cafaro said that after NY police found the bodies of Caponigro and Alfred Salerno, Fat Tony said he was glad he didn't get involved.

PHIL LEONETTI'S BRUNO AFTERMATH STORY

Phil Leonetti is the nephew of the infamous Nicky Scarfo of Philadelphia, a Capo to Angelo Bruno. Years later, Leonetti rolled over after receiving a 45-year sentence. He then told the following story about Bruno.

Leonetti version as told to Scarfo by Genovese Consigliere Bobby Manno

April 17, 1980

After the Bruno hit, the Genovese Family administration called Caponigro to Gigante's Triangle Social Club. They told his brother-in-law, Alfred Salerno, to wait in a nearby Italian restaurant. Then Caponigro met Gigante, Tieri, Salerno, and Bobby Manno in another location to explain the Bruno killing. Finally, some mutts took Caponigro to the basement, where they brutally tortured him to reveal the names of the other plotters. After killing Caponigro, they summoned Alfred Salerno and repeated the torture process.

April 18, 1980

NY police found Caponigro's body stuffed in a mortician's bag in the trunk of a car in the South Bronx at 2:15 AM. They discovered Salerno's body about four miles away in an empty lot. The coroner estimated that Caponigro was dead for three to five hours.

April 18, 1980

Genovese Soldier Vince Napoli traveled to Atlantic City to tell Scarfo that Caponigro and Salerno were dead.

April 19, 1980 (Date unsure)

Testa and Scarfo went to New York to meet with Gigante et al. Gigante said Testa was the new Philadelphia Boss.

June 6, 1980

A jury found Marco Mucciolo not guilty of the 1977 murder of Paddy Mac Macchirole, a one-time Genovese power.

June 30, 1980

A four-count indictment named Tieri as head of the Genovese Family and accused him of taking part in extortion of the Korvette stores, voting for a murder contract, and tax evasion. Prosecutor Nathan H Akerman said, "He is the boss of the largest crime family in La Cosa Nostra in the US." First, Tieri pled not guilty; then Judge Pierre Leval set bail at $75,000, which Tieri met.

October 20, 1980

The prosecution and the defense agreed on a jury for the Tieri trial. In addition, Judge Griesa sequestered the jury to prevent them from being tainted by the massive publicity the event had generated.

October 27, 1980

The Federal trial of Frank Tieri began before District Court Judge Thomas Griesa, with the government accusing him of being the Boss of a secret criminal organization known as La Cosa Nostra. (They were wrong.)

October 28 and 29, 1980

Famous turncoat Jimmy Fratianno testified that he asked Tieri to help retrieve $1.4 million a friend invested in the bankrupt Westchester Theater. Also, Fratianno said there was a La Cosa Nostra and that Tieri was not only the Boss of the Genovese Family but a member of the Commission.

Tieri collapsed in court, and an ambulance rushed him to the Beckman Downtown Hospital.

November 3, 1980

The Tieri trial resumed after his collapse on October 29.

November 7, 1980

Mobster Ralph Picardo testified that, in 1974, he witnessed Soldier Sal Briguglio giving Tieri $25,000 from extortion of the Korvette stores.

November 11/12 1980

Mob Associate Herbert Gross described how Pasquale "Paddy Macchirole" ordered him to a sit-down with Tieri at the back of a joint called Spring Sales in Little Italy in the mid-sixties. The group of men stood around a table while they discussed the problem. Eventually, Tieri ruled that Gross had to pay Macchirole $14,000 first.

November 15, 1980

Turncoat Colombo Associate Joe Cantalupo testified about Tieri threatening his uncle, who wanted to start selling pizza from his Eddie Arcaro restaurant. Tieri had an interest in the nearby Sbarro's and would brook no competition and said the uncle would end up in a funeral home if he disobeyed. Not surprisingly, Cantaluppo said uncle was terrified and quickly sold his part of Arcaros.

Cantalupo also told the jury that he hosted a meeting of Tieri, Colombo Family Boss Joe Colombo, and Gambino Boss Carl Gambino in 1969. Notably, Cantalupo testified that there was a La Cosa Nostra and that Tieri was the Boss of the Genovese Family.

November 19, 1980

Assistant US Attorney Barbara Jones summed up the government's case against Tieri and said, "Threats and violence are the hallmarks of Frank Tieri." Next, defense attorney Jay Goldberg focused on the criminal lives of the four main witnesses against Tieri; Jimmy Fratianno, Ralph Picardo, Herbert Cohen, and Joe Cantaluppo.

November 21, 1980

A federal grand jury convicted Tieri of racketeering conspiracy in the extortion of the Korvette chain, racketeering, and racketeering conspiracy in the fraudulent bankruptcy of the Westchester Theatre. Historically, they declared that there was a La Cosa Nostra, and Tieri was the Boss of the Genovese Family. However, they found him not guilty of tax fraud. Judge Griesa continued Tieri on his $75,000 bail despite the prosecution's objection.

January 23, 1981

In a surprise move at his sentencing, Tieri approached Judge Griesa, showed him his stomach scars, and said, "I am a very sick man; I am in your hands." The prosecution reminded the Judge that they believed Tieri was responsible for the murders of; Genovese Soldier Vincent DiLeo (1980), Boss Angelo Bruno of Philadelphia (1980), Philadelphia Capo Antony Caponigro (1980), Philadelphia Soldier Salerno (1980), Genovese Capo Pasquale Macchirole (1977), and Genovese Soldier Anthony Russo (1979). The Judge reacted by sentencing Tieri to 10 years in the slammer and a $60,000 fine. Then Judge Griesa gave Tieri a gift by permitting him to continue on bail while he appealed.

GIGANTE TAKES OVER AS BOSS

1981

Vincent "Fish" Cafaro later told the FBI that Gigante, Manna, and Santora visited Salerno and Lombardo individually in the hospital and notified them that Gigante was taking over.

March 15, 1981

Tieri entered Mount Sinai hospital

TIERI DIES

March 29, 1981

Funzi Tieri died in the hospital. He was 77.

April 1, 1981

Tieri's family held his funeral at the St Mary Mother of Jesus Church, 3226 84th Street in Brooklyn.

Note:

Tieri died before he could appeal, which legally meant his conviction no longer existed.

CONCLUSION

Frank "Funzi" Tieri was a powerful member of the Genovese Family but never as influential as the media and lawmen suggested. He became famous for being the Boss when he was the Underboss responsible to Boss Phil Lombardo. However, few historians would be writing much about him if not for his high-profile trial in 1980 when the feds put the wrong label on him.

CHAPTER TEN

Anthony "Fat Tony" Salerno

Salerno made a fortune with gambling and loansharking. In 1972 Boss Phil Lombardo promoted Salerno to Consigliere, then six years later moved him up to Underboss with the added responsibility to pretend to be the Boss of the Family in order to protect Lombardo. Unfortunately for Salerno, the feds indicted him as the Genovese Boss and a jury convicted him as such then the Judge sentenced him to 100 years. A summary of his life follows.

DOB
August 15, 1913
NYC

DOD
July 27, 1992
Springfield Medical Center for Federal Prisoners

Physical
5' 8"
180-260 lbs.
Brown eyes
Part of the left ring finger missing

Father

Alfio

Brothers

Alfred

Angelo

April 24, 1945

Providence police arrested Salerno as a suspicious person.

1946

An informer told the FBI that Salerno owned the Roxy Automatic Music Corporation. (I presume this refers to jukeboxes.)

1947

Salerno stayed at the Wofford Hotel in Miami Beach and 1014 Gerard Ave in the Bronx.

April 1947

Salerno told an FBI Agent that he ran Metro Urban Music Company for the last seven years.

April 3, 1947

Miami police arrested Salerno for draft dodging but released him the next day when they realized they had the wrong person.

March 31, 1950

FBI informant MM T-12 told his handler that Salerno was a partner of (Capo) Mike Coppola and frequented the Carib Hotel and the Tahiti Bar in Miami.

May 11, 1954

An FBI report indicated that Chicago Outfit power Paul DeLucia purchased Salerno's Miami Beach home at 4385 Pinetree Drive.

1958

Salerno was involved in the following businesses:

Metro Urban Music Company of 2228 1st Ave, NYC.

Raleigh Dress of Poughkeepsie, NY.

The Play Room Bar of 130 W 58th Street, NYC.

Salerno was a member of Local 1690 of the Automatic Coin and Vending Machine Union and the Retail Clerks International Association.

May 14, 1958

FBI informant MM T-4 reported that Salerno was close to (Capo) Mike Coppola and used to run his operations in New York.

July 5, 1958

FBI informant MM T-12 said Salerno was involved with (Capo) Mike Coppola in the numbers (gambling) in Harlem.

August 26, 1958

FBI informant MM T-13 told the FBI that Salerno controlled numbers (A form of gambling) in New York and was also involved in narcotics.

November 1958

The FBI was investigating whether they should list Salerno in their new Top Hoodlum program.

SALERNO AND BOXING

For many decades boxing was a shady business with lots of participation by organized crime figures. What follows is a tiny window into that world that involves Salerno and the famous 1959 heavyweight championship bout between champ Floyd Patterson and Swedish challenger Ingemar Johansson.

May 13, 1958

Fight manager Herman Wallman told a grand jury that without the support of mobster Frankie Carbo, there was no chance of holding a fight at Madison Square Gardens, the mecca of boxing.

January 1959

Someone invited veteran boxing promoter William Rosenshon to the exclusive Hampshire House on Central Park for a meeting about a possible Floyd Patterson, Ingemar Johannson fight. In attendance were; Salerno, big-time gambler Gil Beckley, and Charlie Black, who represented Patterson's manager Gus D'Amato.

Beckley told Rosenshon that his group would promote the fight but would give him 1/3 of the pie. Eventually, Salerno introduced Rosenshon to lawyer Vincent Velella who gave him $25,000 of Salerno's money to set up Rosenshon Enterprises Inc. (REI), the vehicle to promote the fight. In the agreement, Rosenshon would have 1/3 of the REI shares, while Velella would control 2/3 on behalf of Salerno. In addition, Charlie Black would get a cut from Velella's/Salerno's piece.

Note:

The agreement could not include Salerno's name since everyone knew him as a hood.

January ?, 1959

Rosenshon later testified that famous boxing promoter Jim Norris secretly contacted him on behalf of notorious mobster Frankie Carbo who was also interested in promoting the match.

January 29, 1959

Ingemar Johansson and champ Floyd Patterson signed a contract for a fight at Madison Square Garden. William Rosenshon, a veteran of the boxing business, would promote the fight using his company William Rosenshon Enterprises Inc. (REI.)

June 26, 1959

Challenger Ingemar Johansson won the heavyweight championship by defeating Floyd Patterson at Madison Square Gardens.

August 10, 1959

Before a grand jury, Vincent Velella denied he witnessed Tony Salerno giving William Rosenshon $10,000 in expense money.

August 13, 1959

Detective Frank Marrone from the New York DA's Office told the FBI that Rosenshon said representatives of the underworld had handled the Patterson/Johnson promotion.

September 15, 1959

Before the New York Athletic Commission, Vincent Velella denied he witnessed Tony Salerno giving William Rosenshon $10,000 in expense money.

October 19, 1959

Gus D'Amato, Floyd Patterson's manager, denied knowing Tony Salerno, Frankie Carbo, and Frank Erickson. He also declared no interest in Rosenshon Enterprises, which promoted the fight.

December 10, 1959

An indictment charged lawyer Velella with two counts of perjury. Before a grand jury and the New York Athletic Commission, he denied witnessing Tony Salerno giving William Rosenshon $10,000 in expense money. Judge Charles Marks issued a bench warrant for Velella's arrest.

Note:

The Johansson/Patterson/Mob story is far more complicated than I have outlined above.

August & September 1960
An FBI informant said Salerno frequented the Midtown Restaurant in Miami Beach, where he gambled on horses and sports.

November 23, 1960
A New York Detective assigned to the DA's office told the FBI they would try to shut down Salerno's gambling operations.

1961
Salerno lived at 2242 1st Ave in apartment 4-s.

January 21, 1962
In Miami Beach, Salerno used a white 1957 Caddy registered to Cleveland Soldier John Tronolone.

April 25, 1961
An IRS memo indicated that Salerno entered New England Baptist Hospital in Roxbury, Massachusetts.

May 1, 1961
Staff a New England Baptist Hospital discharged Salerno.

1962
Salerno lived at 1041 Venetian Way in Miami Beach.

1962
An FBI informant reported that Salerno was back from a European trip.

April 1962

An informant told the Miami FBI that Salerno had moved his gambling operation to the Sea Gull Motel.

May 1, 1962

Informant MM T-3 told the FBI that (Capo) Mike Coppola and Salerno controlled the numbers operation in Harlem, with Joe and Vince Rao doing the work.

July 20, 1962

Informant NY T-4 told his handler that Phil "Ben" Lombardo was Salerno's immediate Boss.

1962

An FBI report said Salerno was driving around in a new green Oldsmobile registered to John Tronolone.

July 12, 1962

Informant MM T-6 told his FBI handler that Coppola and Salerno supervised a joint loansharking operation of the New York, Chicago, and Detroit Mafia in the Miami area.

December 27, 1962

FBI informant NY T-5 reported that Salerno was a Capo.

February 1963

Informant MM T-36 told the FBI that Salerno, Mike Coppola, and Alex Rosato had each invested $100,000 in a legitimate loan company.

April 1963

Informant MM T-5 told his FBI handler that (Capo) Mike Coppola was semi-retired and that Salerno took over his gambling operations. He also mentioned that Salerno was friends with Cleveland member John "Peanuts" Tronolone.

August 15, 1963

When a New York FBI Agent approached Salerno, he stopped to talk and mentioned he was trying to sell his Rhinebeck farm. (He never did.) Salerno also said he had recently appeared before a grand jury investigating gambling but took the 5th to all questions. Finally, Salerno admitted to being a gambler all his life and added that he never made a quarter gambling in Miami.

1963

FBI informant MM T-6 told his handler that Salerno was the hidden owner of the Paddock bar at 50th Street and Broadway in NY.

October 1965

A Palm Springs, California grand jury was investigating a possible link between a gathering of men, including Salerno and two casino executives, and Las Vegas gambling.

July 17, 1966

An informant told the FBI that Salerno purchased the largest number of points in Caesar's Palace in Las Vegas.

Note:

A Las Vegas point indicates how much its owner gets of the skim money from a particular hotel.

October 22, 1968

A grand jury handed down was investigating a large-scale numbers racket and possible bribery of police officers. Eleven men associated with the gambling surrendered to DA Frank Hogan to face criminal contempt charges after they refused to testify despite the DA granting them immunity. Salerno was a person of interest but was not among the 11 charged.

November 1969

The Miami Herald ran a big spread on Mafia guys in Florida. They rated Salerno as the 52nd-highest mobster.

January 9, 1970

During a racketeering trial of Genovese Capo Ray DeCarlo, the government's chief witness named Anthony Salerno as one of the men involved in a large stolen and counterfeit bond scheme. Salerno was not a defendant in the DeCarlo trial.

March 4, 1970

A federal grand jury indicted Salerno and eight other men for conspiracy to transport stolen and counterfeit bonds.

October 17, 1970

Federal prosecutors severed Salerno from a bond trial after the chief witness, Zelmanowitz privately told them that he could not identify Salerno.

November 1970

The Miami Herald revisited their story on Mafia guys in Florida, but they had a map showing where mobsters like Salerno lived this time.

May 30, 1973

Before Justice Jacob B Grumet, Salerno pled not guilty to an indictment charging him with controlling loansharking and gambling in New York and Florida.

May 3, 1977

A grand jury indicted Salerno, Vince Cafaro, and others in a vast $10 million gambling ring and charged Salerno with failing to pay federal tax on about $100,000. The prosecutor said Salerno was a Capo in the Tieri (Genovese) Family.

May 13, 1977

Before Federal Judge J Whitman Knapp, Salerno and six other defendants pled not guilty to being involved in a gambling ring. Salerno also denied federal tax evasion. As a result, Judge Knapp released Salerno on $100,000 bail.

June 19, 1977

The Miami Herald ran a profile of Salerno and gave his address as 2899 Collins Ave in Miami.

August 24, 1977

A grand jury in Miami investigated extortions, beatings, and threats in Southern Florida connected to gambling. Salerno was one of many who appeared. He didn't say much.

September 20, 1977

In the prosecutor's opening statement in Salerno's tax trial, he claimed that he spent an average of $100,000 yearly while his income was $40,000. To demonstrate Salerno's spending, the prosecutor pointed out that he owned three homes and drove a new Caddy every two years.

Defense lawyer Roy Cohn countered by claiming the prosecutor was using bias and emotion against his client. He said there was no crime in spending more than you earned.

October 7, 1977

Judge William Knapp declared a mistrial when the jury couldn't reach a unanimous verdict in Salerno's federal tax case.

October 9, 1977

Jimmy Breslin wrote a column about meeting Salerno as he waited for his second tax trial verdict. Considering the trial purpose, Breslin asked Salerno about his expensive clothes and jewelry. Salerno replied, "They say I got so much money; how could I come dressed as a bum?"

Breslin quoted Salerno commenting on a prosecution witness whom he knew. The 360-pound man told Judge Knapp that he used to box at 107 pounds. After that, Salerno claimed the Judge never believed another word the witness said.

December 15, 1977

Judge William Knapp declared a mistrial in Salerno's second trial on income tax evasion after the jury failed to reach a verdict after three days of deliberation. The infamous Roy Cohn again did an excellent job as his defense lawyer.

February 21, 1978

Salerno pled guilty to two counts of tax evasion and one count of interstate gambling before Federal Judge Charles H Tenny.

April 19, 1978

Judge Tenny sentenced Salerno to six months in prison and a fine of $25,000 for tax fraud and illegal gambling.

SALERNO AND THE TEAMSTER ELECTIONS

August 24, 1981

The Cleveland Plain Dealer completed a two-part series on local and national Teamster power Jackie Presser which accused him of being an FBI informant. That was a death sentence for Presser if the paper didn't rescind the story.

Background:

In 1982 it looked like Teamster President Ray Williams was going to be convicted of a crime and would have to resign. Accordingly, supporters of other candidates started to round up support. First, Cleveland's Jackie Presser was a strong candidate, and the Cleveland Family secretly backed him. Next, John "Peanuts" Tronolone, then the Cleveland Consigliere and influential non-member Milton Rockman, went to Chicago to petition the Chicago Outfit leaders for support. The Chicago guys raised the issue of whether Presser was an informant. But the Cleveland guys eventually convinced them otherwise and gained their blessing for Presser.

Tronolone and Underboss Angelo Lonardo went to NYC and met with Salerno, seeking his backing. They explained the worries that Presser was an informant due to the Plain Dealer story, and Salerno agreed to try to get the paper to retract their claims.

He did this thru the infamous Roy Cohn—he had connections everywhere, including knowing the owner of the Plain Dealer. So the paper retracted the story, and Presser became the Teamsters' leader. Salerno was so pleased with his influence that he sent a copy of the retraction to the Chicago Bosses. Oops!

June 6, 1984

A Los Angeles Times story revealed that Presser was indeed an FBI informant. The same day the FBI bug in the Palma Boy Social Club caught this exchange: Salerno said, "Did you read in the papers that Jack Presser is a stool pigeon for the government?" "I think those fucking Chicago guys are going to knock my brains in." (They never did.)

Note:

Presser remained the Teamster President from 1983 until his death on July 9, 1988. Afterward, his backstabbing, long-time informing (Since 1972) womanizing, and plundering union funds became well known.

December 7, 1983

Lucchese Family Capo Neil Migliore, Lucchese Family Underboss Salvatore Santoro and Lucchese Family Consigliere Chris Furnari met with Salerno at the Palma Boy Social Club.

December 13, 1983

Neil Migliore returned to the Palma Boy Social Club and gave Salerno the $20,000 Fat Tony owed him by Migliore and construction man Biff Halloran.

January 31, 1984

Salerno, Lucchese Underboss Sal Santoro, and Lucchese Consigliere Chris Furnari met at the Palma Boy Social Club and discussed the Bonanno Family's wish to rejoin the Commission. There needed to be some clarification about the positions of Bosses Paul Castellano and Carmine Persico. Still, there was no doubt Salerno didn't want the Bonannos on the Commission due to their drug dealing.

May 1984

Cleveland Consigliere John Tronolone visited New York to see who Salerno wanted to replace, a secretary-treasurer of the Teamsters. Salerno put him off because he wasn't the real Boss, and the decision wasn't up to him.

May 1984

Salerno and Gambino Family Boss Paul Castellano ate in the Vivolo Restaurant on 74th Street, and FBI Agents Charlotte Land and Corrine Higgins were also there.

October 7, 1984

Salerno met Cleveland Consigliere John Tronolone and Buffalo Consigliere Joe Pieri Sr about the Buffalo leadership. Pieri was hoping to get the Commission to back his bid to become the new Buffalo Boss but needed Tronolone to introduce him to Salerno and to show that the Cleveland Family supported him.

October 8, 1984

Buffalo's Joe Pieri and Tony Salerno discussed the Buffalo leadership dispute in Salerno's social club. Pieri told Salerno that Buffalo Boss Sam Frangiamore wanted to step down. Pieri claimed that Junior Persico, Boss of the Colombo Family, blessed Pieri Sr. to be the new Boss. However, Buffalo Underboss Joe Todaro disputed this interpretation of Persico's position.

Note:

It remains to be seen whether Pieri thought Salerno was the Genovese Boss and thus a Commission member or understood he had to go through Salerno to get to the real Boss Vince Gigante.

Note:

The Commission approved Joe Todaro Sr as the new Buffalo Boss, with his son Joe Jr the Underboss and Joe Pieri Sr. as the Consigliere.

December 12, 1984
Salerno and Lucchese Boss Tony Corallo met at the Palma Boy Social Club. Salerno related the story of a dispute where Phil Lombardo interfered which greatly frustrated Salerno. He felt his superiors gave him a job and prevented him from accomplishing it.

Note:

This transcript is confusing because the information from Vincent Cafaro was that Vince Gigante had demoted Phil Lombardo in 1981, yet here he was making a decision in 1984.

January 8, 1985
Salerno, Cafaro, and Zingaro met at the Palma Boy Social Club, and Zingaro revealed that the good guys had 800 hours of Lucchese Boss Tony Lucchese tapes from a bugged Jaguar.

SALERNO'S THREE TRIALS

Salerno faced three trials in a row. To make the material easier to read, I have given each entry an appropriate label: The Commission Trial, the Genovese Family Case, and the New Jersey Genovese Case.

Commission Trial

February 25, 1985

The feds conduct a series of arrests for the Commission trial. Below is a summary of the FBI taking Salerno into custody.

FBI Agents: Dave Binney, Kate Ball, Bob Tolan, and Peter Kelleher buzzed Salerno's apartment and identified themselves, so Vincent Cafaro let them in. They find Salerno in a bathrobe at the head of a table; six other mutts were also there, and no one had started eating the delivered food.

Cafaro called Salerno's lawyer Ray Cohn.
Cohn talked to FBI Agent Binney—he wants more time—no dice
Quotes from old Pepe Sabato
"Tough guys, fucking FBI."
Some FBI Agent responded,
"Put a cork in it, okay, Pepe?"

Soon Salerno was in an FBI car headed to FBI HQ, and an Agent later said, "Fat Tony seemed to find the view (across the East River) engrossing. He kept his face pressed to the car window during the entire trip downtown."

Commission Case

February 27, 1985

US Magistrate Michael Dollinger set Salerno's bail at $2 million, which he posted later that day.

Genovese Family Case

March 20, 1986

The feds announced the Genovese Family indictments. It included charges of murder (Joseph Ullo and Philly Capo John Simone), extortion, gambling, bid rigging, and fixing the election of Teamster president Roy Williams. In addition, the indictment labeled the Genovese Family a criminal enterprise under the RICO Law, with Tony Salerno named Boss.

Genovese Family Case

March 29, 1986

Federal Judge John Walker denied bail for Salerno and Cafaro after the prosecution convinced him they were a danger to the community.

Genovese Family Case

April 2, 1986

The Judge amended the no-bail order for Salerno and Cafaro.

Genovese Family Case

April 11, 1986

New Judge Mary Johnson Lowe upheld the no-bail ruling for Salerno and Cafaro.

Genovese Family Case

July 3, 1986

The Second Court of Appeals reversed the no-bail ruling for Salerno and Cafaro.

September 1986

After having a dispute with Salerno, Soldier Vince Cafaro decided to become an informer.

September 26, 1986

Cafaro saw a doctor as part of a deception plan to release him as an informer.

Commission Trial

September 1986

The Commission trial started with Salerno as a defendant and Lucchese Boss Tony Corallo, Colombo Boss Carmine Persico, and others.

Commission Trial

September 24, 1986

Former Cleveland Underboss Angelo Lonardo told the Commission jury that he traveled to New York several times to consult Salerno for the Cleveland Family was responsible to the Genovese Family. For example, Lonardo asked Salerno to approve Kansas City Roy Williams to the Teamster Presidency. He returned a year later to seek approval for Cleveland's Jackie Presser to head the Teamsters after Williams got legally jammed up. Finally, Lonardo sought support from Salerno for the Cleveland Family to induct new members. Cleveland Consigliere John Tronolone arranged each visit since he had known Salerno for decades.

October 24, 1986

Fortune Magazine rated Salerno as the richest Mafia member. This conclusion was just a wild guess.

October 1986

Officials temporarily freed Cafaro for medical reasons.

Commission Trial

November 19, 1986

The Commission trial ended with convictions for Salerno et al. The feds did not use Cafaro as a witness. Salerno went down on one extortion conspiracy, 12 counts of extortion or attempted extortion, plus six labor bribery violations. Under the RICO law, these are called "predicate acts," and at least two of them are required, within ten years of each other, to prove RICO conspiracy and substantive RICO. The latter two means the defendant is guilty of conspiring (planning) and participating to benefit a criminal enterprise. (The Commission.)

December 27, 1986

Cafaro pulled off a sting drug buy for $210,000.

Commission Trial

January 13, 1987

Judge Richard Owen sentenced Salerno to 100 years and a fine of $240,000. The other defendants got similar terms.

Note:

For an in-depth look at the Commission Trial, please see my book, "The Commission."

Genovese Family Case

January 15, 1987

The feds charge Salerno and other Genovese guys with various counts, including murder, extortion, gambling, bid rigging, and fixing a Teamster presidential election.

March 19, 1987

Cafaro buys a kilo of heroin for $210,000 in marked bills. Police arrested Luchese Soldier Ralph Tutino, Leoluca Guarino, and Sal Larca.

March 20, 1987

The drug arrests above revealed Cafaro's informer status. The prosecution pressures him to testify against Salerno, but he resists. Cafaro finally agrees to plead to one count but no charges against his son.

Genovese Family Case

April 1987

The feds announced a superseding indictment in the Genovese Family trial.

Genovese Family Case

April 6, 1987

The Genovese Family trial started, but the prosecution did not use Vincent Cafaro because they feared the defense would claim they used Cafaro to determine the defense's strategy.

Genovese Family Case

May 4, 1987

Former Cleveland Underboss Angelo Lonardo told the jury that Cleveland Associate Milton Rochman got the Chicago Outfit to support the candidacy of Jackie Presser as the new Teamster President. Then Lonardo and Rochman traveled to New York to convince Salerno to do the same.

Genovese Family Case

May 18/19, 1987

Former Los Angeles member Jimmy Fratianno testified in the Genovese Family trial. He said Cleveland Teamster power Jackie Presser told him he did not make any move without checking with Cleveland Boss Jack Licavoli. In addition, Fratianno told the jury that he was present at a meeting in New York where Salerno and others voted to kill a mobster (Joseph Ullo) who absconded without paying a debt. Ironically, in court, Fratianno mistakenly identified another defendant as Salerno.

Genovese Family Case

May 26, 1987

By a 6-3 vote the US Supreme Court upheld the constitutionality of the 1984 Bail Reform Act. They felt it was reasonable for the government, in very strict cases, to keep a defendant in custody to protect the public.

This decision meant Salerno was not getting out while he appealed his convictions.

Genovese Family Case

June 1, 1987

Former Teamster President Roy Williams testified in the Salerno trial that Kansas City boss Nick Civella controlled him.

1987

The State of New Jersey estimated that the Genovese Family had 275 members and 600 Associates.

Genovese Family Case

September 23, 1987

The Second Circuit Court of Appeals affirmed the no-bail ruling for Salerno and Cafaro.

October 01, 1987

Cafaro's deal folded because he is upset by the adverse reaction of his wife, son, and girlfriend to his rolling over. In response, the feds sent him back to jail, and a bank put a lien on his girlfriend's home.

April 1988

Cafaro testified before Congress with no deal. He publicly revealed that Salerno was just a Front Boss. Cafaro recounted that Frank Tieri made him in 1974. He also said Salerno was hassling him about a gambling debt which made him initially turn to the government.

Genovese Family Case

May 4, 1988

The Genovese Family trial ended with nine convictions. Key figures included: Capo Vince DiNapoli, Louis DiNapoli, Capo Matty Ianniello, former Underboss/Front Boss Anthony Salerno, and Capo Aniello Migliore. But Salerno, Cleveland Associate Milton Rockman, and Cleveland Consigliere John Tronolone were found not guilty of rigging the Teamster election. Also, the jury declared Salerno and Tronolone not guilty of the murder of Philadelphia Capo John Simone.

Businessmen Nick Auletta (S&A Concrete), Biff Halloran (Transit Mix and Certified Concrete), Alvin Chattin (an employee of Halloran), and Richard Costa (Marathon Foods) were also convicted. The feds also confiscated Halloran's Transit Mix and Certified Concrete.

Genovese Family turncoat Vincent Cafaro pled guilty to two counts and signed his cooperation deal with the government. He also admitted to conspiracy in Newark.

New Jersey Genovese Case

April 10, 1989

Before Judge John W Bissell, Salerno tearfully pled guilty to:

Trying to take control of a Morris County, NJ, gravel pit.

Tried to extort $450,000 from the gravel pit owner.

Racketeering charges associated with accusations against Genovese members in NJ where they tried to eliminate competition for a shopping center development. Salerno was an unindicted co-conspirator in this last guilty plea.

New Jersey Genovese Case

September 7, 1989

Judge Bissell sentenced Salerno to five years for his New Jersey Genovese Family convictions. Salerno would serve this term once he completed his sentences in the Commission and Genovese Family trials.

June 28, 1991

The Second Court of Appeals overturned Salerno's conviction in the Genovese Case. They ruled that the Judge refused to include evidence favorable to the defense. This ruling had no effect on Salerno's freedom.

1992

The US Supreme Court reversed the Second Court of Appeals ruling that overturned the convictions in the Genovese Case.

July 18, 1992

Salerno suffered a stroke in the Springfield Medical Center for Federal Prisoners, and staff took him to a local hospital for treatment.

July 25, 1992

Salerno returned to the Springfield Medical Center for Federal Prisoners.

July 27, 1992
Salerno died of a heart attack in Springfield.

CONCLUSION

The feds sent Salerno to prison for being the Boss of the Genovese Family when he was not. It is interesting that Salerno never rolled over in the hopes of regaining his freedom before he died. However, Salerno participated in discussions of murder and selecting Teamster presidents along with a host of other crimes. He may not have been Boss but he, at various times, was Consigliere, and Underboss of the Genovese Family which made him a major Mafia criminal who deserved to be in the slammer.

CHAPTER ELEVEN

Phil "Ben" Lombardo

Historians know less about Lombardo than just about any La Cosa Nostra leader. Vito Genovese must have anointed him prior to dying in prison in 1969. Since the feds never focused on Lombardo he did not have an extensive criminal record from which to mine information. From informants we do know that he was in the crew of Capo Mike Coppola in the 1960s and was involved in gambling. He did serve time for a narcotics conviction back in the 1940s but there is no evidence he continued in that racket afterward. Below I've summarized what little I know about Lombardo.

DOB
October 5, 1908
NYC

DOD
April 1987
Hollywood, Florida

Description
5' 6"
Black balding hair
Brown eyes
Small build

His left eye was crossed, which led to a derogatory nickname, "Cockeyed Ben."

Father

Filipi

Mother

Eleanor Roto

Daughters

Three.

Son

Philip Lombardo Jr.

Residences

1926-1930 303 E 107th Street, NY.

1933 2187 Washington Ave, Bronx.

1934 1213 Lawrence Ave, Bronx.

1935 1218 Elder Ave, Bronx.

1936 1343 Purdy St, Bronx.

1950 324 Audubon Road, Englewood, NJ.

1942

A jury convicted Lombardo of selling and possessing narcotics. A Judge gave him a six-month sentence.

1959

An FBI report said Lombardo and another man had the hat check operation at the Copacabana. They had made a $30,000 profit, but Boss Vito Genovese demanded the money because he had financial problems.

1960

Lombardo acted as a witness in the marriage of Pasquale (Patsy Jerome) Genese.

1960

The owner of Cottone Construction Company told the FBI that Lombardo worked for him in a foreman position and received a salary of $250 weekly plus bonuses. His primary duties were ensuring the other employees were doing the work properly.

February 22, 1962

FBI informer MM T-11 said that Lombardo sometimes brought New York numbers money to (Capo) Mike Coppola in Miami.

June 20, 1962

Informer NY T-4 told the FBI that Lombardo was Tony Salerno's Boss. (Not the Family Boss.)

September 6, 1962

FBI informer NY T-1 said that Lombardo was tight with a guy from the Bronx named Jerome. The FBI speculated that this was Michael Giorano.

September 28, 1962

Informer NY T-8 told his FBI handler that Lombardo was running things in NY while Mike Coppola was in prison.

October 1964

The Lombardo's called the State Police after a break-in at their Englewood home.

October 9, 1964

An FBI bug caught Acting Underboss Tommy Eboli relating a conversation with Acting Boss Jerry Catena. They were preparing for a pre-Commission meeting to discuss the Joe Bonanno problem, and Eboli suggested that Capo Phil Lombardo should be part of the conclave. This tape suggests Lombardo was already an influential figure in 1964. Turncoat Vince "Fish" Cafaro testified in 1988 that Boss Vito Genovese appointed Lombardo as his stand-in back in 1959.

1967

The FBI filed a report that indicated Lombardo spent the winter months in Hollywood, Florida, and that Tommy Eboli was a good friend.

July 24, 1969

The FBI spoke to Lombardo as part of their efforts to find fugitive Genovese Soldier Sammy Granello.

August 13, 1970

The Hackensack Record carried a story that identified Lombardo as the Acting Underboss in the Jerry Catena Family.

December 23, 1977

An FBI bug caught Genovese Soldier Anthony "Little Pussy" Russo stating that Lombardo was the real Boss of the Genovese Family.

July 9, 1981

Bouncers at the Surf nightclub in Orthley Beach, NJ, threw an unruly Phil Lombardo Jr, son of Genovese Boss Phil Lombardo, out of the facility. He allegedly responded by returning and spraying off-duty NJ State Trooper Denis McDowell in the face with a mace-like product. McDowell and others chased Lombardo down then McDowell placed him under arrest. The trooper later testified that Lombardo was ranting about being connected and that his father ran NJ and New York. If convicted, Lombardo Jr faced up to fifteen years in prison. His friends decided they had to act to protect him.

November 11, 1981

A grand jury indicted seven men for bribing Trooper McDowell. He participated in a State Police sting that included taping the bribery. During the arrests, the police searched Phil Lombardi Sr's home but did not charge him in this incident. After a trial, a jury convicted Lombardo Jr's lawyer and another man.

CONCLUSION

Lombardo's biggest accomplishment was flying under the radar of the FBI while controlling the Genovese Family in the 1970s. He used a series of Underbosses to act as the Boss while he pulled the strings in anonymity. Hopefully further research will flesh out his activities while leading the Genovese Family.

CHAPTER TWELVE

Vince Gigante

Gigante was the Mafia's greatest actor winning the Oscar for best performance from the time he became Boss in 1981 until he admitted faking mental illnesses in 2003. It was an incredible strategy going back into the 1960s when he avoided prosecution by fooling the physiatrists. His personal families and close aides always knew it was an act but made great contributions to keep the show rolling. A summary of his unique life follows.

DOB
March 29, 1928
New York, New York.

DOD
December 19, 2005
Springfield Medical Center for Federal Prisoners

April 2, 1945
The police charged Gigante with criminal receiving (Possessing stolen goods), but Felony Court Judge Ramsgate dismissed the charge.

January 28, 1948

Gigante pled guilty to grand larceny and arson, and General Sessions Judge Goldstein suspended his sentence. However, he would remain on probation until January 27, 1951.

1950s

An informer told the FBI that Gigante was involved in a Cadillac car theft ring, shylocking, and after-hours night clubs.

June 14, 1950

A jury convicted Gigante of conspiracy. (?) Special Sessions Judge Cooper gave him a 60-day sentence.

1951

Gigante lived at 238 Thompson Street.

September 29, 1951

The police arrested Gigante for gambling.

October 5, 1951

Felony Court Judge Orr dismissed Gigante's gambling charge.

February 16, 1953

Special Sessions Judge Thompson sentenced Gigante to ten days in jail and a $75 fine for gambling.

May 2, 1957

Vincent Gigante, acting on orders from Underboss Vito Genovese, attempted to kill Boss Frank Costello but only wounded him. However, Costello quickly made a life-saving deal with Genovese and stepped down as Boss. The NYPD said Gigante's driver was Tommy Eboli and Dom Alongi was also in the vehicle.

1957

Gigante drew two salaries as a building superintendent at the Washington Square Village Corp. The records indicated he received a total of $900 for the year.

July 18, 1957

A Daily News article indicated that the police were looking for a small-time gambler for the Costello shooting. A parking ticket from near the Costello shooting scene led the police to a car owned by Gigante. The reporter described Gigante as a fat ex-pug, an underworld hanger-on, and the Waddler.

August 12, 1957

The NYPD arrested Mario and Ralph Gigante after a traffic stop. Mario got into an altercation with a police officer, and they charged Ralph with vagrancy.

August 13, 1957

A Magistrate held Mario Gigante on charges of vagrancy, felonious assault, and weapons violations and set bail at $3,000. Police found a hatchet and a baseball bat in Mario's vehicle.

August 14, 1957

Magistrate Harry G Andrews, from the Manhattan Arrest Court, dismissed Ralph Gigante's vagrancy charge.

August 19, 1957

Gigante turned himself in, and the police booked him for attempted murder. Frank Costello was brought in at 4:45 PM to look at the suspect in his shooting. Actor Phil Kennedy, with Costello on the night of the shooting, also visited the police station but denied identifying anyone when he left.

August 20, 1957

Officials arraigned Gigante in Felony Court before Magistrate Reuben Levy, who set bail at $150,000. Gigante's lawyer David M Markowitz stated that his client first heard about the Costello shooting on TV. He then filed a writ of habeas corpus to be served on the City Prison Warden to show why Gigante should not be released on reasonable bail.

August 21, 1957
Superior Court Justice George M Tilzer reviewed Gigante's writ of habeas corpus but ruled that Gigante "has shown an open defiance of law and order" and kept bail at $150,000.

August 22, 1957
A grand jury indicted Gigante in the Costello shooting.

August 23, 1957
Officials hauled Gigante before Magistrate Reuben Levy in Felony Court, who ordered a formal arraignment the following day.

August 29, 1957
Gigante pled not guilty in the Costello shooting.

September 13, 1957
Gigante's lawyer asked for a bail reduction from $100,000 to $25,000, but General Sessions Judge Mitchell Schwetzer refused the request.

September 18, 1957
General Sessions Judge Mitch D Schweitzer reduced Gigante's bail to $100,000, which his family and friends posted. However, the police arrested Gigante as he exited the courthouse and hauled him before Chief Magistrate John M Murtaugh in Traffic Court. Murtaugh fined Gigante $500 for ten outstanding traffic tickets.

April 28, 1958
The Gigante trial started and then recessed.

May 5, 1958

FBI informant NY T-3 said Genovese powers Tony Bender and Tom Eboli, plus lesser lights, met in the Savannah nightclub to figure out how they would pay for Gigante's defense.

May 14, 1958

Phil Kennedy testified he didn't see anyone leave the building after the shooting. Kennedy was in the taxi with Costello but stayed behind to settle the fare when Costello entered his apartment building.

May 15, 1958

Norval Keith, the doorman at Costello's apartment building, gave the following testimony before Judge John A Mullen.

He opened the door to Costello's taxi.

He saw a big back vehicle parked nearby.

He watched Costello enter the building.

A big man brushed by him and followed Costello into the apartment lobby.

He heard the big man say, "This is for you, Frank!" as he fired one shot at Costello.

He said the gunman weighed about 20 to 40 pounds more than the defendant.

He had previously identified Gigante in a 12-man lineup.

He admitted that one of his eyes was useless.

He identified the time on a clock that was sixty feet away.

May 16, 1958

Norval Keith continued his testimony before Judge John A Mullen. Costello's defense lawyer hammered him with accusations of drinking on the job and having poor eyesight. Fortunately for Gigante, it was an effective cross-examination. The Daily News described Gigante as "hulking and thick-lipped."

In the hopes of supporting Keith's testimony, the prosecutor put Detective Edward W Lehane on the stand. The police officer explained that he had known Gigante for a long time and had seen him in 1957 when he was very fat and had long hair. Then, when Gigante surrendered, the Detective said he had lost between 30-40 pounds and now had a brush cut.

May 20, 1958

Costello testified that he heard a loud firecracker-like sound, then turned around and saw nobody. At this point, Frank felt a wetness on the right side of his head and discovered it was blood. Costello said he couldn't figure out why anyone would shoot him. The prosecutor had both Gigante and Costello stand and asked the latter to take a good look at the defendant. Costello put on his glasses but said he had never seen this person before.

A doctor testified that Costello must have been facing his attacker, for the bullet went from front to back on the right side of his head, passing through his hat.

Two Detectives testified about suspecting Gigante about two weeks after the shooting and described their fruitless search for the gangster. One said he visited Gigante's wife about 15-20 times and questioned other relatives and friends. The prosecutor used this testimony in an attempt to show that Gigante was on the run, thus indicating guilt.

May 21, 1958

A detective who knew Gigante testified that the gangster was much bigger in the past. The prosecutor hoped this testimony bolstered that of the doorman, who said Gigante was smaller than when the shooting happened.

May 27, 1958

Prosecutor Alexander Herman's case was severely damaged when Costello claimed he couldn't identify his attacker. In his summation, Herman blasted Costello as a "brazen liar, a hoodlum, and a gangster" who knew who shot him.

Defense attorney Maurice Edelbaum also castigated Costello as a mug whom the cops should have dragged down to their headquarters to look at pictures of possible suspects. Instead, the police showed Costello all kinds of respect by taking photos to his apartment. Edelbaum described the doorman as someone who drank and had the DTs in the courtroom. He then made fun of Norval Keith's red nose.

The Judge gave the case to the jury, who returned a not-guilty verdict at 11:45 PM. Gigante's family and supporters erupted in wild cheers, and his parents were in tears. However, Gigante appeared very relaxed and told the press, "I knew it had to be this way because I was innocent."

COMMENT

Gigante did shoot Costello, but his lawyer Edelbaum did a great job casting doubt on the witness testimony of the doorman. Costello had little choice but to refuse to identify Gigante, for it was the code of LCN, plus he had gained a pass from Vito Genovese by retiring. Allegedly, after Costello refused to identify Gigante and left the stand, Gigante said, "Thanks Frank," as Costello passed the defense table.

1958
Gigante and his family lived at 134 Becker Street.

July 6 or 7, 1958
According to information provided by hitman Harold Konigsberg in 1965, Gigante attended a meeting where Family leaders decided to kill John Michael Earle. Capo Tony Bender, Dom DeQuatro, Dom Alongi, Mario Gigante, Larry Denticio, George Martinelli, and Konigsberg were in attendance. Konigsberg was the shooter.

June 18, 1958
Harold Konigsberg killed hood John Earle in a cafeteria at 8th and 57th Avenue.

October 1, 1958

Someone killed local union hood John Scanlon in NJ. On May 27, 1965, FBI informer NY T-6 told his handlers that Gigante attended a meeting that OK'd the hit.

July 7, 1958

Federal Narcotics Agents arrested Genovese and Gigante after a federal grand jury indicted them and others on a narcotics conspiracy. The agents found Gigante at the Lexington Social Club at Spring and Sullivan Streets. Authorities took the two men to the Federal House of Detention.

July 8, 1958

US Attorney Paul Williams opened the narcotics conspiracy indictment. Then arraigned Gigante and the others before Federal Judge Alexander Bicks, who set Gigante's bail at $35,000.

1959

Gigante was involved with the Try-Ann Vending Company with Tommy Eboli.

April 3, 1959

A federal jury convicted Gigante and others of a narcotics conspiracy. Judge Bicks continued Gigante on his original $35,000 bail.

April 17, 1959

Judge Bicks sentenced Gigante to seven years.

Note:

Please see more details on the trial and sentences in the Genovese chapter.

January 2, 1960

The Second Court of Appeals rejected the appeal of Genovese, Gigante, et al.

February 18, 1960
Gigante arrived at Lewisburg Penitentiary to begin serving his seven-year narcotics conspiracy sentence.

May 1, 1960
Judge Brick refused to order a new trial for Genovese, Gigante, et al.

May 16, 1960
The US Supreme Court refused to hear an appeal from Genovese, Gigante et al.

June 12, 1960
Judge Brick refused a new trial for Genovese, Gigante et al.

May 9, 1961
Gigante's father died.

1963
The Second Court of Appeals refused a new trial for Genovese, Gigante, et al. The defense claimed the chief prosecution witness had recanted his testimony.

October 21, 1963
The US Supreme Court ordered the Second Circuit Court of Appeals to review their rejection of a new trial for Genovese, Gigante, et al.

October 16, 1964
The Second Circuit Court of Appeals decided that there were insufficient grounds for a new trial.

February 7, 1964
The Lewisburg prison staff gave Gigante an excellent report on his conduct.

October 16, 1964

The Parole Commission released Gigante.

1965

Gigante was operating out of the Vicarl Social Club at 207 Sullivan Street. Reports said he was involved in horse booking and numbers.

March 1, 1965

The US Supreme Court refused to hear an appeal from Genovese, Gigante et al. for a new trial.

May 27, 1965

FBI informer NY T-6 told his handler that Gigante was involved in planning the separate murders of John Scanlon and John Earle in 1958.

MENTAL HEALTHY STRATEGY

1966

Gigante and his family lived at 5 Arrowhead Road in Old Tappan, NJ. Gigante claimed to be a dispatcher for the P&G Motor Freight Company in the Bronx.

January 1966

FBI Director J Edgar Hoover ordered his New York Office to refocus on Gigante.

October 27, 1966

In 1971 Dr. Michael J Scolario testified that Gigante began seeing him for a "character disorder."

1967

In later testimony, Gigante said he worked as a salesman for the Scott Novelty Company of Newark, NJ, at a salary of $15,000 yearly. The company made ladies' hats at the time.

1967

An Old Tappan detective introduced Gigante to the Police Chief at the request of Gigante's friend Michael Zuppas.

December 1967

Gigante gave Chief Schuh $100 in a Christmas card.

January 1968

Ten-day stay in a hospital.

June 1968

An informer told the FBI that Gigante was a Genovese Family Capo.

December 1968

Gigante gave Chief Schuh $100 to be split with the rest of the five-person police force.

February 14, 1969

Boss Vito Genovese died in the Springfield Medical Center.

At some point, the Family elected Capo Phil Lombardo as their new Boss.

June 27, 1969

The FBI observed Gigante meeting with Capo Phil Lombardo.

July 14-18, 1969

The Bergin County Prosecutor's Office began surveillance of Gigante.

July 18, 1969

Gigante complained about the surveillance to Detectives near his home.

August 20, 1969-August 29, 1969

"Feels depressed, trouble concentrating."

Late December 1969

Olympia Gigante went to the Old Tappan Police Station and handed out money to the officers.

December 1969

Gigante and Michael Zuppas met with Chief Schuh and requested that he inform them of upcoming surveillance of Gigante by Bergin County detectives. They promised to "take care of him."

January 19, 1970

Zuppas met Chief Schuh and asked about surveillance on Gigante. He passed on a card containing $100 and said it was from Mr. and Mrs. Gigante.

February 1970

A prominent article in "The Record" detailed Gigante's past and alleged bribery of the Old Tappan Police Force.

February 17, 1970

Gigante's friend, Michael Zuppas, met with the Old Tappan Police Chief to complain about the surveillance of Gigante.

February 25, 1970

The Old Tappan Police Chief told the Bergin County Prosecutor that he had accepted two gifts of $100 from Gigante but felt it was an everyday practice at Christmas. The City Council later suspended the Chief.

February 27, 1970

Michael Zuppas again met with the Old Tappan Police Chief about Gigante's surveillance.

March 17, 1970

A grand jury indicted Gigante, Chief Schuh, four constables, and Olympia Gigante on bribery-related charges.

March 19, 1970

Gigante and his mistress Olympia pled not guilty to charges related to the Old Tappan Police Force. County Court Judge Benjamin P Galanti set bail of $25,000 for Gigante and $10,000 for Olympia.

March 19, 1970

Reverend Louis Gigante held a press conference on the courthouse steps claiming that the Bergin County Prosecutor was railroading his brother. He said a negative article in "The Record" upset Gigante's family and friends.

April 27, 1970-June 19, 1970

"Want to sleep forever."

May 12, 1970

Gigante was supposed to appear for trial for failing to register as a convicted narcotics trafficker, but he was in the hospital.

September 28, 1970-October 9, 1970

Gigante's wife wrote on the admission form,

"My husband needs care but doesn't realize it."

December 9, 1970

Superior Court Judge J Morris Pashman rejected an appeal from Gigante's lawyer that pretrial publicity infringed on Gigante's right to a fair trial.

January 13, 1971-February 19, 1971

Gigante in a hospital.

September 20, 1971-October 19. 1971

Gigante in a hospital.

September 22, 1971
Gigante agreed to let a court-appointed psychiatrist examine him at St Vincent's Hospital.

January 13, 1971
"I feel very sick again. I can't sleep; I can't think or do anything."

December 4, 1972-December 14, 1972
"I feel very nervous all the time."

March 13, 1973
A jury found Michael Zupa not guilty of bribing the Old Tappan Police Force.

April 24, 1973
Superior Court Judge J Morris Pashman dismissed bribery charges against Gigante.

June 13, 1973
Louis Gigante won the election to New York City Council.

April 1, 1975
FBI informer NY T-2 reported that Gigante was using an insanity ploy.

June 13-June 14, 1975
The FBI surveilled the Gigante social club and saw little.

June 11, 1977
Judge Morris Malech ruled that Gigante was incompetent and couldn't face bribery charges. However, he also ordered that there would be another hearing on September 17.

GIGANTE IS THE NEW BOSS

1981

Vincent "Fish" Cafaro later told the FBI that Gigante, Manna, and Santora visited Salerno and Lombardo individually in the hospital and notified them that Gigante was taking over. However, Gigante permitted Salerno to continue as the "Front Boss."

Olympia Esposito bought a home on East 77th near Park Avenue for $490,000.

1983

A New Jersey Crime Report tagged Genovese Soldier John DiGilio as a power on the docks. The report claimed DiGilio was involved in labor extortion, stevedoring, loansharking, cargo thefts, gambling, and other rackets.

GIGANTE DODGES COMMISSION INDICTMENT

On February 25, 1985, the feds announced an indictment of Bosses and Associates involved with the Mafia Commission. However, they did not name Gigante in this indictment or any of the superseding indictments, even though he was the official Boss of the Genovese Family. Instead, the feds mistakenly called Soldier and Front Boss Anthony Salerno the Boss.

1987

John Gotti sent Sammy Gravano to see Genovese Underboss Venero Mangano to get a piece of the windows replacement program for the New York Housing Authority.

February 1988

Father Gigante applied to Superior Court to have his brother Vincent declared incompetent.

Summer 1989

Gigante had heart surgery.

GIGANTE DODGES THE WINDOWS TRIAL

May 30, 1990

A grand jury indicted Gigante and 14 others for ripping off the New York Housing Authorities window replacement plan since 1978.

May 31, 1990

Gigante went to the NY Downtown Hospital complaining of chest pains. The doctors admitted him and prescribed nitroglycerin.

June 29, 1990

Doctors released Gigante from the hospital after heart treatment.

Gigante admitted himself to St Vincent's Hospital for psychiatric evaluations by two physiatrists he picked and two selected by the court.

November 27, 1990

Doctors released Gigante from St Vincent's Hospital.

March 11, 1991

Four court-appointed psychiatrists found Gigante unfit to stand trial.

December 9, 1991

The FBI set up a camera to observe Gigante's residence for his mistress at 505 LaGuardia Place.

January 24, 1992

The FBI camera near Gigante's residence began operation.

April 2, 1992

A jury convicted John Gotti of racketeering.

GIGANTE DOWNFALL BEGINS

June 10, 1993

A grand jury brought down a six-count indictment charging Gigante with racketeering and conspiracy to murder. However, Gigante didn't appear in court because he was a patient at St Vincent's Hospital.

July 1993

Judge Nickerson ruled that Gigante had to live with his mother and confine himself to a ten-block radius around her home.

October 28, 1994

An Assistant US Attorney asked Judge Eugene Nickerson to put Gigante in the Metropolitan Correctional Center for a 28-day psychiatric evaluation.

September 11, 1995

A court-appointed psychiatrist, Dr. Daniel Swartz, said it was impossible to evaluate Gigante, for he claimed God told him not to answer any questions. In addition, the Doctor said he was no longer sure his previous evaluation that Gigante had a psychotic disorder was correct.

March 1996

Turncoats Sammy Gravano and Al D'Arco testified that they felt Gigante was competent.

May 1996

Judge Nickerson said that Gigante ran his crime Family from 1970 through 1991 and asked the psychiatrists to review their previous findings of incompetence.

June 10, 1996

The Feds arrested Acting Boss Barney Bellomo, Acting Underboss Michael Generoso, and Consigliere James Ida.

June 24, 1996

A garbage racket indictment included Mario Gigante and a bunch of companies.

August 28, 1996

Reviewing their previous assessments, two psychiatrists changed their opinions and ruled Gigante ready for trial. Two others stuck to their belief he wasn't. Finally, Judge Nickerson ruled Gigante was OK for trial.

September 6, 2006

Officials arraigned Gigante before Judge Nickerson in the Brooklyn Federal Courthouse. He pled not guilty.

December 9, 1996

James La Rosa, Gigante's lawyer, announced that Gigante had checked into Mount Sinai Hospital for a heart operation.

January 1997

Gigante had heart surgery.

May 1997

Judge Nickerson revoked Gigante's bail.

June 25, 1997

Gigante's trial finally began.

July 2, 1997

Former Philadelphia Underboss Phil Leonetti testified that Gigante ordered the murders of six men who violated Commission rules by killing two Philadelphia Bosses.

July 3, 1997

The prosecution played FBI tapes of Gigante talking coherently with Olympia Esposito in her home.

July 25, 1997

The jury found Gigante guilty of racketeering, bid rigging, extortion, and running the Family. However, they ruled him not guilty of six Philly-related murders but guilty of conspiring to murder John Gotti and Peter Savino.

December 18, 1997

Judge Weinstein sentenced Gigante to 12 years and a fine of $1.2 million. He also refused bail and ordered authorities to turn Gigante over to Federal Correctional Authorities on January 5; meanwhile, he would stay in the Westchester Medical Center's prison ward.

July 26, 1998

News accounts report that Capos Punchy Illiano and Lawrence Dentico were running the Genovese family after the imprisonment of Gigante.

January 22, 1999

The Second Court of Appeals upheld Gigante's conviction.

December 2000

Judge Weinstein denied a request to bring Gigante back to New York from Texas for medical tests.

January 23, 2002

A 14-count indictment included Gigante and his son Andrew. The feds alleged that Gigante continued to run his Family from behind bars and used his son Andrew to pass messages. In addition, they accused Gigante of obstruction of justice by faking mental illnesses for decades.

January 25, 2002

Magistrate Steven Gold released Andrew Gigante on $2.5 million bail.

February 7, 2002

Before Judge I Leo Glasser, Gigante pretended he could not enter a plea in the January 23, 2002 indictment. Prison officials had brought Gigante to New York from a prison medical facility in Fort Worth, Texas.

March 13, 2002

Judge I Leo Glasser rejected Gigante's plea to be transferred to a hospital rather than remain in prison.

March 20, 2002

Prosecutors played a series of audio tapes of Gigante talking to his wife and girlfriend from his prison cell in Fort Worth. They also revealed videotapes of Gigante during visits with his son Vincent and a doctor. All showed a very coherent Gigante.

April 23, 2002

Judge I Leo Glasser ruled that Gigante was competent to stand trial.

April 7, 2003

Genovese Family Boss Vincent Gigante pled guilty to obstructing justice by misleading psychiatrists and psychologists evaluating his mental competence to influence their testimony in prior cases. GIGANTE's guilty plea agreement called for a three-year sentence after he completed a 12-year term from another conviction. Prison officials took him back to Fort Worth.

August 1, 2003

Prison officials transferred Gigante to the Springfield Missouri Medical Center for Federal Prisoners so he could get more intensive health assistance.

October 16 and 17, 2005

Gigante's son Vincent visited him in the Springfield medical facility and found Gigante in a near comatose state.

November 2005
Prison officials moved Gigante to the St. John's Medical Center in Springfield because of heart and kidney problems.

November 23, 2003
Prison officials brought Gigante back to the Springfield Medical Center for Federal Prisoners.

December 19, 2005
Gigante died in the Springfield Medical Center of a heart attack.

December 22, 2005
The family of Gigante's legal wife held a memorial service in NJ., but without Gigante's body.

December 23, 2005
Gigante's mistress' family held a second funeral at St. Anthony of Padua Church. Gigante's brother Reverend Louis Gigante led the funeral mass with the body present.

OTHER MAJOR EVENTS DURING GIGANTE'S REIGN

February 10, 1997
Acting Boss Bellomo and Acting Underboss Generoso pled guilty in the San Gennaro Festival case.

CONCLUSION

Gigante had a long run at the top of the Genovese Family by balancing a crazy act to fool the good guys and a sane persona to run the Family. In addition he juggled two wives and sets of kids. Gigante sanctioned murders and all kinds of criminal activity while he ruled his Genovese Soldiers and Capos. An outsider might find it strange that Gigante never travelled and enjoyed his money but for him, dominating one of American's most powerful organized crime organizations was his nirvana.

CHAPTER THIRTEEN

Ruggiero "Richie the Boot" Boiardo

Boiardo was a long time New Jersey Capo in the Genovese Family who became famous thanks to the media. Life Magazine ran a spread of picture of his odd estate complete with statues of all his family members. Hidden bugs captured other Mafiosi talking about Boiardo's legendary "fire pit" where he allegedly disposed of the bodies of Mafia victims. The fact that Boiardo was active in mob affairs deep into his 80s also created wonder and attention. A summary of his life in the Mafia follows.

DOB
November 8, 1890
Naples

DOD
October 29, 1984
New Jersey

Physical
5' 7 1/2"
Gray hair

Son
Anthony

Residences
240 Broad Street North, Newark

Before 1930
35 Newark Street
1930-1946
328 Beauford Ave, Livingston, NJ

1900
He entered the United States through Philadelphia

PROHIBITION

1925-1928
Boiardo managed illegal stills with the Mazzocchi gang.

1928
Boiardo split off from his gang and started to operate stills independently. In addition, he and his crew allegedly hijacked Abner Zwillman's liquor trucks and battled with his former partners, the Mazzocchi brothers.

1930
Rumors stated that Al Capone brokered a peace meeting between Boiardo and Zwillman.

1930
Boiardo lived at 242 Broad Street in Newark.

GANG WARFARE

November 4, 1930
Two gangsters shot John Passelli in his bed at Newark General Hospital. Doctors had admitted him for injuries from a beating. When they wanted to release him, Passelli paid for a private room and stayed on. Unfortunately,

this move didn't save him from his enemies. The police told the press that Passelli was a chief lieutenant of Boiardo.

November 26, 1930

Two gunmen, firing from a rented apartment across the street, blasted Boiardo as he exited his armored car in front of his home in Newark. He had been out with another friend whom the driver, Joseph Juliano, dropped off before going to Boiardo's home. As the shooting took place, Juliano raced away. A milkman found Boiardo, and an ambulance took him to the hospital with ten shotgun pellets in the head and six in the chest/neck. It was Boiardo's bad luck that the police found a revolver in his clothing, leading to a charge of illegal gun possession.

February 4, 1931

A jury found Boiardo guilty of illegal gun possession, but Judge Flannagan released the gangster on $25,000 bail until sentencing.

March 9, 1931

Judge Dallas Flannagan sentenced Boiardo to 21/2 years in prison and a fine of $1,000 for illegal gun possession.

March 20, 1931

Someone shot and killed Phil Rossi behind the bar at the Ringside Athletic Club. The police believed it was revenge for the Boiardo hit attempt on November 26, 1930.

August 6, 1931

The press discovered a police and prison investigation into alleged wild drinking and carousing parties at the Crosswicks State Prison farm where Boiardo was a prisoner.

1932

Boiardo began an elimination campaign against members of his crew who had taken over his operations while he was in prison.

March 2, 1934

A taxi driver found a seriously wounded Joseph Juliano staggering down a Newark Street and rushed him to St Michael's Hospital. With wounds in his chest, shoulder, and groin Juliano stuck to the code and said he had no idea who shot him. Juliano was Boiardo's driver the night he was ambushed.

June 18, 1934

Police found the bodies of three men in a vehicle on Fern Road in East Brunswick, NJ. The rumors were they were hijacking stills, and we later learn that Boiardo ordered the hit and got hell for doing so.

July 2, 1934

NJ Troopers found the body of Jerry Rullo lying on a car seat in a field in New Providence. Later they discovered his blood-stained vehicle in a garage in Newark. Police speculated that Rullo was part of the still-raiding gang found dead on June 18, 1934.

1933-1937

Boiardo owned a funeral car service on Stone Street in Newark.

1937

Boiardo and a partner owned the Vittorio Castle restaurant at 8th Ave and Summer Ave in Newark.

1938

The New Jersey State Alcohol and Beverage Control Commission granted Boiardo a permit to work at the Vittorio Castle restaurant because he had a clean record for five years.

January 10, 1939

A federal grand jury indicted Boiardo for income tax evasion.

November 10, 1939

A federal grand jury indicted Boiardo and seven others for violating federal liquor law, and the authorities described Boiardo as a Newark home wrecker contractor. Judge Phillip Forman set trial for November 20, 1939.

April 10, 1940

A federal jury found Boiardo not guilty of income tax evasion involving an illegal still.

October 26, 1946

Boiardo held a funeral for his wife, Jennie. It took 31 vehicles to carry the flowers to Holy Cross Cemetery in North Arlington.

1948

Boiardo and his partner sold the Vittorio Castle restaurant, although some authorities felt he remained a hidden owner.

May 19, 1948

During an FBI interview, Boiardo stated he owned the Boiardo Construction Company, but he was the only employee. In addition, he said he was a salesman for Primo Motor Company and had the Sorrento Restaurant on Park Ave in Newark.

1935-1948

Boiardo was involved in a lottery whose winning number came from an Italian lottery. But, in 1948, word spread that the Boiardo crew was pulling a scam by picking their number, thus ensuring few people won.

1950

Six hundred guests attended the reception for Anthony "Tony Boy" Boiardo and his wife at the prestigious Essex House in Newark. Future Genovese Family Acting Boss Jerry Catena was the best man, and Underboss Willie Moretti appeared.

February 3, 1951

William "Billy Jenkins" Cardinal's family reported him missing. Police found his nephew's vehicle in Clark Township near Rahway with Jenkin's glasses and driver's license in the front seat. Allegedly "Billy Jenkins" was involved in the 1934 murder of three hoods.

In the early 1960s, an FBI bug heard Capo Ray DeCarlo and Soldier Anthony Russo discussing the "Billy Jenkins" hit. DeCarlo related that Boss Vito Genovese told him they hit Jenkins because he ignored warnings from Vito to stay out of politics in Keansburg. In addition, DeCarlo said Boiardo asked Underboss Willie Moretti's permission to kill Jenkins.

Interestingly, DeCarlo again discusses the Jenkins hit a few days later and says Boiardo did it without an OK. The story was that he asked his Capo Mike Miranda but did not go higher up the authority chain. DeCarlo also claimed he had saved Jenkins on two occasions. Anthony Russo recalled that after the hit, Ritchie Boiardo said, "Well, we got revenge on one already."

December 1951

The FBI files state that Boiardo owned the Harrison Fuel company in Passaic, NJ.

1952

The FBI files said Boiardo was involved in gambling in Newark and Harrison. Also, he controlled the Ladies Garment Workers Union in Newark.

May 1953

Boiardo opened the upscale El Sorrento Club in Newark.

June 9, 1953

The INS contacted the FBI as part of their efforts to denaturalize Boiardo.

March 28, 1956

FBI Agents interviewed Boiardo at their Newark office. He stated he avoided narcotics and vice, although others didn't. Boiardo denied he was beholding to a man whose name the FBI blacked out in the file but that he was responsible to someone but not Lucky Luciano.

September 23, 1960

John Russo, James Calabrese, and Pasquale Antonelli were wounded in a wild shootout at the Freemont Club in Newark. From his hospital bed, Antonelli admitted shooting the two men but refused to say why.

October 17, 1960

Doctors released John Russo from the Martland Medical Center, but the authorities held him on $100,000 bail.

October 18, 1960

John Russo appeared before a grand jury investigating the Freemont Club shooting.

December 1, 1960

Judge Walter H Conklin found Anthony Boiardo in contempt after he refused to testify before a grand jury about the September 23 gun battle.

The Judge released Anthony to the custody of his lawyers until his sentencing later in the month.

September 13, 1961

Essex County Prosecutor Brendan Byrne announced he would question Anthony Boiardo about the disappearance of bartender Natale Lento. In addition, he was to be a key witness against John Russo, who was involved in a shooting at the Club Freemont. The prosecutor charged Russo with perjury from his grand jury appearance about the event after Lento testified.

1962-1967

Anthony Boiardo joined the Valentine Electrical Company, and their gross sales rose from $1 million to $10 million thanks to many Newark City contracts.

January 25, 1962

The FBI bug in Ray DeCarlo's office caught him complaining that Anthony Boiardo gave Newark mayoralty candidate Hugh Addonizio $5,000 directly instead of going through himself. DeCarlo wanted to be the sole source of contact between Addonizio and the mob.

1962

An illegal FBI bug overheard Capo Ray DeCarlo and Anthony Russo discussing their favorite topic, the Boiardos. DeCarlo recalled Underboss Willie Moretti sarcastically saying to Boiardo after he requested permission to kill one of his men:

"Look, get them all together and kill them all at once! Here, every six months, you want to kill another of your guys. You killed Zip (David Zipper killed in 1930), you killed Johnny Rusek, and you killed Swack. You tried to kill Casey. Here you want an OK for Bill Jenks."

February 23, 1963

The FBI hidden bug caught DeCarlo, Anthony Boiardo, Decavalcante Family Boss Sam Decavalcante, and his Capo Louie Larasso discussing old mob hits. DeCarlo said they should have given Underboss Willie Moretti a lethal dose of poison rather than gunning him down in public. They batted that idea around a bit before moving on to the killing of a "Little Jew." Anthony Russo said his father hit the victim on the head with a hammer, and he went down. Then Russo claimed he whacked the guy on the head with a crowbar eight times, and the guy swore at him.

February 26, 1963

DeCarlo discussed the murder of the "Little Jew" with Anthony Russo. In his version, Russo lured the victim to some location, and he, his brother John, and Anthony Boiardo beat him badly, with Anthony Russo completing the job by strangling him with a chain. Russo said Richie Boiardo was not present.

September 4, 1963

The FBI overheard Capo Ray DeCarlo relate information passed on to him by an NJ State Trooper. According to the lawman, all Valachi had to say about New Jersey was that Jerry Catena took his place when Genovese went away.

October 21, 1963

Among the witnesses subpoenaed to testify before a grand jury were: Jerry Catena, Ritchie Boiardo, Bonanno Soldier Tony Riela, and others.

November 15, 1963

Ritchie Boiardo and his son Anthony appeared before an Essex County grand jury investigating crime. Anthony had attempted to have his subpoena quashed, but Judge Alexander P Waugh denied his request.

August 9, 1966

Boiardo testified before a grand jury investigating the shooting of two teenagers on his estate. The kids testified that they were looking for a haunted house before they were wounded. Boiardo complained to the press that people were hounding him because of his name.

February 2/3, 1967

Federal agents raided the Altruist Club in Newark, looking for gambling paraphernalia. Federal tax agents arrested Boiardo for failing to register as a gambler by buying a federal gambling stamp plus conspiracy to avoid paying federal taxes on his gambling receipts. The magistrate released Boiardo on $1,000 bail.

1967

Boiardo had major stomach surgery.

April 18, 1968

US Attorney David Satz Jr sought dismissal of the gambling charges against Boiardo. The US Supreme Court had ruled that requirements that gamblers have a gambling stamp and pay a special gambling tax were unconstitutional. However, the government decided to use the same evidence in a state trial.

1969

A grand jury indicted Boiardo and 18 others for violating the state lottery laws. The charges stemmed from the February 1967 raid on the Altruist Club.

1969

The New York Times ran an article on New Jersey and included a description of Anthony "Tony Boy" Boiardo's split-level home at 65 Avon Drive in Essex Falls.

April 11, 1969

During the Boiardo gambling trial, an IRS undercover agent testified that one of the defendants called Boiardo "The Boss of the Eastern Seaboard."

April 28, 1969

A jury convicted Boiardo and 18 other men of conspiracy to violate the New Jersey State gambling laws. Judge Fusco released Boiardo on $5,000 bail until sentencing.

Secretly Superior Court Judge James R Giuliani ordered a probe after three jurors independently reported someone approached them during the trial. (Presumably, in an attempt to bribe them.)

June 11, 1969

Judge James Giuliano sentenced Boiardo to 2 1/2 to 3 years for his conspiracy to violate the New Jersey gambling laws. He gave the other defendants a variety of terms. Trial Judge Ralph Fusco was also present for this legal action.

December 17, 1969

A US grand jury indicted Anthony Boiardo, former Newark Mayor Hugh Addonizzio, and others for conspiracy to extort contractors who won city contracts, plus many individual crimes.

April 30, 1970

Anthony Boiardo and his co-defendants won a small victory when District Court Judge Barlow ruled that their trial should take place in Trenton rather than Newark due to adverse publicity for the defendants. However, the Judge rejected moves to dismiss the indictment or severe the defendants so they could have individual trials. In addition, he rejected Boiardo's claims that the government might have undisclosed electronic surveillance to use against him. The Third Circuit Court of Appeals upheld Judge Barlow's decisions.

June 23, 1970

In the racketeering trial of former Newark Mayor Hugh Addonizio, the chief prosecution witness, Paul Riga, described a series of encounters with Anthony Boiardo. Riga testified that defendant Anthony LaMorte introduced him to Boiardo, who insisted that Riga kickback 10% on any city contract he won. LaMorte described Boiardo as, "This is the man who really runs Newark." Riga added that Boiardo told him he took care of the mayor and city council.

June ?, 1970

Judge Barlow revoked Anthony Boiardo's $50,000 bail, which put the gangster in the Somerset County Jail while the Addonizzio trial proceeded.

July 5, 1970

Anthony Boiardo suffered a heart attack in the Somerset County Jail, and an ambulance rushed him to St Francis Hospital in Trenton. Later, Judge Barlow severed Boiardo from the trial.

November 1971

Parole officials freed Capo Ritchie Boiardo from a 21/2 to 3-year gambling conviction after he completed 13 months.

January 7, 1973

In an FBI-bugged conversation between Genovese Capo Ray DeCarlo and Soldier Anthony Russo, they recalled a 1934 hit where Boiardo had three men killed for hijacking stills. They also mentioned that Billy Jenks was involved. Someone murdered him back in 1951.

March 24, 1978

Anthony Boiardo died of a heart attack in the Community Hospital in Montclair.

April 24, 1978

The Boiardo family held a funeral for Anthony Boiardo at the Megaro Funeral Home, followed by burial at Gate of Heaven Cemetery in East Hanover. It was a low-key affair, with about 50 in attendance.

February 1980

Federal Judge Frederick B Lacey ruled that Capo Ritchie Boiardo was too weak to stand trial for skimming the Jolly Trolley casino in Las Vegas. A State Judge, Michael R Imbrani, came to a similar conclusion and dropped Boiardo from a trial alleging murder, robbery, extortion, and conspiracy.

QUOTES ABOUT BOIARDO

New Jersey Assistant Attorney General John J Bergin

"Boiardo is the final arbitrator of disputes, territorial fights, and other problems" in gambling in Newark.

Anthony "Little Pussy" Russo talking about the Boiardos

"They're bad, Ray, they're bad people."

Capo Ray DeCarlo

"They're wastrels." (Boiardo father and son.)

CONCLUSION

Boiardo's long reign as a Genovese Capo involved gambling, loansharking, political corruption, and some murders. He never was a serious factor in the leadership of the Family but his vote would have been an important one. From illegal bugs it was clear that some fellow Mafiosi feared Boiardo and did not like his son "Tony Boy.' Boiardo remained active into his 1980's before a mental decline made him a non-factor.

CHAPTER FOURTEEN

Angelo Prisco

Prisco was a powerful Genovese Capo who couldn't stay out of legal problems. He rose to power when Genovese leaders ordered a hit on their New Jersey Capo John DiGilio. Then Boss Vince Gigante wanted low-level Associate Angelo Sangiuolo murdered which Prisco arranged. Seventeen years later that event came back to bite Prisco and he spent the rest of his life behind bars. A short summary of his life follows.

DOB
August 1, 1939
New York

DOD
June 21, 2017
In prison.

1979
Vince Gigante sponsored Angelo Prisco's induction into the Genovese Family.

1984
The Genovese Family leaders ordered a hit on their violent New Jersey Capo John DiGilio. Prisco soon became a New Jersey Capo in his place.

June 3, 1992

The NYPD found the body of Genovese Associate Angelo Sangiuolo in the backseat of a van parked at a McDonald's in the Bronx.

September 29, 1994

A New Jersey grand jury indicted Prisco and 12 others for racketeering, including murder, arson, extortion, and selling guns.

June 1997

Capo Angelo Prisco pled guilty to arson and racketeering before Judge Edward J Turnbach. A man burned down the Mud Shots bar in Garfield, NJ but claimed those who hired him never paid. Prisco admitted he tried to help the arsonist get his money.

February 20, 1998

Judge Edward J Turnbach sentenced Prisco to twelve years for his arson conviction.

September 1998

Prisco confessed to his role in the conspiracy to extort the Scores strip club.

1999

A Judge sentenced Prisco to two years for his role in the extortion of the Scores strip club. Luckily for Prisco, it ran concurrently with his previous 12-year sentence.

July 2000

The NJ Parole Board refused to release Prisco, and he also lost an appeal of this decision.

January 2002

The NJ Parole Board refused to release Prisco because he would not admit to being a mobster.

Mary 2002

Two of Prisco's lawyers met with the Chairman of the NJ Parole Board.

May 17, 2002

The New Jersey Parole Board erased its denial of Prisco's application for release. Later a board member claimed the Chairman said they should do it as a favor for the governor's office.

May 23, 2002

The parole board agreed to release Prisco to his wife's home no later than October 21, 2002.

June 6, 2002

Prisco's lawyer asked the parole board to release him earlier to his aunt's home in New Jersey.

July 10, 2002

The parole board agreed to an earlier release for Prisco.

August 21, 2002

The parole board released Prisco, who stated he planned to work three days a week as a cook. He had completed four years of his 12-year sentence.

March 2003

The New Jersey media had a field day with the story of Prisco's early release and the suggestion the New Jersey governor may have played a role. The governor vehemently denied these suggestions.

December 17, 2003

New Jersey banned Angelo Prisco from all their casinos.

May 2004

The New Jersey State Commission of Investigation declared that Prisco had returned to his criminal life.

June 2004

Prisco helped the son of the late John DiGilio obtain the lighting contract at the St Gennaro Feast. The son made two $2,500 payments to Prisco in return.

February 10, 2005

Parole agents arrested Capo Angelo Prisco for unauthorized travel and violating his parole. They returned him to prison.

September 2005

Parole officials released Prisco from his parole violation term.

March 7, 2006

A grand jury indicted Prisco and two others for extortion at the St. Gennaro Festival. A contractor, asked Prisco to convince another electrician to drop his contract to supply and service lights at the popular event. If this gambit were successful, the new contract holder, John Capelli, would kick back to Prisco.

May 17, 2007

Prisco pled guilty to the St Gennaro Festival extortion conspiracy. Later Judge Joseph Greenway sentenced him to five years.

April 27, 2009

A jury found Capo Angelo Prisco guilty of extortion, conspiracy to murder, robbery, racketeering, and illegal gambling. The murder conspiracy involved the January 3, 1992 hit of his cousin Angelo Sangiuolo. Boss Vince Gigante ordered the murder because Sangiuolo robbed Genovese-connected gambling joints.

Prisco lured Sangiuolo to his Giglio Boy's Social Club and ordered the victim to go with Paul Gacciolone and John Leto in a van. When the vehicle drove under an elevated subway Leto used the noise to turn around and fill the unsuspecting Sangiuolo with lead. Gacciolone parked the van in a McDonald's in the Bronx, and Prisco picked up the two killers with his Caddy. Leto and others eventually rolled over and doomed Prisco.

August 18, 2009

Judge Naomi Reice Buchwald sentenced Prisco to life in prison for his April 2009 convictions.

September 2, 2010

The Second Court of Appeals affirmed the judgement of conviction against Prisco.

June 21, 2017

Angelo Prisco died in Coleman Prison in Florida.

CONCLUSION

Capo Angelo Prisco had a series of legal problems going back into the 1990s. Despite spending time in prison Prisco didn't leave the Mafia life behind but kept soldiering on resulting in a conviction that left him to rot behind bars until he died. For an outsider this kind of life doesn't seem to make sense but it didn't take the Genovese Family long to replace Prisco.

PRISCO LEGAL DOCUMENTS

PRISCO APPEAL

No. 09-3705-cr United States Court of Appeals, Second Circuit U.S. v. Prisco 391 F. App'x 920 (2d Cir. 2010) Decided Sep 2, 2010 No. 09-3705-cr. September 2, 2010. Appeal from the United States District Court for the Southern District of New York (Buchwald, J.). ON CONSIDERATION WHEREOF, it is hereby ORDERED, ADJUDGED, and DECREED that the judgment of the district court be and hereby is AFFIRMED. Roger L. Stavis, Gallet Dreyer Berkey, LLP, New York, NY, for Defendant-Appellant. Elie Honig, Assistant United States

Attorney (Katherine Polk Failla, Assistant United States Attorney, on the brief), for Preet Bharara, United States Attorney for the Southern District of New York, New, York, NY, for Appellee. Present: ROBERT A. KATZMANN, PETER W. 921 HALL, DENNY CHIN, Circuit Judges. *921 SUMMARY ORDER Defendant-Appellant Angelo Prisco appeals from a judgment of conviction entered on August 20, 2009, following a jury trial on a nine-count superseding indictment, S2 08 Cr. 885(NRB), for racketeering conspiracy, the substantive racketeering offense (and specific racketeering acts), conspiracy to commit home invasion robberies, possession of firearms in the furtherance of the robberies, extortion conspiracy, substantive extortion, interstate transportation of stolen property, and the operation of an illegal gambling business. On appeal, Prisco argues that: (1) a previous plea agreement in the District of New Jersey should have precluded the prosecution of certain charges in the Southern District of New York that were "covered" under the District of New Jersey plea agreement; (2) the district court erred in declining to suppress the defendant's statements to a jailhouse informant and in declining to hold an evidentiary hearing thereon; and (3) the district court violated the defendant's right to confrontation in admitting an expert report by a medical examiner who had not performed the autopsy of the murder victim. We assume the parties' familiarity with the facts and procedural history of the case. On February 15, 2007, the defendant entered into a plea agreement in the District of New Jersey, which stated, in relevant part, that the "agreement is limited to the United States Attorney's Office for the District of New Jersey and cannot bind other federal, state, or local authorities." Though Prisco encourages this Court to turn a blind eye to this language, it is the law of this Circuit that a plea agreement in one U.S. Attorney's office does not, unless otherwise stated, bind another. See United States v. Annabi, 177 F.2d 670, 672 (2d Cir. 1985) (per curiam) ("A plea agreement binds only the office of the United States Attorney for the district in which the plea is entered unless it affirmatively appears that the agreement contemplates a broader restriction."); see also United States v. Salameh, 152 F.3d 88, 120 (2d Cir. 1998) (per curiam) (stating that reference to the "the Government" in a plea agreement binds only the office in which the agreement was made unless "there [is] evidence to show that [a prosecutor] [i]s attempting to evade its own 1 obligations . . . by transferring a prosecution to another office") (alterations in original) (internal quotation marks omitted). In the absence of any language in the New Jersey plea agreement to suggest otherwise, and with no compelling reason to infer any intent to the contrary, see United States v. Russo, 801 F.2d 624, 626 (2d Cir. 1986), we decline to extend the New Jersey plea agreement beyond its clearly stated terms. The defendant also moved pursuant to Massiah v. United States, 377 U.S. 201, 84 S.Ct. 1199, 12 L.Ed.2d 246 (1964), to suppress certain testimony by a jailhouse informant, Michael Sparfven, with whom Prisco had conversations about his offense conduct while incarcerated. In accordance with the holding in that case, it is undisputed that there is no Sixth Amendment violation of the right to counsel to the extent that none of Sparfven's notes written on or after September 17, 2008 (the date of the indictment) was admitted. Upon our review of Sparfven's notes, and in light of the fact that Prisco failed to raise any objection to the accuracy or authenticity of the notes or their dating, we are satisfied that the district court did not commit clear error in admitting notes taken before September 17, 2008. Accordingly, the district court also appropriately declined to hold an evidentiary hearing. See Puglisi v. United States, 586 F.3d 209, 215 (2d Cir. 2009). Finally, the defendant challenges the admission of the autopsy report of the *922 murder victim, Angelo Sanguilo, pursuant to Melendez-Diaz v. Massachusetts, ____ U.S. ____, 129 S.Ct. 2527, 174 L.Ed.2d 314 (2009). We need not reach that question here because the admission of the report was harmless error in any event. The government's case against the defendant was very strong, and the minor factual discrepancies upon which the defendant seizes are readily reconcilable upon closer inspection of the record. 922 We have considered the defendant's remaining arguments and find them to be without merit. For the foregoing reasons, the judgment of the district court is AFFIRMED

INFORMANT JEFF SANTINI
TAPES ANGELO PRISCO

Jeff Santini rolled over on the Genovese Family and helped the FBI by taping some of his conversations. Below is the transcript of his talk with Angelo

Prisco as Santini drove him to a meeting with Acting Boss Danny Leo on December 24, 2004.

Angelo Prisco
Drop me off at the Glen Rock (Inn, a restaurant in Glen Rock, New Jersey in Bergen County). And Rocky's gonna take me someplace. I don't know what they want. I think it's to give me money, Jeff, I'm not sure.

Other than that, I wouldn't have even went. But what else could it be on Christmas Eve, it couldn't even wait. They want to give me something for the holiday.

Remember I said something about the lump I was supposed to get? I don't know if I told you; this might be it. Like the guys that were around me when I got pinched. They're not around me. It was absorbed.

But I'm a good man, so I don't make no big thing out of it. Hey, when I was away and (I told them) if this guy (Chin) was home, this never would've happened. I'm a good man, know what I mean? I didn't do nothing wrong. I'm no fucking rat. I did my time. I did my 12 years when I was 58 years old. I'm a man.

So why should I have to lose these fucking guys.

Know what I told them? "Oh we thought you gave them up." No, I didn't give nobody up. Even if I'm not having them make no money, I don't give nobody up.

So ever since then, they've been giving me, like, $1,000 to $1,500 a month. They said they were gonna give me a lump -- this might be it, you know. What couldn't wait til Monday if it was something else?

Jeff Santini
I'm gonna drop you off? Mike told me not to leave your side.

Angelo

Well, listen, Rocky is gonna be there.

Jeff

Mike said don't leave you alone for a second.

Angelo

He gets paranoid. I said, Mike I didn't do nothing wrong; if they want me, I ain't got no dirty mind. There's no deep dark secrets where they're gonna say you did this, you did that.

Jeff

Who is this guy?

Angelo

It's my family. Matter of fact, matter of fact, he's one of the guys I put in.

Jeff

We can't let nothing happen to you.

Angelo

No, I don't think it's anything like that. But, hey, it's my life, that's my life -- there's nothing you can do about it.

Jeff

Shut up. I'll be right there. I'll run them all over.

Angelo

I'm too good a man in everyone's eyes. There's no reason for this.

Jeff

Forget about the lump sum; what about the continuation?

Angelo

What I told them was, this guy was around, yes, but this guy's not with me no more. So, OK, fine, I'm a good soldier. But they knew, they knew, I said, look, I'll take care of my own shit, nobody has to do anything for me. They've been doing the right thing by me so far, and this might be, who knows..

Jeff

How come they didn't give you the car?

Angelo

They had to give him a name.

Jeff

It's his place ....

Angelo

This guy is with the Gambinos. I didn't like them and I ....but anytime they needed something from me, or whatever, they would send him to me because they knew he was my friend. We'd be hugging and kissing and I'd say, what do you want? "Ang, what can I tell you, they sent me." Of course they sent you -- they're not gonna send someone I don't like. They got so many f****** rats in that group.

Jeff

Sammy got what was coming to him. He got that pinch for ecstasy. And then he's got a hold in New Jersey here because of the Ice Man. The Ice Man didn't give him up, but kind of implicated him....

Angelo
Oh.

Jeff

And look at the son -- he was getting out in September.

Angelo
What kid?

Jeff
John Junior (Gotti).

Angelo
I don't think Sammy the Bull had anything to do with that. That was something else -- that was Mikey Scars. "He's my right-hand man," he told me. He talked to me inside about him. "You should've made him your left hand man." He ain't a bad kid that kid.

Jeff
But he's caught in the mix. I don't know if he could handle that.

Angelo
Let me explain something to ya. Everybody thinks, "Our family is different." And they are, in lots of ways ....Say I gotta do something and I take you with me. That's it, nobody else knows. The only one that knows anything is the boss. These guys (the Gambinos), the whole family, they all know something happened.

We were taught, if it's done --- the old timers tell you, if someone's gotta go, they become a cockroach. What do you do with a cockroach? You kill the cockroach, you step on the cockroach, and you go about your business. You don't go calling people up and saying, "Hey, I took on a cockroach last night." They had to make it that way, but that's the way it is.

Angelo
Couple of months before I made parole, I thought they were gonna slam me with something else.

Jeff

The skeleton in your closet.

Angelo

Whatever, ya know. But they didn't. But they let me go, then they were gonna put me back because of that Steven Seagal.

Jeff

He didn't send you the Christmas cards, did he?

Angelo

He wants to see me, but I'm not -- he ain't a bad guy, and when it happened, Jeff, I told them, "Listen, you're pushing this f****** guy to the wall. He's an actor. He's a Jewish actor."

Jeff

Jewish, I didn't know that.

Angelo

He's a Jewish actor, he's not a f****** tough guy. They sent word back to me, "We'll do whatever we want with him. He's our piece of cheese, and we'll cut him up anyway we want." I said, OK. Then he came to see me, I said, "Steven, I can't help you." So he ratted, and now once he ratted, all their lawyers -- one guy named Larry Bronson, he's a Jersey lawyer.

Jeff

Hackensack.

Angelo

He came to see me. I says, "Yeah, Larry, what's up?" He says, "You know who sent me here, don't ya?" I said, "Who?" He says, "I can't tell ya." "You can't tell me?" I grabbed him by his throat and I twisted his tie and he was turning purple -- I says, "You can't tell me, you mother*****?" Like I got insulted. "You wanna come and talk to me and you don't tell me who's" -- and I twisted his f****** tie and he says, "SONNY CICCONE!"

I said, what does he want? He said maybe you could talk to Steven, he's ratting. I said, when I sent the message that you're pushing this guy to the wall, I was told to mind my f***** business -- you know what? Get the f*** out of here -- tell him to go f*** himself. I'm minding my business.

I couldn't stop it, you know what I mean? I'm looking to go for parole in another six to eight weeks, and you want me to tell the guy to drop a lawsuit -- a case against them? They'll never let me out of here! Get the fck out of here! I hate them f****** guys. I don't do nothing for the Gambinos -- as soon as I hear them, my asshole goes like this......

They think who the f*** they are. They think they're the number one in the world, ya know? Everybody else is shit on their shoe.

Jeff
Peter (Gotti) just got convicted.

Angelo
Who?

Jeff
Peter

Angelo
F****** imbecile. Jerk off.....You wanna send two guys to kill a guy who ratted on your brother... Kill him before he rats! You know what I mean, Jeff?....Kill him before, don't kill him after! That's compounding the felony! Stupid, ya know? He wasn't the sharpest knife in the draw, anyway.

All of them -- I hate them f****** gangsters -- they singlehandedly destroyed this whole life.

Jeff

You think it was his downfall the flashiness? I mean, I don't wanna bring up --

Angelo

His downfall was his ego. That was his downfall. All the tapes they got of him in the woman's apartment. OK, he didn't know they were being taped, but you got Sammy the Bull there who's your underboss – you got this other guy, Frankie Loc, who's your consigliere.

You gotta explain to them the life? He put himself in there. You gotta explain to them about this life? About this is ours and our thing? You don't talk to underlings -- you don't talk to a boss -- an underboss and a consiglieri like that. Why, they don't know?

Jeff

How did they get their rank?

Angelo

He did it. That's neither here nor there. I said, look, I don't want to see anyone (unintelligible). I feel bad for them. They throw rocks at the (??) to draw attention to themselves. Stupid. What are you gonna do, that's life.

Without guys like us they wouldn't need the FBI, the cops – surveillance and all that. Who they gonna watch?

Jeff

Terrorists.

Angelo

Yeah.

CHAPTER FIFTEEN

Arthur "The Little Guy" Nigro

In the early 2000s Nigro had a brief run as Acting Boss of the Genovese Family when his predecessors had legal problems. In his youth Nigro served honorably in the US Armed forces but went another way when he returned to civilian life. For years few knew his name but with the 2003 murder of Connecticut Capo Al Bruno brought him into the limelight. His story follows.

February 12, 2001
An FBI Agent later testified that he was having a conversation with Capo Al Bruno on this date when he mentioned that Emilio Fusco became an inducted member while Bruno was in prison. This admission was shocking to the agent who recorded it in the files.

2003
A jury found Emilio Fusco guilty of some crimes, and before sentencing, the court required a report on his background. To Fusco's shock, it included the FBI Agent's account that Bruno had outed Fusco as a made guy.

Soldier Emilio Fusco complained to Soldier Anthony Arliotta about Bruno's revelation to an FBI Agent that he was a made man. Arliotta passed the message on to Soldier Felix Tranglese. Then Tranglese has a series of meetings with Acting Boss Arthur Nigro at the Nebraska Steak House in the Bronx. After presumably conferring with other Genovese Family powers Nigro told Tranglese, during a walk/talk, he approved the proposed hit on Bruno but that Fusco and Arillota had to do it with Tranglese remaining in the background.

Arliotta discussed the hit with gangster brothers Fotios (Freddy) and Ty Geas. Then Fotios gave local hood Frankie Roche $10,000 to do the killing. Roche had a further incentive, for he had busted up a Bruno-controlled bar, and Bruno was demanding compensation.

Note:

The FBI only knew the details of the above information years later. I have placed it here in the hopes of avoiding confusion.

May 19, 2003
On the orders of Nigro and with the cooperation of his brother Fotios, Ty Geas shot union official Frank Dadabo nine times but failed to kill him. Nigro was in a union dispute with Dadabo.

November 23, 2003
Genovese Capo Al Bruno exited the Our Lady of Mount Carmel Society facilities in Springfield after his weekly card game. As he was about to enter his vehicle, a gunman shot him six times, ending Bruno's life.

Bruno had been in charge of the Genovese Connecticut crew since the natural death of Capo Frank Scibelli in 2000. Bruno ruffled feathers by increasing the shakedowns of illegal activities in his territory. On one occasion, a local barber, in debt to Bruno, attempted to kill him in the same parking lot where Bruno died. Unfortunately, many others did not appreciate Bruno's methods.

May 18, 2007
Nigro pled guilty before Judge Louis A Kaplan to a charge of extorting an apartment complex owner to rent commercial space to a Nigro friend for

less than market value. The original indictment named 34 members and Associates of the Genovese Family.

September 28, 2007
Judge Louis A Kaplan sentenced Nigro to 51 months for extortion.

April 1, 2011
A jury convicted Arthur Nigro, Fotios Geas, and his brother Ty of several crimes, some of which are listed below:

The 2003 killing of Capo Al Bruno.

The attempted murder of union official Frank Dadabo.

The attempted murder of Louis Santos. (Suspected informant).

Extortion.

The jury convicted Ty and Fotios Geas for the murder of Gary Waterman.

September 12, 2011
Judge P Castel sentenced Nigro to life and gave the same terms to brothers Fotios and Ty Geas.

June 6, 2011
Judge P Castel rejected the appeal of Nigro and the two Geas brothers for a judgment of acquittal.

May 24, 2019
Nigro died in prison.

CONCLUSION

Arthur Nigro became well known when he was indicted for the 2003 murder of Capo Al Bruno. In hindsight that killing, based on Bruno telling an FBI

Agent about an Associate being made by the Family, was a mistake. Nigro and others were looking for an excuse for they coveted Bruno's extensive rackets in Connecticut. As usual, trusted men rolled over on Nigro and he spent the last eight years of his life locked up.

NIGRO DOCUMENTS

NIGRO SUPERSEDING INDICTMENT

MANHATTAN U.S. ATTORNEY FILES ADDITIONAL CHARGES AGAINST FORMER ACTING BOSS OF GENOVESE ORGANIZED CRIME FAMILY AND FOUR OTHERS

PREET BHARARA, the United States Attorney for the Southern District of New York, announced the unsealing of a Superseding Indictment charging three additional individuals for their involvement in the alleged racketeering, murder, and other criminal activities of the Genovese Organized Crime Family.

FELIX TRANGHESE and TY GEAS were arrested this morning in Springfield, Massachusetts. EMILIO FUSCO remains at large. Defendants ARTHUR NIGRO, the alleged former Acting Boss of the Genovese Organized Crime Family, and FOTIOS GEAS, an alleged Family associate, -- who were incarcerated on other charges when the underlying indictments in this case were unsealed -- were previously transferred to the Southern District of New York for prosecution.

An underlying indictment in this case previously charged NIGRO and FOTIOS GEAS with racketeering and the 2003 murder of ADOLFO BRUNO, among other crimes. The Superseding Indictment unsealed today charges TRANGHESE, an alleged Capo, FUSCO, an alleged made member, and TY GEAS, an alleged associate, each of the Genovese Organized Crime Family, with racketeering and participating in the same murder. In addition, FUSCO, FOTIOS GEAS, and TY GEAS, are charged with the November

4, 2003, murder of GARY WESTERMAN, whose body was uncovered in Agawam, Massachusetts, in a coordinated search by the FBI and the Massachusetts State Police in April 2010. NIGRO, FOTIOS GEAS, and TY GEAS, are also charged with the May 19, 2003 attempted murder of FRANK DADABO, and with conspiring to murder LOUIS SANTOS in Fall 2003. According to an Indictment unsealed earlier today in Manhattan Federal Court: In their capacities within and associated with the Genovese Organized Crime Family, NIGRO, TRANGHESE, FUSCO, FOTIOS GEAS, and TY GEAS conspired to murder and aided and abetted in the November 2003 murder of ADOLFO BRUNO, to maintain and increase their position in the Genovese Organized Crime Family as well as to prevent BRUNO from providing information to law enforcement about crimes committed by members and associates of the Genovese Organized Crime Family.

Similarly, FUSCO, FOTIOS GEAS, and TY GEAS conspired to murder and murdered GARY WESTERMAN on November 4, 2003, to maintain and increase their position in the Genovese Organized Crime Family as well as to prevent WESTERMAN from providing information to law enforcement about crimes committed by members and associates of the Genovese Organized Crime Family. A conference in this case is scheduled before United States District Judge P. KEVIN CASTEL on July 26, 2010, at 11:00 a.m.

Mr. BHARARA praised the work of the Joint Organized Crime Task Force -- including agents of the Federal Bureau of Investigation and detectives of the New York City Police Department. Mr. BHARARA also thanked the United States Attorney's Office for the District of Massachusetts, the Hampden County District Attorney's Office, and the Massachusetts State Police for their valued assistance in the investigation. Manhattan U.S. Attorney PREET BHARARA said: "For years, the Genovese Organized Crime Family allegedly has terrorized the city of Springfield, Massachusetts, with a series of violent crimes. It has been nearly seven years since Adolfo Bruno was murdered on a city street in Springfield and Gary Westerman was murdered and buried in the woods in Agawam. Today, through the tireless and coordinated efforts of numerous law enforcement agencies, the defendants stand accused of an array of racketeering and murder charges that stretched far beyond Springfield." This case is being prosecuted by the Office's Organized Crime Unit. Assistant United States Attorney MARK LANPHER is in charge of the prosecution. The charges contained in the Indictment are merely accusations, and the defendants are presumed innocent unless and until proven guilty.

NIGRO CONVICTION

Former Acting Boss of Genovese Family and Two Associates Convicted in Manhattan Federal Court for Multiple Murders, Racketeering, and Extortion

U.S. Attorney's Office • **Southern District of New York** (212)
April 01, 2011   637-2600

PREET BHARARA, the United States Attorney for the Southern District of New York, announced that ARTHUR NIGRO, former acting boss of the Genovese organized crime family of La Cosa Nostra; and FOTIOS GEAS and TY GEAS, associates of the Genovese organized crime family, were convicted today after a three-week jury trial of various crimes, including multiple murders, attempted murder, murder conspiracies, racketeering, racketeering conspiracy, extortion, and loansharking. All three defendants were convicted for their participation in the November 2003 murder of Adolfo Bruno in Springfield, Massachusetts. FOTIOS GEAS and TY GEAS also were convicted of the November 2003 murder of Gary Westerman in Agawam, Massachusetts.

Manhattan U.S. Attorney PREET BHARARA said: "The jury's swift verdict in this case takes some very dangerous men off the streets—men who clearly did not think twice about killing anyone who got in their way. Today's verdict makes it clear that those who so flagrantly and repeatedly violate the law will be punished."

According to the trial evidence and other documents filed in the case:

In the early 2000s, NIGRO rose to the position of acting boss of the Genovese organized crime family. As acting boss, NIGRO supervised and oversaw the Genovese Family's operations in the Bronx, New York and Springfield, Massachusetts, among other places, where he profited from the criminal activities of Genovese Family soldiers and associates. FOTIOS GEAS and TY GEAS were Genovese Family associates in Springfield, Massachusetts.

On November 23, 2003, Adolfo Bruno, a captain in the Genovese organized crime family, was gunned down in downtown Springfield, Massachusetts, on orders from NIGRO. NIGRO ordered the hit to increase his power and position in the Genovese Family, and to punish Bruno for having spoken with the Federal Bureau of Investigation. FOTIOS GEAS and TY GEAS planned the Bruno murder, and ultimately enlisted a shooter to kill Bruno. On November 4, 2003, FOTIOS GEAS and TY GEAS shot and killed Gary Westerman in Agawam, Massachusetts, because they believed Westerman was cooperating with the Massachusetts State Police. The defendants buried Westerman's body in the woods, where it remained until April 2010, when the FBI excavated the hole in connection with the investigation in this case and found Westerman's remains.

All three defendants were also convicted of the attempted murder of Frank Dadabo. NIGRO ordered the murder because of a union-related dispute they had been having. Acting on NIGRO's orders, on May 19, 2003, TY GEAS approached Dadabo on a street in the Bronx and shot him nine times. FOTIOS GEAS helped planned the hit, and drove the getaway car. Despite being shot nine times, Dadabo survived.

All three defendants were also convicted of conspiring to murder Louis Santos, and FOTIOS GEAS and TY GEAS were convicted of conspiring to murder Giuseppe Manzi. The Manzi murder was planned to eliminate the leader of a rival criminal faction in Springfield, while the Santos murder was planned because the defendants believed that Santos was cooperating with law enforcement.

NIGRO, FOTIOS GEAS, and TY GEAS all face mandatory sentences of life in prison. Sentencing has been scheduled for June 23, 2011.

Mr. BHARARA praised the work of the FBI's New York Field Office and the FBI's Springfield, Massachusetts, Resident Agency. Mr. BHARARA also thanked the United States Attorney's Office for the District of Massachusetts; the Massachusetts State Police; the Hampden County District Attorney's Office; the Springfield Police Department; and the New York City Police Department.

Assistant U.S. Attorneys MARK LANPHER, ELIE HONIG, and DANIEL GOLDMAN are in charge of the prosecution

NIGRO APPEAL

Opinion

S5 09 Cr. 1239 (PKC).

June 6, 2011

MEMORANDUM AND ORDER

P. CASTEL, District Judge

Following an approximately three week trial, defendants Arthur Nigro, Fotios Geas and Ty Geas were each convicted of various counts under superseding indictment S5 09 Cr. 1239 (the "Indictment"). At the close of the Government's case-in-chief, each defendant moved for a judgment of acquittal under Rule 29, Fed.R.Crim.P., and I reserved decision on the motions. Each defendant has now indicated that he will rest on his prior motions, objections and arguments in lieu of submitting further briefing or argument.

Each defendant based his Rule 29 motion on the claim that the evidence was insufficient to establish his guilt on the charged counts. A defendant challenging the sufficiency of the evidence to support his conviction under Rule 29 "bears a heavy burden."United States v. Abdulle, 564 F.3d 119, 125 (2d Cir. 2009) (internal quotation marks omitted). A motion for judgment of acquittal "should be granted only if the district court concludes there is 'no evidence upon which a reasonable mind might fairly conclude guilt beyond a reasonable doubt," and the defendant shows that "no rational trier of fact could have found him guilty." United States v. Irving, 452 F.3d 110, 117 (2d Cir. 2006) (quoting United States v. Taylor, 464 F.2d 240, 243 (2d Cir. 1972)).

In evaluating a motion under Rule 29, the court must view the evidence "in the light most favorable to the government. "Abdulle, 564 F.3d at 125 (internal quotation marks omitted). "The government need not negate every theory of innocence." United States v. Autuori, 212 F.3d 105, 114 (2d Cir. 2000). Moreover, the court must "defer [] to the jury's evaluation of the credibility of the witnesses, its choices between permissible inferences, and its assessment of the weight of the evidence. "United States v. Jones, 482 F.3d 60, 68 (2d Cir. 2006); see also United States v. Florez, 447 F.3d 145, 156 (2d Cir. 2006) ("We will not attempt to second-guess a jury›s credibility determination on a sufficiency challenge."). Where "the court concludes that either of the two results, a reasonable doubt or no reasonable doubt, is fairly possible, [the court] must let the jury decide the matter." Autuori, 212 F.3d at 114 (internal quotation marks omitted) (alteration in original).

All three defendants were convicted of Racketeering Conspiracy, Racketeering, Murder in Aid of Racketeering, and Extortion Conspiracy. Arthur Nigro and Fotios Geas were convicted of Interstate Travel in Aid of Racketeering. Fotios Geas and Ty Geas were also convicted of a second count of Murder in Aid of Racketeering. All three defendants were found not guilty of Murder for the Purpose of Obstructing Justice.

The evidence before the jury included the testimony of four cooperating witnesses who testified that they were members or associates of the Genovese Organized Crime Family. Each testified about one or more of the defendants' participation in the conspiracy or other charged crimes. The Government also presented tape recordings of the defendants' own statements, the testimony of an attempted murder victim, testimony from law enforcement officers, physical evidence, phone records, and surveillance photographs.

Having presided over the trial, being thoroughly familiar with the record and upon review and consideration of the evidence, I conclude that the Government's proof was sufficient to sustain all of the convictions and there is no basis for relief. The motions of defendants Arthur Nigro, Fotios Geas and Ty Geas for a judgment of acquittal under Rule 29 are DENIED.

SO ORDERED.

CHAPTER SIXTEEN

Liborio "Barney" Bellomo

When Boss Vince Gigante got jammed up on legal charges in 1990, he named Capo Liborio Bellomo his Acting Boss. Then Bellomo had his problems and did time in prison with others taking over the role of Acting Boss. Below is a summary of Bellomo's life in La Cosa Nostra.

DOB
January 8, 1957

1976
In a careless move, Bellomo left his gun and some policy slips in his vehicle, where a cop saw them. He later pled guilty, and the Judge gave him three months' probation.

1977
The Genovese administration inducted Bellomo into the Family with future turncoat Soldier Vince Cafaro as his sponsor. In addition, Soldier Salvatore "Toddo" Bellomo, Liborio's father, watched the ceremony at the First Ave Pizzeria in East Harlem.

1987
Bellomo made Ralph Coppola the chief Carpenters Union shop steward at the Jacob Javits Center.

1990 (Best guess)
Boss Vince Gigante named Liborio Bellomo as his Acting Boss.

September 16, 1990
The US Attorney for the Southern District of New York launched a civil racketeering suit against the District Council of Carpenters and its leading officials.

1991
Federal officials removed Ralph Coppola, chief steward at the Javits, because they identified him as a Genovese Family agent. Bellomo's brother-in-law, Anthony Fiorino, replaced him as a District Council representative.

March 1993
Bellomo agreed to stay away from the Carpenters Union.

1994
The Carpenters Union and its top officials signed a consent decree with the government, permanently enjoining the defendants from racketeering or associating with known members of organized crime.

December 15, 1994
A phone tap of Consigliere Joe Ida told of an upcoming administration meeting, and a tracking device on his vehicle led the good guys to the sit-down.

December 1994
Bellomo, Generoso, and Ida met to discuss grand jury subpoenas of Soldiers and Associates of Capos Malangone and Gangi crews.

March 1995
Kenneth Conboy, the federal monitor for the Carpenters Union, brought charges against Anthony Fiorino, claiming he was the Genovese Family

representative at the Javits Center. Conboy said Fiorino ran a corrupt hiring list and threatened a member who complained about a contract violation.

The Independent Hearing Panel accepted Conboy's information and expelled Fiorino from the Union for life. Later, Judge Haight affirmed the decision, ruling that Fiorino favored a small group of individuals over other union members looking for work.

June 11, 1996

The feds announced a 68-count grand jury indictment that involved Acting Boss Bellomo, Acting Underboss Mickey Generoso, Consigliere Joseph Ida, and others. One of the main complaints was that the Genovese Family skimmed the famous Feast of San Gennaro through the supposedly non-profit Society of San Gennaro Naples and Suburbs Inc.

The indictment also charged Bellomo, Generoso, and Ida with the murder of Ralph DeSimone, whose body the police found at JFK on June 12, 1991. It also alleged that Ida took part in the murder of Soldier and suspected informer Antonio "Hickey" DiLorenzo on November 25, 1988. There were a series of other counts, which I won't list here. The Judge refused bail for Bellomo, Generoso, and Ida.

December 20, 1996

Bellomo passed a third polygraph saying he knew nothing of the hit on Ralph DeSimone. One of the purposes of these tests was to convince Judge Kaplan that he was not a danger to society and, thus, would be eligible for bail. However, Judge Kaplan stated that Bellomo's Mafia rank proved he was a danger, so Bellomo remained locked up until his trial.

February 10, 1997

Bellomo agreed to a ten-year deal and forfeited $250,000 for conspiracy to extort $215,000 from a Connecticut waste hauling company. Generoso decided to plead to conspiracy to extort and control Local 46 of the Mason

Tenders Union and their District Council. Four other men pled guilty to crimes involving the San Gennaro Festival.

September 22, 1997

Judge Lewis Kaplan sentenced Bellomo to ten years for extortion and a fine of $250,000. Acting Underboss, Generoso got a term of 18 months and a fine of $250,000 for conspiracy to extort and control the Mason Tenders District Council and its Local 46.

September 16, 1998

Capo Ralph Coppola disappeared. He had pled guilty to using bid rigging to extort $1.2 million from the Men's Apparel Guild of California.

January 23, 2002

A grand jury indicted Vince Gigante for conspiracy to obstruct justice with his crazy act. In addition, the indictment charged Gigante, Bellomo, and others for gaining control of locals of the International Longshoremen's Association and extorting companies on the New York and Miami docks.

April 7, 2003

Bellomo and others pled guilty to extorting companies on the docks of New York and Miami.

July 31, 2004

Lawyer Peter Peluso allegedly told Genovese Capo John Ardito that Bellomo Ok'd the Ralph Coppola hit.

February 23, 2006

An indictment charged Bellomo with mail fraud and ordering the murder of Capo Ralph Coppola.

June 2007

Bellomo pled guilty to mail fraud after the feds dropped the Ralph Coppola murder charge.

July 2007
Judge Lewis Kaplan sentenced Bellomo to one year and one day for his guilty plea to mail fraud.

July 2008
Parole officials moved Bellomo to a halfway house.

December 1, 2008
Parole officials released Bellomo.

February 2016
Jerry Capeci wrote that his sources told him Bellomo was now the official Boss of the Genovese Family. In addition, Capeci said Bellomo had Capo Peter DiChiara acting as his Street Boss.

CONCLUSION

As of this writing (2023) Bellomo is the official Boss of the Genovese Family. He has served his dues by spending time in prison without talking. Most sources say he is well respected by his Soldiers and probably won't face any internal revolt. His real problem will be the FBI who surely are already focused on his activities. Only time will tell how long he remains free.

CHAPTER SEVENTEEN

Danny Leo

Leo was a respected Genovese Capo who held the position as Acting Boss from 2005 to 2009 (Approximate). Legal troubles forced Leo to step down otherwise his reign would have continued.

DOB
January 16, 1928
NYC

November 24, 1978
The police found the bodies of Maurice Anzis and his girlfriend.

December 13, 1978
The DA received permission to bug the interior of the Antonio Social Club.

December 19, 1978
Police begin surveilling Danny Leo, John Santaniello, and others outside the Antonio Social Club.

January 11, 1980
The DA received permission to continue to bug the Antonio Social Club.

April 22, 1980

The DA presented Leo with a notice he had been eavesdropped on and handed him a grand jury subpoena.

May 5, 1980

Leo appeared before the grand jury and asked to see a Justice so he could rule on the legality of the eavesdropping. Justice George Roberts then ruled that the bugs were legal and ordered Leo to testify before the grand jury.

June 4, 1980

Leo appeared before the grand jury again, and the DA informed him he had immunity, but Leo refused to testify. Finally, the DA hauled him before Justice Roberts, who repeated his order that Leo must testify.

Note:

If the grand jury grants a witness immunity, the good guys can't use any of his testimony against him in future proceedings.

June 5, 1980

Leo appeared before the grand jury but refused to testify.

June 10, 1980

The grand jury indicted Leo on eight counts of contempt.

June 11, 1980

The DA informed Leo of his indictment.

June 12, 1980

Officials arraigned Leo on his indictment charges before Justice Roberts.

Later, in pretrial action, Justice Roberts dismissed one contempt count but upheld seven others.

June 22, 1981

Justice Shirley R Levitan found Leo guilty of two counts of contempt but dismissed five others.

October 1999

Leo, Ernie Muscarella, and Dentico inducted fifteen men into the Genovese Family. The FBI overheard this using a bug on Salvatore Asparo a few days after the ceremony.

2005

Danny Leo became the Acting Boss of the Genovese Family.

May 30, 2007

A grand jury indictment charged Leo and his nephew, Joe Leo, with threatening a livery driver over payments on a $150,000 loan and extorting illegal gambling operators. Federal Judge Lewis Kaplan denied bail.

October 31, 2007

Before Judge Kaplan, Leo and his nephew pled guilty to threatening a livery driver over lack of payments on a loan.

January 3, 2008

Judge Kaplan sentenced Danny Leo to five years for threatening a livery driver over loans.

February 4, 2009

A grand jury indicted Danny Leo and others for racketeering offenses. (Please see the Indictment below.)

2009 (Best guess)

Danny Leo stepped down as the Acting Boss of the Genovese Family.

January 10, 2010

Leo pled guilty to racketeering involving overseeing the extortion of a Jersey City business, aiding the takeover of a Manhattan bar when the owner could not repay a loan and illegal gambling. (Please see below.)

March 2010

Judge Ronald L Ellis sentenced Leo to 18 months and a fine of $1.3 million.

January 25, 2013

Parole officials released Leo from Coleman Prison in Florida.

CONCLUSION

Danny Leo had his fifteen minutes of fame when he was the Acting Boss of the Genovese Family. Like so many other leaders he ended up behind bars but thankfully for him, the term was not too long and he was back on the streets in 2013. It would be interesting to know how much of his $1.3 million forfeiture has been paid.

LEO DOCUMENTS

DANNY LEO INDICTMENT FEBRUARY 4, 2009

U.S. CHARGES FORMER ACTING BOSS AND 12 OTHER MEMBERS, ASSOCIATES OF THE GENOVESE ORGANIZED CRIME FAMILY LEV L. DASSIN, Acting United States Attorney for the Southern District of New York, JOSEPH DEMAREST, Assistant Director-in-Charge of the New York Office of the Federal Bureau of Investigation ("FBI"), and RAYMOND W. KELLY, Police Commissioner of the City of New York ("NYPD"), announced the unsealing today of a 38-count Indictment (the "LEO Indictment") against 12 defendants, including DANIEL LEO, former Acting Boss, and various members and associates of the Genovese Organized Crime Family of La Cosa Nostra.

The LEO Indictment charges the defendants with racketeering and other offenses, including violent extortions of individuals and businesses, loansharking, narcotics trafficking, and the operation of illegal gambling businesses.

DANIEL LEO, CHARLES SALZANO, JOSEPH LEO, and VINCENT COTONA are already in federal custody on other charges. According to the LEO Indictment, unsealed today in Manhattan federal court: DANIEL LEO, CHARLES SALZANO, ROCCO PETROZZA, FELICE MASULLO, PATSY AVERSA, VINCENT COTONA, JOSEPH LEO, JOSEPH PETULLO, ANTHONY MASULLO, and ANGELO MASULLO participated in racketeering offenses related to the affairs of the Genovese Organized Crime Family.

DANIEL LEO served as Acting Boss of the Genovese Family beginning in approximately 2005; during the time he served as Acting Boss, he supervised racketeering crimes of his own "crew" of Genovese Family members and associates, including Soldier CHARLES SALZANO and associates JOSEPH LEO and ARTHUR BOLAND.

SALZANO and JOSEPH LEO are charged with various racketeering offenses, including loansharking and the operation of an illegal gambling business. Additional charges against defendants named in the Indictment include making and collecting extortionate loans to small business owners and other individuals, including owners and operators of bartending schools in New York City and New Jersey, and threatening victims with physical harm if they did not repay the loans.

In 2006, DANIEL LEO placed long-time Soldier and Acting Capo ANTHONY PALUMBO in charge of the New Jersey operations of the Genovese Family. PALUMBO and other New Jersey-based Family members and associates under his supervision, including his driver FELICE MASULLO and Soldier ROCCO PETROZZA, are charged with, among other offenses, forcibly taking over a small business in Jersey City, New Jersey, to collect payment on a loan shark loan. PETROZZA and associates PATSY

AVERSA, VINCENT COTONA, and JOSEPH PETULLO are charged with extortion of the owners and operators of this same business.

FELICE MASULLO -- who served as PALUMBO's driver and was proposed as a member of the Genovese Family -- is charged with his brothers, ANTHONY MASULLO and ANGELO MASULLO, with racketeering offenses, including the trafficking of cocaine and -2 crack cocaine, loansharking, and operating an illegal sports- betting business.

Acting Boss of Genovese Crime Family Pleads Guilty in Manhattan Federal Court to Racketeering Offenses U.S. Attorney's Office

January 27, 2010
· Southern District of New York

PREET BHARARA, the United States Attorney for the Southern District of New York, announced that an Acting Boss of the Genovese Organized Crime Family, DANIEL LEO, a/k/a "The Lion," and his nephew and primary lieutenant, JOSEPH LEO, pleaded guilty to racketeering charges today in Manhattan federal court.

According to the Indictment filed in Manhattan federal court:

Beginning in about 2005, DANIEL LEO became the Acting Boss of the Genovese Organized Crime Family, from his previous post as a member of the Family's ruling panel. During the time DANIEL LEO served as Acting Boss, he continued to supervise a "crew" of Genovese Organized Crime Family members and associates, including JOSEPH LEO and others, who committed loansharking, extortion, and illegal gambling offenses under DANIEL LEO's direction.

Both defendants pleaded guilty today to Counts One and Two of the Indictment, which charged them with participating in, and conspiring to participate in, the affairs of the Genovese Organized Crime Family through a pattern of racketeering activity. Specifically, both defendants admitted during today's plea proceeding that they participated in the affairs of the Genovese Organized Crime Family by engaging in loansharking, and that they conspired to operate an illegal gambling business.

These two defendants entered their guilty pleas before United States Magistrate Judge RONALD L. ELLIS. They are scheduled to be sentenced by United States District Judge RICHARD J. HOLWELL on April 2, 2010. Each defendant faces a maximum sentence of 40 years in prison and a maximum fine of $250,000 or twice the gross gain or loss from the offense. DANIEL LEO and JOSEPH LEO are currently serving prison sentences of 60 months and 46 months, respectively, based on their prior convictions in Manhattan federal court on extortion charges in October 2007.

Three other defendants charged in the Indictment have pleaded guilty: FELICE MASULLO, ANTHONY MASULLO, and ANGELO MASULLO. Each of them pleaded guilty on November 6, 2009, before Magistrate Judge THEODORE H. KATZ, to a superseding information captioned United States v. Felice Masullo et al., S2 08 Cr. 874 (RJH) (the "Information").

As alleged in the Information, FELICE MASULLO was an associate of the Genovese Organized Crime Family who had been proposed to be made a Soldier. FELICE MASULLO was charged with participating in, and conspiring to participate in, the affairs of the Genovese Organized Crime Family through a pattern of racketeering activity. In connection with his plea, FELICE MASULLO admitted that he participated in the affairs of the Genovese Organized Crime Family through his participation in a conspiracy to distribute cocaine, a conspiracy to extort a victim (identified as Victim-8 in the Information), and a conspiracy to operate an illegal gambling business. In addition, two of FELICE MASULLO's brothers—ANTHONY MASULLO and ANGELO MASULLO—also pleaded guilty to participating in a conspiracy to extort Victim-8.

FELICE MASULLO, ANTHONY MASULLO, and ANGELO MASULLO are scheduled to be sentenced by Judge HOLWELL on February 19, 2010. FELICE MASULLO faces a maximum sentence of 40 years in prison and a maximum fine of $250,000 or twice the gross gain or loss from the offense. ANTHONY MASULLO and ANGELO MASULLO face maximum sentences of 20 years in prison and a maximum fine of $250,000 or twice the gross gain or loss from the offense.

Mr. BHARARA praised the efforts of the Federal Bureau of Investigation and the New York City Police Department in this investigation.

Assistant United States Attorneys DAVID B. MASSEY, AVI WEITZMAN, BRIAN JACOBS, and SHARON FRASE are in charge of the prosecutions.

LEO SENTENCING ON MARCH 23, 2010

FORMER ACTING BOSS OF GENOVESE CRIME FAMILY SENTENCED IN MANHATTAN FEDERAL COURT TO 18 ADDITIONAL MONTHS IN PRISON PREET BHARARA, the United States Attorney for the Southern District of New York, announced that former Acting Boss of the Genovese Organized Crime Family, DANIEL LEO, a/k/a "The Lion," was sentenced today for conspiracy and participation in the affairs of the Genovese Organized Crime Family through a pattern of racketeering activity, including loansharking and illegal gambling offenses. DANIEL LEO was sentenced to 18 months in prison and ordered to forfeit $1.3 million as the proceeds of the Genovese Family's illegal gambling business.

LEO's sentence was ordered to run consecutively to his 60-month sentence based on his conviction in Manhattan federal court on extortion charges in October 2007. DANIEL LEO and his primary lieutenant and nephew, JOSEPH LEO, pleaded guilty to the offenses for which DANIEL LEO was sentenced today on January 27, 2010, before United States Magistrate Judge RONALD L. ELLIS.

JOSEPH LEO is scheduled to be sentenced tomorrow at 12:30 p.m. before United States District Judge RICHARD J. HOLWELL, who also imposed the sentence today in Manhattan federal court. According to the Superseding Indictment to which the defendants pleaded, other documents filed in this and related cases, and statements made in court:

Beginning in about 2005, DANIEL LEO became the Acting Boss of the Genovese Organized Crime Family, from his previous post as a member of the Family's ruling panel. During the time DANIEL LEO served as Acting Boss, he continued to supervise a "crew" of Genovese Organized Crime Family members and associates, including JOSEPH LEO, CHARLES SALZANO, and others, who committed loansharking, extortion, and illegal gambling offenses under DANIEL LEO's direction.

Six other defendants charged in the Indictment have pleaded guilty: FELICE MASULLO, ANTHONY MASULLO, ANGELO MASULLO, VINCENT COTONA, CHARLES SALZANO, and ARTHUR BOLAND. FELICE MASULLO, ANTHONY MASULLO, and ANGELO MASULLO pleaded guilty on November 6, 2009, before Magistrate Judge THEODORE H. KATZ, to a superseding Information.

FELICE MASULLO was an associate of the Genovese Organized Crime Family who had been proposed to be made a Soldier. FELICE MASULLO was charged with participating in, and conspiring to participate in, the affairs of the Genovese Organized Crime Family through a pattern of racketeering activity. In connection with his plea, FELICE MASULLO admitted that he participated in the affairs of the Genovese Organized Crime Family through his participation in a conspiracy to distribute cocaine, an extortion conspiracy, and a conspiracy to operate an illegal gambling business.

In addition, two of FELICE MASULLO's brothers -- ANTHONY MASULLO and ANGELO MASULLO -- also pleaded guilty to participating in an extortion conspiracy. FELICE MASULLO, ANTHONY MASULLO, and ANGELO MASULLO are scheduled to be sentenced by

Judge HOLWELL on April 9, 2010. FELICE MASULLO faces a maximum sentence of 40 years in prison and a maximum fine of $250,000 or twice the gross gain or loss from the offense. ANTHONY MASULLO and ANGELO MASULLO face maximum sentences of 20 years in prison and a maximum fine of $250,000 or twice the gross gain or loss from the offense.

VINCENT COTONA and CHARLES SALZANO pleaded guilty on March 3 and 5, 2010, respectively, before the Honorable JAMES C. FRANCIS IV, to superseding Informations charging that COTONA and SALZANO knowingly received the proceeds of extortion. SALZANO also pleaded guilty to operating an illegal gambling business, and agreed to forfeit $200,000 as the proceeds of that offense. COTONA and SALZANO are scheduled to be sentenced by Judge HOLWELL on March 25 and June 9, 2010, respectively. COTONA faces a maximum possible sentence of three years in prison and a maximum fine of $250,000 or twice the gross gain or loss from the offense. SALZANO faces a maximum possible sentence of eight years in prison and a maximum fine of $500,000 or twice the gross gain or loss from the offense. COTONA is currently serving a prison sentence of 24 months based on his prior conviction in United States District Court for the District of New Jersey on money laundering conspiracy charges in January 2008. SALZANO recently completed a 37 month prison sentence based on his prior conviction in -2 Manhattan federal court on extortion charges in September 2007.

ARTHUR BOLAND pleaded guilty on February 19, 2010, before the Honorable KEVIN NATHANIEL FOX to loansharking, and is scheduled to be sentenced by Judge HOLWELL on May 21, 2010. BOLAND faces a maximum possible sentence of 20 years in prison and a maximum fine of $250,000 or twice the gross gain or loss from the offense. At the time of his plea, BOLAND agreed to forfeit $20,000 as the illegal proceeds of his loansharking offense.

Mr. BHARARA praised the work of the Federal Bureau of Investigation and the New York City Police Department in this investigation. This case is being handled by the Office's Organized Crime Unit. Assistant United States Attorneys DAVID B. MASSEY, AVI WEITZMAN, BRIAN JACOBS, and JASON HERNANDEZ are in charge of the prosecutions.

CHAPTER EIGHTEEN

Anthony "Tony Pro" Provenzano

Provenzano is a famous Mafia figure due to the mistaken belief that he was directly involved with the disappearance of former Teamster President Jimmy Hoffa in 1975. Tony Pro dominated Local 560 of the Teamsters in New Jersey for many decades, much to the frustration of law enforcement. If they succeeded in sending him off to prison one of his loyal brothers quickly filled his slot. Finally intense FBI pressure caused some of his loyalists to break and Provenzano spent the rest of his life behind bars. His story follows below.

DOB
May 7, 1917
NYC

DOD
December 12, 1988
At a civic hospital near
Lompoc Prison, California

July 6, 1959
Provenzano appeared before the Senate Rackets Committee but took the Fifth to most questions about kickbacks for labor peace. Ironically, his future murder victim, Anthony Castellito, a Teamster Local 560 officer, also took the Fifth to the same queries.

Hoboken truck fleet owner Arthur Pitman testified that he paid Provenzano $2,500 in December 1954 for labor peace. Another trucking company executive, Walter Dorn, told the Committee that he paid Hudson County Deputy Prosecutor Michael Communale $200 a month from 1953 until 1959 at the insistence of Provenzano. When questioned about this, Communale admitted taking the money but said he never passed any funds on to Provenzano.

September 2, 1959

A court-appointed monitor of the Teamsters Union called on Jimmy Hoffa to remove Tony Provenzano from his position because Provenzano was corrupt. In addition, the monitor wanted a Teamster board to try Provenzano on charges developed in US Rackets Committee testimony.

November 15, 1960

A New Jersey grand jury indicted Provenzano. The indictment is below:

The Grand Jury in and for the District of New Jersey, sitting at Newark, charges:

1. That Anthony Provenzano was an officer of Local 560, International Brotherhood of Teamsters, Chauffeurs, Warehousemen, and Helpers of America, whose principal place of business was located in Hoboken, New Jersey.

2. Dorn's Transportation, Inc. was a corporation that had its principal office in Rensselaer, New York, which said corporation is from now on sometimes referred to as the 'Dorn Company.'

3. 'Dorn Company' was engaged in the business of a common carrier of general commodities in interstate commerce.

4. On or about January 1, 1952, the 'Dorn Company' opened a terminal within the State of New Jersey at Secaucus, New Jersey.

5. That from on or about January 1, 1952, to and including June 1, 1959, within the State and District of New Jersey, Anthony Provenzano did willfully, knowingly, and unlawfully obstruct, delay and affect interstate commerce by extortion and the said Anthony Provenzano did obtain from the 'Dorn Company ' and Walter A. Dorn, and officer of the 'Dorn Company,' and with their consent, the sum of $17,100.00, the payment of said amount having been induced by the said Anthony Provenzano by the wrongful use of fear of financial and economic injury to the business of the company above in the interstate transportation of general commodities.

1960

The Judge dismissed the indictment ruling on a technicality.

March 20, 1961

The Supreme Court of New Jersey reversed the trial Judge's ruling on the indictment and re-instated it.

1961

Genovese Soldier Sal Briguglio and Genovese Associate Salvatore Sinno strangled Teamster Local 560 secretary-treasurer Anthony Castellito to death at his summer cottage near Kingston, NY. They were acting on orders from Tony Provenzano, who wanted to get rid of a rival. Also present were Bonanno Associate Harold Konigsburg, along with Ed Skowren.

March 24, 1963

Someone killed New Jersey Teamster Walter Glockner.

May 1963

Teamster members re-elected Tony Provenzano, president of Joint Council 73.

June 11, 1963

A jury found Provenzano guilty of extorting $17,100 from the Dorn Company. Federal Judge Robert Shaw released Provenzano on $15,000 bail.

July 11, 1963

Judge Robert Shaw dismissed Provenzano's lawyers' application for a new trial and sentenced the Teamster leader to seven years in prison and a fine of $10,000. The Judge continued Provenzano on bail while he appealed.

December 1963

Teamster members nominated Tony Provenzano for the Presidency of Joint Council 73. He was unopposed. After a complaint to the Labor Department in September, the Teamsters decided to re-run the May election.

January 21, 1964

Tony Provenzano won re-election to the Presidency of Teamster's Joint Council 73, winning the support of 142 of the 175 voters.

February 24, 1964

One thousand people paid $50 each to attend a dinner honoring Tony Provenzano. A scholarship fund named after his mother would receive the profits.

March 12, 1964

The Third Circuit Court of Appeals heard arguments on the Provenzano appeal and reserved judgment.

June 30, 1964

The Third Circuit Court of Appeals upheld Provenzano's July 11, 1963, extortion conviction.

March 30, 1965

Judge Shaw of the District Court denied Provenzano's motion for a new trial. Provenzano claimed the anti-Provenzano biases of a juror prevented a fair trial, and the government didn't release all the relevant information about Provenzano.

May 1966

Provenzano began serving this extortion conviction sentence.

1970

Parole officials released Provenzano after he completed his extortion conviction sentence from 1963.

Kickback case

December 9, 1975

A Southern District of New York grand jury indictment, charged Provenzano and Anthony Bentro violated an anti-kickback statute by offering a bribe to an official of the Utica Teamsters Benefit fund in return for approval of a loan to renovate the Woodstock Hotel in NYC.

Castellito case

June 23, 1976

A grand jury indicted Provenzano, Salvatore Briguglio, and Harold Konigsberg for conspiracy to murder and the murder of Teamster official Antony Castellito.

November 1976

Provenzano's ban from the Teamster ended after serving a four-year term for extortion plus waiting out a two-year ban.

Kickback case

September 21, 1977

The grand jury returned a superseding indictment charging Provenzano and Bentro with conspiracy to offer a bribe to a union official in return for loan approval.

Kickback case

November 11, 1977

Judge Bonsal dismissed the original and superseding indictments against Provenzano and Bentro without prejudice to the government, which meant they could try again.

Kickback case

December 19, 1977

On its third try, the grand jury got it right when they indicted Provenzano and Bentro for illegally offering a kickback to a union official to approve a loan.

Kickback case

March 17, 1978

Provenzano's kickback trial began before Judge Metzner.

March 21, 1978

A shooter killed Genovese Soldier Sal Briguglio as he walked down a street in Little Italy. He was a defendant along with Provenzano and Konigsberg in the Albert Castellito murder case.

Kickback case

March 25, 1978

The jury convicted Provenzano and Bentro of conspiracy to offer a bribe to a union official in return for approval of a loan to renovate the Woodstock Hotel in NYC.

Castellito case

June 14, 1978

The jury convicted Provenzano and Harold Konigsberg of the murder of Anthony Castellito. A key prosecution witness was Salvatore Sinno, who admitted to strangling Castellito with Sal Briguglio on behalf of Provenzano. Other devastating testimony came from a neighbor who fingered Sinno and Konigsberg as two men he saw around Castellito's cottage on the day of his murder. In a strange set of circumstances, the neighbor stopped when he noticed a vehicle on the side of the road and heard digging sounds from the forest. He went home but returned shortly afterward and met three men who said they were looking for properties to buy. Since he had homes for sale, the neighbor drove the three killers around looking at places. The infamous Ralph Picardo, a Provenzano Associate who rolled over on Provenzano, also made an appearance for the prosecutors. Picardo claimed that Provenzano told him he ordered the death of Castellito.

Castellito case
June 21, 1978
Judge John Clyne sentenced Provenzano and Konigsberg to life for the 1961 murder of Anthony Castellito.

Kickback case
July 11, 1978
Judge Metzner sentenced Provenzano to four years for his conspiracy to bribe sentence but ruled it would run concurrent to his murder conviction sentence. He set bail at $25,000.

Seatrain case
February 22, 1979
A grand jury indicted Provenzano, Gabe Briguglio, Steve and Thomas Andretta, and Ralph Dellechico for extorting the Seatrain Transportation Company.

Seatrain case
May 25, 1979
A jury convicted Provenzano, Steve Andretta, and Thomas Andretta for extorting the Seatrain Transportation Company. However, the Judge released them on bail until sentencing. Provenzano was on bail of $175,000 from this and other convictions.

Castellito case
June 7, 1979
The Appellate Division of the NY Supreme Court threw out Provenzano's murder conviction in the Castellito case. They had no problem with the trial evidence. Still, they ruled that the Judge's refusal to remove a juror due to her association with the prosecutor forced the defense to unfairly use up one of their exclusions to remove the potential juror.

Seatrain case

July 3, 1979

Provenzano filed a motion requesting a hearing on some of the evidence and questioned the sequestering of the jury in the Seatrain trial.

Seatrain case

July 6, 1979

The Judge refused to question the jurors as requested by Provenzano.

Seatrain case

July 10, 1979

The Judge sentenced Provenzano to twenty years and a fine of $20,000 for his Seatrain extortion conviction. He gave Thomas Andretta twenty years and his brother Steven ten. He ruled there would be no bail for the men who were dangerous to the community.

Seatrain case

August 21, 1979

The Third Court of Appeals upheld the trial Judge's ruling of no bail for Provenzano and Thomas Andretta in their Seatrain extortion conviction.

Kickback case

January 16, 1980

The Second Court of Appeals upheld Provenzano's kickback conviction.

Provenzano's lawyers claimed the government did not release all the appropriate government documents to them, but the Judges disagreed.

Seatrain case

May 8, 1980

The Third Circuit Court of Appeals denied Provenzano a new trial and affirmed his conviction in the Seatrain case.

Seatrain case

October 14, 1980

The US Supreme Court declined to hear Provenzano's appeal of his Seatrain conviction.

Castellito case

December 31, 1980

The Court of Appeals of New York previously rejected that failing to dismiss a potential juror who was an associate of the DA in the Castellito murder case was grounds for a reversal of Provenzano's conviction. Instead, they sent the case back to the Appellate Division of the New York Supreme Court for further review. On this date, the Appellate Division upheld the murder conviction of Provenzano but granted defendant Harold Konigsberg a new trial.

PART OF THE APPELATE DIVISION'S RULING ON PROVENZANO'S CASTELLITO VERDICT

Anthony Provenzano and Harold Konigsberg were charged with the murder of one Anthony Castellito approximately 15 years after he disappeared in June of 1961. Although Castellito's body was never discovered, the defendants were jointly tried and convicted upon proof consisting of admissions, accomplice testimony and circumstantial evidence. Our review of the trial record persuades us to the view that the only part of the transcript requiring discussion is that relating to accomplice testimony. Salvatore Sinno, a participant in the Federal witness relocation program, testified for the People. He stated that he agreed to participate with three others in luring Castellito to his farm in Kerhonkson, New York, for the purpose of murdering him in a rural area. The plan was effectuated and about a week later Sinno testified that he met with Provenzano in his office along with Konigsberg and Salvatore Briguglio, the other participant in the murder. At that meeting, Sinno stated, Provenzano gave Konigsberg a sealed envelope, a fact which Sinno related to Provenzano's earlier statement to him that Konigsberg would be paid $15,000 for his efforts. Provenzano claims that corroboration of this testimony was inadequate and that reversal is, therefore, required. The People's corroborating witness, Ralph Picardo, also a participant in the Federal witness relocation program, and an alleged murderer, testified that he met with Provenzano in North Bergen, New Jersey, in late 1972 or early 1973 and, further, that Provenzano stated that Castellito had been killed as a result of a power struggle in the Teamsters Union and that he, Provenzano, had ordered the killing. Clearly, if self-incriminating extrajudicial statements made by a defendant constitute sufficient corroborative evidence, the requirements of CPL 60.22 (subd 1) to the effect that "A defendant may not be convicted of any offense upon the testimony of an accomplice unsupported by corroborative evidence tending to connect the defendant with the commission of such offense" has been substantially met in this case. This is so even if, as here, the accomplice is a person of disrepute or may have received a promise of reduced exposure to criminal liability by promising to implicate others *(People v. Daniels,* 37 N.Y.2d 624). Such proof, i.e., a defendant's extrajudicial statements of complicity, has been held to constitute sufficient corroborative testimony so as to permit the question to go to the jury *(People v. Ozarowski,* 38 N.Y.2d 481 [defendant›s statement "We think we killed a Spic last night"]; see, also, *People v. Peller,* 291 N.Y. 438; *People v Buchalter,* 289 N.Y. 181, affd 319 U.S. 427; *People v. Feolo,* 284 N.Y. 381). Accordingly, we conclude that the testimony of witnesses Salvatore Sinno and Ralph Picardo adequately established the accessorial culpability of defendant Provenzano for the crime of murder in the first degree. Therefore, pursuant to section 20.00 Penal of the Penal Law, **the conviction of Provenzano for the murder of Anthony Castellito can be affirmed**

1981

Members of Local 560 voted to give Tony Provenzano an annual pension of $28,000.

Seatrain case

January 13, 1981

Provenzano filed a motion for a new trial claiming new evidence would affect the verdict in the Seatrain case.

Seatrain case

May 11, 1981

Judge H Curtis Meaner heard and reserved a decision on Provenzano's motion for a new trial based on the claim the government did not reveal to the defense that they allegedly promised witness Picardo he would not have to face a retrial in his murder conviction that an appeal court overturned.

Seatrain case

May 18, 1981

Provenzano asked the Judge for a delay in the decision on his motion for a new trial.

Seatrain case

June 5, 1981

Provenzano's lawyers filed a recusal motion with Judge Meaner. They wanted a new Judge.

Seatrain case

June 22, 1981

Judge Meaner denied Provenzano's recusal motion. Accordingly, he would remain as Judge.

Seatrain case

September 5, 1981

Judge Meaner ruled that there would be no new trial for Provenzano and Thomas Andretta in the Seatrain case. He rejected their claims that the government withheld information that would have discredited witness Ralph Picardo.

PROVENZANO DEATH

December 12, 1988
Provenzano died of heart problems in a civic hospital near the Lompoc
Federal Penitentiary in California.

PROVENZANO AND HOFFA

GANGLAND NEWS

ASK ANDY

July 7, 2016
THE FBI BOUGHT A BILL OF GOODS FROM LITTLE RALPHIE PICARDO

After 41 years, no one believes that anyone will find Jimmy Hoffa — alive
or dead. But even if someone does discover his body, it's a safe bet that the
usual suspects from New Jersey and Pennsylvania, whose names had nothing
to do with Hoffa's demise or the disposal of his remains.

These suspects include Pennsylvania Mafia boss Russell Bufalino, Genovese
Capo Anthony (Tony Pro) Provenzano, Soldier Salvatore (Sally Bugs)
Briguglio, Teamsters Union official Frank (The Irishman) Sheeran, and
Philip (Brother) Moscato, the mob-connected owner of a dump on the
Hackensack River where the bad guys supposedly disposed of Hoffa's body
more than 40 years ago.

I say this with all due respect to the FBI, and my good friend Dan Moldea,
who has written extensively about the subject and knows more about the late
Teamsters Union president than anyone. But, unfortunately, I believe they,
the media, and the entire law enforcement community were all taken in by
Ralph (Little Ralphie) Picardo, a low-life murderer with ties to Tony Pro

who came up with a tall tale to get out of a 17-to-23 years prison term for the slaying of a New Jersey man.

To begin with, it makes no sense that someone would give the North East mob families the task of whacking Hoffa, whose murder was likely sanctioned by the Mafia Commission since he was such a prominent national figure. Moreover, he was an Associate of the Detroit Family. So they could do it without raising Hoffa's suspicions. And too many things could go wrong with a plan involving a New Jersey hit team traveling to Detroit, killing Hoffa, and then transporting his body 600 miles for burial in the Garden State.

The only so-called evidence that links Tony Pro's guys to the hit is the words of Picardo, who told the FBI he learned about Hoffa's demise from gangster buddy Steve Andretta in August of 1975, less than a month after Hoffa disappeared. At the time, Picardo was not a happy camper. Nevertheless, he had a powerful motive to find a way to freedom. When Picardo was in jail, Tony Pro's crew had taken his business interests. The only thing of value he had was his connection to Tony Pro and the suspicion he was involved in the Hoffa hit. Andretta's visit after the Hoffa murder provided the link.

Isn't it implausible that Andretta would tell Picardo about the sensational killing of Hoffa while he was on one side of a glass partition talking to him on a prison phone that officials could easily bug? It's hard to believe that any gangster, even the dumbest alive, would do such a thing.

The FBI, floundering around and making no progress, was delighted with the Hoffa story Picardo told them four months later in November. There is no report of him passing a polygraph exam, but even if he did, no one has found any evidence confirming his account.

With Picardo's information, the FBI developed this theory on the Hoffa murder: Bufalino, the Boss of the tiny Northeast Pennsylvania Family, had given the contract to Tony Pro. Detroit mob Capo Anthony (Tony Jack) Giacalone lured Hoffa to a fake peace meeting with Provenzano. Hoffa was picked up by his associate, Charles (Chuckie) O'Brien, and taken to a home where Tony Pro's guys killed him.

Provenzano Associate Briguglio, his brother Gabe, and Thomas Andretta had all flown to Detroit by private plane and did the job, the theory goes. In addition, some allege that Frank Sheeran was involved in some way. Hoffa's body was placed in a 55-gallon drum and driven to Jersey City for disposal by a Gateway Transportation truck. Neither the FBI nor anyone else has come up with any evidence to support this theory.

Even the feds realized it was nuts to think that gangsters would drive a body from Michigan to New Jersey to dispose of it. So in January of 1976, a little more than a month after the FBI got a federal judge to authorize a search of Brother Moscato's dump, the Department of Justice announced it had decided not to bother.

The FBI could not place Provenzano or his three cohorts in Detroit on July 30, when Hoffa disappeared. Despite the pressure that included a 63-day contempt sentence, Steve Andretta denied the Hoffa murder story and telling it to Picardo. Giacalone had a solid alibi and rejected the idea of planning to meet Hoffa. The feds found evidence that Frank Sheeran drove into Detroit the next day with Bufalino but could not prove that either man was in town on July 30. Finally, Picardo's claim that Bufalino was an Acting Genovese Family Boss with tremendous clout was false.

Here's my take on the plot.

Tony Giacalone lured Hoffa to a supposed peace meeting. The evidence for that is a reminder note Hoffa left on his desk. In addition, Hoffa told others about this meeting. Outside the Machus Red Fox restaurant, Hoffa was picked up, probably by Giacalone's brother Vito "Billy Jack" Giacalone, maybe with a few others. Billy Jack's presence would make sense to Hoffa since he was to meet with his brother. Unfortunately, the FBI could not pinpoint Billy Giacalone's location that day. Hoffa may have been killed in the car or somewhere else. His killers most likely buried the body in the Detroit area. It was a tiny group which significantly decreased the likelihood that an informer could learn the details and spill the beans.

All the Detroit characters are dead; thus, there is little chance we will ever get a complete account of the famous hit, let alone find Hoffa's body.

There is no hard evidence to support my theory, either. But it makes more sense than the elaborate, convoluted plan that Little Ralphie concocted.

I also dismiss the claim by Frank Sheeran that he flew into Detroit on a private plane to join up with the New Jersey mobster at a home where he killed Hoffa. Other than his words, no evidence of his flight in and out of Pontiac, Michigan, or any further details he supplied, have been proven.

CONCLUSION

Anthony Provenzano was a very important figure in the Genovese Family and the Teamsters Union. His power caused many trucking firms to cave in and pay to avoid labor problems. Everyone who wanted to be Teamster President had to court Provenzano due to his union influence on the east coast. When one of his Associates rolled over on Provenzano his long reign came to a slow end.

CHAPTER NINETEEN

Matty "The Horse" Ianiello

Ianniello was an old school Mafioso. He was involved in the rackets from a young age and progressed to a Capo position fairly quickly. His involvement or alleged connection to many Manhattan bars, restaurants, and sex clubs created a lot of notoriety. But Ianniello also had his hand in extortion, union racketeering and the like. Matty the Horse had endless legal battles, but all things considered he did a minimum amount of time behind bars considering his life time devotion to the "life." A quick summary of the major events in his Mafia life follows starting in the 1960s.

Contempt Case
June 11, 1964
Ianniello appeared before a New York County grand jury probing police corruption. (See details below.)

Contempt Case
June 18, 1964
Ianniello appeared again before a New York County grand jury probing police corruption. (See details below.)

Contempt Case

RELATED DOCUMENTS

Ianniello, owner of "two licensed bars and grills" in the sensitive mid-town area, was called before the Grand Jury on June 11, 1964. At the outset, he refused to be sworn on the ground that he was a defendant in a pending misdemeanor prosecution. He was then told by an assistant district attorney that he was called "solely in the role of a witness" in the Grand Jury's investigation of a bribery conspiracy involving police and officials of the State Liquor Authority. After he was told by the prosecutor, before the Grand Jury, that the "grand jury is ready to confer immunity upon you should you consider any answers that you might have to give [incriminatory]," and after he had said that he understood the nature of this advice, he consented to being sworn. Defendant was thereafter questioned about conversations concerning investigations of police payoffs, which he allegedly had had with one Benny Cohen in 1963. When he stated that he could not recall such conversations, he was reminded that the Grand Jury had "voted to confer immunity" upon him, and that he was legally obligated to give truthful testimony. Pressed to affirm or deny that the conversations had taken place, defendant asked: "Could I excuse myself to see my attorney for a minute? * * * I want to ask him if it's a proper question." This request was denied and, after defendant persisted in his request, the prosecutor suggested that they "go in open court * * * and make an application." This course was not pursued, however. Instead, the Grand Jury foreman, at the prosecutor's request, directed the witness to answer. He thereupon answered that he did not recall the conversations.

The questioning then turned to the subject of defendant's alleged meeting in September, 1963 with one O'Shea, a police sergeant. Although the conversation allegedly involved a confidential investigation pending against defendant's friend, Benny Cohen, defendant persisted in stating that he did not "recall" the conversation and could not affirm or deny that it had ever occurred. This testimony was the basis for one of the four contempt charges in the indictment.

The other three counts of the indictment dealt with testimony given when defendant was recalled, a week later, on June 18, 1964. They too involved defendant's purported inability to recall conversations in the recent past. Thus, defendant stated that he could not recall whether anyone had, within the previous six months, told him to stay away from Sergeant O'Shea because the officer was under investigation. Nor could he recall having entertained police officers, other than a police captain, at his farm.

Finally, three of the contempt counts refer to testimony given after a week's recess, during which defendant had extended opportunity to consult with his lawyer and undoubtedly did so, and hence are free of taint. The appearance before the Grand Jury a week after the first meeting is critically important. By that time defendant had the fullest opportunity to consult with counsel. Actually, the only area in which he still needed proper lawful advice was with respect to his status as a witness given transactional immunity. The Grand Jury was still insisting unequivocally that it was giving him immunity or was ready to do so, and there was no assertion by anyone or implication from anything that he had waived any rights to his privilege against self-incrimination or that he was not entitled to the fullest immunity allowed by the statute. His conduct on his second appearance before the Grand Jury, therefore, presents no difficulty in assessing it as contemptuous and is highly persuasive in confirming that his purpose in asking to speak with his lawyer on the first occasion was specious and without legal basis.

Contempt Case
February 3, 1965
Superior Court Justice Abraham N Geller handled the preliminary steps when Ianniello faced a charge of criminal contempt before a grand jury investigating police bribery. The prosecutor claimed Ianniello was evasive and also gave false answers to questions. Judge Geller set bail at $25,000 until trial.

Contempt Case

1966

Justice Mark dismissed the criminal contempt charge against Ianniello. He ruled that the grand jury refused to let Ianniello leave the room to consult his lawyer. DA Frank Hogan appealed to the Appellate Division which confirmed the indictment's dismissal stating that since the grand jury had Ianniello as a target he was immune from contempt. Hogan appealed to the Second Circuit Court of Appeals.

Contempt Case

February 21, 1968

The Second Court of Appeals ruled that Ianniello's rights were not violated and that the court must reinstated the criminal contempt charge. At this point Ianniello's lawyer obtained 39 postponements of the case over the next three years.

Contempt Case

April 16, 1971

A jury convicted Ianniello of criminal contempt but Justice Harry Birns handed down a one year suspended sentence. Later the Justice stated that he did so based on Ianniello's positive probation report and, in addition, two jurors recommended leniency.

Umberto Case

April 7, 1972

A group of three hoods gunned down reengage Colombo Soldier Joey Gallo in Ianniello's Umbertos Clam House. Gallo bodyguard Pete Diapoulos showed a gun in Matty's face in the mistaken belief Matty Ianniello had set Gallo up. Luckily for Ianniello, Diapoulos' gun was empty.

March 31, 1975

A small group of men failed to obtain a liquor license when they planned to re-open the famous Copacabana Club. The famous night spot, located at 10

East 60th Street closed in 1973 when its long-time manager, Jules Podell died. The State Liquor Authority denied the license.

May 9, 1975

Justice George Pestel ruled that the SLA needed more evidence to support their claim of hidden owners at the Copacabana. The Authority argued that the three owners were fronts for Ianniello.

October 15, 1975

A grand jury indicted Ianniello and seven others with bribery, extortion, and conspiracy in the garment center. The Judge released Ianniello on $25,000 bail.

November 17 1976

A jury found Ianniello and two others not guilty of bribery, extortion, and conspiracy involving the garment center.

Umberto Case
February 28, 1985

Ianniello pled not guilty to an indictment charging him and others with a wide spread skimming racket of a number of night clubs and bars.

Umberto Case
December 30, 1985

A jury convicted Ianniello and eight others of tax fraud and racketeering involving hidden ownership of nightclubs. The jury also ordered Ianniello and two others to forfeit $2 million.

Umberto Case
February 13, 1986

Judge Edward Weinfeld sentenced Ianniello to six years and a fine of $61,000 for racketeering, racketeering conspiracy and fraud involving hidden ownership and skimming of nightclubs. Judge Weinfeld ordered

Matty Ianniello to forfeit $666,666.67. The Judge also sentenced seven co-defendants.

Umberto Case
DOCUMENT

Ianniello and a partner secretly controlled and profited from a group of bars and restaurants in New York City: the Peppermint Lounge (at various times known as Hollywood and G.G. Barnum's); the New Peppermint Lounge; the Mardi Gras; the Haymarket; the Grapevine; and Umberto's Clam House. The "heart of the enterprise was [a] scheme to skim cash on a massive scale" from the businesses.

The jury convicted Ianniello on thirty-five counts of mail fraud and six counts of tax evasion. The jury also found that Ianniello committed every one of the forty-four acts of mail fraud submitted to it by the trial court for consideration as predicate RICO acts, and convicted Ianniello of substantive and conspiracy violations of RICO. Judge Weinfeld sentenced Ianniello on the RICO counts to concurrent six year prison terms and separate $10,000 fines, and on the remaining counts to concurrent five year prison terms, separate $1,000 fines, and two years of probation.

The government established the following facts at trial:

—Ianniello and his partner skimmed cash from bar and admission receipts of the businesses, and failed to report the income on personal tax returns.—The books, records and tax returns of the businesses were falsified to conceal the diversion of money and to avoid payment of taxes by the businesses.—The Peppermint Lounge underwent chapter 11 bankruptcy proceedings and was obligated to file monthly financial statements with the bankruptcy court. Cash was skimmed during this period and the statements filed with the court were falsified. The interests of Ianniello and his partner were concealed from State liquor licensing authorities in furtherance of the cash skimming scheme. The facilities of the New Peppermint Lounge were acquired when the original Peppermint Lounge was closed for fire code violations. The transaction was concealed from State liquor licensing authorities. Ianniello and his partner ran the scheme from the offices of C & I Trading at 135 West 50th Street in Manhattan.

Umberto Case
February 21, 1986
The Feds launched a Civil RICO case to remove the Ianniello brothers from the restaurant business and force them to sell any holdings in restaurants and bars.

Umberto Case
April 1986
Judge Haight denied the governments motion to appoint a receiver for Umberto's Clam House but did so without prejudice. That meant the government could try again if it has more evidence. Consequently the feds began an in depth study of Umberto's finances.

May 13, 1986
A jury found Ianniello not guilty for extorting a company to obtain the contract to remove Consolidated Edison's garbage.

Genovese Case
May 15, 1986
A grand jury indicted Ianniello, Salerno, and others for participating in the concrete club and extortion in the food business. (I refer to these proceedings as the Genovese Case.)

Umberto Case
May 22, 1986
Using the financial records it has accumulated the feds again approached Judge Haight seeking the appointment of a receiver.

Umberto Case

June 3, 1986

Judge Haight again denied the feds request to appoint a receiver for Umbertos but ordered more hearings to determine the merits of the government's case.

Umberto Case

September 30, 1986

Judge Haight accepted the government's motion to appoint a receiver for Umbertos. He said the criminal records of the Ianniellos, the government's financial investigation, and the refusal of the Ianniello's to answer questions about Umbertos were the key factors in his decision.

Umberto Case

November 14, 1986

Judge Haight appointed a receiver for Umbertos but he/she could not fire employees nor sell the business.

Umberto Case

December 4, 1986

The Second Court of Appeals denied the Ianniello's appeal.

Umberto Case

February 20, 1987

The Ianniellos filed a motion to remove the receiver but withdrew the appeal and asked for the reinstatement of their appeal of December 4, 1986.

Umberto Case

July 21, 1987

The Second Court of Appeals rejected the Ianniellos motion to remove the receiver but rejected the feds appeal to not have to cover the cost of the receivership.

Genovese Case

May 14, 1988

A jury found Ianniello, Tony Salerno and others guilty in the Genovese Family trial.

June 10, 1988

Authorities arrested Ianniello and Salerno in an extortion conspiracy over control of a sand pit. (See March 15, 1989)

Genovese Case

October 13, 1988

Federal Judge Mary Johnson sentenced Ianniello to 13 years for his role in the Family's concrete racket and the extortion of sales of hot dogs to stores and stands. The Judge rejected Ianniello's motion for a new trial.

Genovese Case

February 23, 1989

The Second Court of Appeals ruled the Judge Mary Johnson may have interfered with the legal process and ordered another District Court Judge to hold hearings.

March 15, 1989

Ianniello pled guilty to extortion, mail fraud, and tax evasion related to a condo project in NJ. In addition he pled to extortion and tax evasion in the takeover of a sand pit. (See December 6, 1989)

Genovese Case

April 26, 1990

Chief District Judge Brieant ruled that Judge Johnson did not interfere with the jurors as an Ianniello appeal alleged. This ruling meant that Ianniello would not get a new trial.

December 6, 1990

A Judge sentenced Ianniello to five years for extortion and racketeering. The jury found him guilty of fraudulently obtaining a $21 million loan for a condo project in Edgewater, NJ.

Genovese Case

June 28, 1991

The Second Court of Appeals overturned the convictions in the Genovese Case. They ruled that the Judge made a serious error by refusing to admit some grand jury testimony by concrete company owners who were not available to testify at trial. The government appealed this ruling to the Supreme Court.

1992

The US Supreme Court reversed the Second Court of Appeals ruling that overturned the convictions in the Genovese Case.

Genovese Case

July 24, 1992

Ianniello filed an appeal for a new trial based on recent rulings by the Second Court of Appeals.

Genovese Case

May 5, 1993

District Judge Stanton dismissed Ianniello's appeal for a new trial.

Genovese Case

November 18, 1993

The Second Court of Appeals refused a new trial for Ianniello.

Umberto Case

1994

The government returned Umbertos to the control of Robert Ianniello. The appointed receiver was unable to run the restaurant to profitably and since the feds were paying the cost of receivership it was a no win situation for the feds.

Umberto Case
November 1996
The Ianniello's closed their Umbertos Restaurant at the corner of Mulberry and Hester in Little Italy. (129 Mulberry). They also sold the building.

1997
When Boss Vince Gigante went to prison he appointed Matty Ianniello as his Acting Boss.

Umberto Case
May 2000
The Ianniellos opened a new Umbertos at 178 Mulberry.

Union Extortion Case
July 28, 2005
A grand jury indicted Ianniello and 18 others for extortion. They accused Ianniello of extorting $100,000 from a medical clinic that did business with Local 1181 of the Amalgamated Transit Union. Magistrate Douglas Eaton set bail at $5,000,000 but allowed Ianniello to go home until a later hearing.

Union Extortion Case
July 29, 2005
At Ianniello's bail hearing Assistant US Attorney Timothy Treaner cited Ianniello's record and also claimed Ianniello still has some control and received some benefits from the San Gennaro Festival. Nevertheless Judge Kimba Woods released Ianniello subject to a further hearing in August.

2005
Ianniello stepped down as Acting Boss after being indicted for extortion.

Garbage Extortion Case

June 9, 2006

A Connecticut grand jury indicted Ianniello and 28 others for a garbage extortion scheme. The indictment alleged that Ianniello received payments from James Galante to enforce the "property rights" system which ensured Galante's companies would have no competition. The Magistrate released Ianniello on a $1 million bond.

Union Extortion Case

September 14, 2006

Before Magistrate Ronald L Ellis Ianniello pled guilty to conspiracy to infiltrate a union and interfering with a grand jury probe. Ianniello agreed to forfeit up to $1 million.

Garbage Extortion Case

December 21, 2006

In New Haven, Ianniello pled guilty before Judge Ellen Bree Burns to extorting James Galante's trash companies in New York and Connecticut and tax evasion. He agreed to forfeit $130,000 that FBI Agents found at his home. Judge Burns continued Ianniello on a $1 million bond.

Union Extortion Case

April 16, 2007

Judge Kimba Woods sentenced Ianniello to 18 months, a fine of $25,000 and forfeiture of $75,000 for his guilty plea for extorting labor payments using Local 1181 of the Amalgamated Transit Union.

Garbage Extortion Case

May 9, 2007

Judge Ellen Bree Burns sentenced Ianniello to two years for his guilty plea in the trash extortion case involving the "property rights" system with the James Galante trash hauling companies in Connecticut and New York.

2009

Prison official released Matty Ianniello from his combined sentences.

2010

The Ianniellos moved their Umbertos a few spots north of the original.

August 15, 2012

Matty Ianniello died at his home in Old Westbury, Long Island. He was 92.

Appendix A

The History of the Genovese Family Administration

CAUTION

Some of the following dates are guesstimates since I do not have primary evidence to support them.

Genovese Family 1900-1911

<u>Boss</u>

Giuseppe Morello

1900-1911

Jailed in 1910 for 25 years

<u>Underboss</u>

Ignatz Lupo

1900-1910

Jailed for 30 years

<u>Consigliere</u>

Unknown

Genovese Family 1911-1914

Boss
Fortunato "Charles" Lomonte
1911-1914
Killed May 13, 1914

Underboss
Tommaso "Joe" Lomonte
1911-1914
Killed October 13, 1915

Consigliere
Unknown

Genovese Family 1914-1916

Boss
Nick Terranova
1914-1916
Killed September 7, 1916

Underboss
Ciro Terranova
1914-1916

Consigliere
Unknown

Genovese Family 1916-1920

Boss
Ciro Terranova
1916-1920

Underboss
Unknown

Consigliere
Unknown

Genovese Family 1920-1931*

Boss
Joe Masseria
1920-1931
Killed April 14, 1931

Underboss
Giuseppe Morello
1921-1930
Killed August 15, 1930

Consigliere
Saverio "Sam" Pollaccia
19??-1931
Disappeared 1932

* This version of the Genovese Family was an amalgamation of the Masseria and Morello Families. They united to fend off the power of the D'Aquila (Gambino) Family.

Genovese Family
1931-1947

Boss
Charles "Lucky" Luciano
1931-1947
Jailed 1936

Deported 1946

Resigned 1947 (?)

Acting Boss

Frank Costello

1936 -1947

Note:

Elected Acting Boss, according to Valachi

Underboss

Vito Genovese

1931-1937

He fled to Italy to avoid a murder charge

Willie Moretti

1937-1947

Consigliere

"Sandino" (According to Valachi)

Note:

Genovese may have been Acting Boss for a short period before he fled to Italy however I cannot find any primary evidence to support this claim. The theory seems logical since he was the Underboss.

Genovese Family

1947-1957

Boss

Frank Costello

1947-1957

Resigned after surviving an assassination attempt.

Note:

This entry is making the unsupported assumption that the Family picked Costello as Boss once it was clear that Luciano would never return to the USA after he was deported from Cuba in 1947.

Note:

A January 19, 1981 FBI bug in the office of New England Underboss Jerry Angiulo overheard him say this about Costello, "You know the mistake he made? He never got himself elected."

Underboss
Willie Moretti
1947-1951
Killed October 4, 1951
Vito Genovese
1951-1957

Consigliere
Unknown

Genovese Family
1957-1969

Boss
Vito Genovese
1957-1969

He was in prison from February 1960 until his death on February 14, 1969

Acting Boss
Jerry Catena
1960-1969

Note:

A 1963 FBI bug overheard Genovese gangsters saying that Genovese had appointed Catena as Acting Boss.

Note:

March 28, 1967

Informer NKT-2 said that Genovese appointed Phil Lombardo as Acting Boss of the entire LCN in 1967.

Underboss
Jerry Catena
1957-1969

Acting Underboss
Tom Eboli
1960-1969

Note:

Acting Boss Jerry Catena was quite comfortable letting Eboli handle most of the day to day business of the Family.

Consigliere
Mike Miranda
1957-1969

Capos 1960:

Vince Aloi, James Angelini, John Biele, Richie Boiardo, Tony Carillo, Gerry Catena, Frank Celano, Salvatore Celembrino, Mike Coppola, Angelo DeCarlo, Peter DeFeo, Cosmo Frasca, Vince Generoso, Tom Greco, Rocco Pellegrino, Anthony Strollo, Frank Tieri.

Note:

Phil Lombardo became Acting Capo for Mike Coppola in the mid-sixties. He quickly rose in power from that point on.

Genovese Family
1969-1981

Boss
Phil Lombardo
1969-1981
Vince Gigante and others forced an ill Lombardo to retire.

Acting Boss
Tommy Eboli
1970-1972
Killed July 16, 1972

Eli Ziccardi
1972-1974
Missing

Frank Tieri
1974-1978
Retired

Anthony Salerno
1978-1981
Stroke—demoted to Soldier

Underboss
Tom Eboli
1969-1972
Killed July 16, 1972

Eli Zeccardi
1972-1974
Disappeared in 1974.

Frank Tieri
1974-1978
Retired due to ill health.

Anthony Salerno
1978-1981

<u>Consigliere</u>
Mike Miranda
1969-1972
Retired

Anthony Salerno
1972-1976
Chin Gigante
1976 according to Sammy the Bull
(Five Families p 538)

Antonio Ferro
1976-1980
Bobby Manna
1980-1981

During this period, the Underboss was presented to the other Families as the "Boss" so Lombardo could keep a low profile.

An FBI informant named Eboli "Acting Boss" after Genovese died.

Capos 69:

Vinnie Alo, Ruggiero Boiardo, Angelo DeCarlo, Antonio Carillo, Sal Celembrino, Frank Celano, Peter DeFeo, Cosmo Frasca, Vincenzo Generoso, Mike Generoso (acting), Thomas Greco, Rosario Mogarvero, Frank Tieri, Harry Lanzo, Rocco Pelligrino, Sal Cufari.

Genovese Family
1981-2005

Boss
Vince Gigante
1981-2005
Died in prison December 19, 2005

Note:

The dates and names of the various Acting Boss are often contradictory. Various US Attorney's, DA's, and the FBI named individuals as Acting Boss for a particular indictment or press release. Unfortunately no agency has provided a complete chronological list that I am aware of.

Acting Boss
Anthony Salerno
1982-1986
Jailed

Note:

During this period Salerno was technically only a Soldier.

Liberio Bellomo
1990-1996
Convicted/ten years

Matty Ianniello

1997-2005
(According to the NY Times)

Committee
1997-1998
Dom Cirillo and Lawrence Dentico

Frank "Farby" Serpico
1998-?

Ernest Muscarella
2000-2002
Indicted

Arthur Nigro
2003

Dom Cirillo
2004-2005

Pled guilty
Danny Leo
2005-2010
Jailed from 2008 until 2013

Underboss
Sammy Santora
1981-1987
Died May 28, 1987

Venero Mangano
1987-1991
Jailed

Acting Underboss
Mickey Generoso
1991-1996
Jailed for 57 months

Ernie Muscarella
1996-2002

Consigliere
Bobby Manna
1981-1989
Jailed

Acting Consigliere
James Ida
1990-1996
Sentenced to life in 1996

Capos mid-80s, according to Cafaro.

Vince Gigante, Dom Alongi, Al Malangone, Louis Gatto, Joey Gatto (replaced his father), Joe Parlivecchio, Angelo Prisco, Ralph Coppola, Al Longo, Sal Aparo, Joe Zito, Pasquale Parello, Rosario Gangi, Joe Dente Jr, Jimmy Masseria, James Ida, Dom Cirillo, Charles Tuzzo, Sal Lombardi, Anthony Baratta.

Genovese Family
2005-2010

Boss

Acting Boss Committee
Paul DiMarco/Liborio Bellomo/Danny Leo

Underboss
Venero Mangano

Consigliere
James Ida
Life in 1996

Acting Consigliere
Dom Cirillo

Genovese Family
2014-

Boss
Liborio Bellomo
2014-

Underboss

Consigliere
Peter Di Chiara
2014-2018
Died March 2018

Appendix B

Testimony of Vincent Cafaro

April 29, 1988
Senate Permanent Subcommittee on Investigations

Senator NUNN. First of all, as I understand it, Mr. Cafaro, you currently remain under Federal indictment on various criminal charges in the Southern District of New York. Is that correct?

Mr. CAFARO. Yes, Senator.

Senator NUNN. Given the fact of that indictment, I want to advise you of your rights as a witness before this Subcommittee, and if there are any questions, you and your attorney certainly can confer, and you can certainly pose those questions to us.

First, you have the right not to provide any testimony which may tend to incriminate you. Do you understand that right?

Mr. CAFARO. Yes, Senator.

Senator NUNN. Do you understand that if you do testify here this morning anything you say here may be used against you in other legal proceedings?

Mr. CAFARO. Yes, Senator.

Senator NUNN. Second, you have the right to consult with an attorney before answering any question or questions before the Sub-committee. Any questions we may pose this morning, you have the right to confer with your attorney before answering that question.

Do you understand that right?

Mr. CAFARO. Yes, Senator.

Senator NUNN. In that regard, I would certainly suggest to both of you that if you do want to confer, and if the attorney feels a need to confer, he is welcome to do that, and we will give you time for that before we require an answer. Mr. Cafaro, the Subcommittee looks forward to your testimony this morning. I know you have previously provided the Subcommittee with a signed, sworn, rather detailed affidavit, which we will not hear in total this morning, but we will make it a part of the record. Is that correct, that you have given us an affidavit?

Mr. CAFARO. Yes, Senator.

Senator NUNN. I understand that you have a shorter prepared statement, and we will be delighted to have you present that statement at this time. Once you complete that statement we will have questions for you. Again, we appreciate your being here this morning, and after Senator Roth, our ranking member, gives his opening statement, we will turn it over to you. Senator Roth.

OPENING STATEMENT OF SENATOR ROTH

Senator ROTH. Thank you, Mr. Chairman. It is fitting that we conclude these hearings on traditional organized crime by focusing on the organized crime capital of this country, New York.

Not only is New York important because it is the home of the most powerful LCN families in this country, but it is also the headquarters for many of our Nation's most important industries.

By exerting undue influence on industry through its control of ancillary businesses and labor unions, organized crime can use its base in New York to wield immense economic power throughout the country.

As we will hear this morning from a former member of one of the New York LCN families, the primary means by which organized crime obtains control over legitimate business is through its control of labor unions, and that is the real power behind the LCN in New York. Organized crime's control of organized labor results in organized extortion. Kickbacks can become just one of the costs of doing business. Of course, most labor unions in New York and elsewhere are not involved with, or under the influence of, organized crime. But in these hearings we are necessarily concerned with those few that are.

Mr. Chairman, I would like to take this opportunity to commend you, and Chief Counsel Eleanore Hill, as well as your staff, for focusing the attention of this Subcommittee and the American people on the problem of organized crime. Under your direction PSI has continued to carry out its important mandate to investigate and eliminate organized crime. Perhaps in 25 years, hearings such as these will be unnecessary, and the only evidence of the LCN will be in crime novels and old movies.

Thank you, Mr. Chairman.

Senator NUNN. Thank you very much, Senator Roth.

Let me just add a word. We are going to hear a good bit about some industries, and some labor unions this morning, and as Senator Roth has just stated, when organized crime does control either organized labor unions, or segments of industry, it is indeed very serious.

I think we need to put it in a broader perspective, however, before we begin. We have had testimony over and over again before this Subcommittee, over the years, that in some cities, and perhaps New York is one of those in which control by organized crime of labor is disproportionate perhaps, but, overall, most labor unions, most labor leaders are honorable, law-abiding citizens.

We are going to hear some exceptions this morning in that context, and I hope we do put it in that context. I think the same thing can be said about business in this country. We are going to hear about corrupt businesses this morning, but that does not mean that all businesses in America or in New York City, or anywhere, are corrupt. So I think we have to put it in context, and where it happens we have to be very concerned about it, but it is important to keep our perspective.

Mr. Cafaro, we are delighted to have you this morning. We are pleased that you are cooperating and we welcome your testimony, so why don't you proceed.

Mr. CAFARO. Good morning, Mr. Chairman, and members of the subcommittee. My name is Vincent Cafaro, known to my friends as the "Fish". Thirty-six years ago, when I was 17 years old, a kid in New York City, I got "pinched' or busted for possession of 2 ounces of "junk," meaning narcotics.

Senator NUNN. Mr. Cafaro, if you want to pull that mike down a little bit, I think it might be easier. Just take your time now. We have got plenty of time. You have got all the time you need. Just take your time as you present your statement.

Mr. CAFARO. Yes, sir. My grandparents went to "Fat Tony" Salerno, at the time a soldier in the Genovese family or "brugad," for help. Fat Tony took me aside and gave me some advice: leave the junk alone; if you need money, go out and steal. Six or 7 years later, around 1958, Fat Tony came to me and asked me if I wanted to work for him in a numbers office. I said yes, and stayed with Fat Tony for the next 25 years. In the end, Fat Tony had become, in many ways, like a father to me. In 1986, the Federal Government charged Tony, myself, and 14 others, amico nostra, for, among other things, racketeering, extortion and conspiracy.

Tony and the others are now awaiting a jury verdict on those charges in New York City. Shortly after the indictment was returned, I began cooperating with the FBI and the U.S. attorney's office. I agreed to and did wear a wire for the FBI for 5 months in New York City. In October 1987, for a number of reasons, including concern for my family, I informed the prosecutor's office that I no longer wished to cooperate, and was placed in custody to await trial.

I am providing this statement independently of any agreement with the U.S. attorney's office. My case and all the charges against me remain pending. I have not been given any immunity by the Federal Government or by this subcommittee.

In 1974 I got "straightened out." In other words, I became a "made" member of the Genovese family or the "brugad," a true amico nostra. This is not something that you ask for. It is something that you are offered by the family, if they feel you are worthy.

Our family or our "brugad" has approximately 400 members, with a definite hierarchy: a boss, an underboss, and a consigliere, followed by 14 caporegimes. Each caporegime has a crew of at least eight.

The boss of the Genovese family is Vincent Gigante, also known as "Chin." Bobby Manna—Louis Manna—is the consigliere. Until his death in April 1987, Sammy Santera was the underboss of our brugad.

Beginning in the early 1980's, Fat Tony Salerno was generally recognized on the streets as the boss of the Genovese family. In fact for years Fat Tony reported back to Phillip Lombardo, also known as Ben or Benny Squint.

In the 1960's, when Vito Genovese went to jail, he had turned over control of our brugad to Lombardo. Lombardo wanted to stay in the background and keep the heat off himself. So over the years, Tommy Ryan, then Eli Zaccardi, then Funzi Tieri, and finally Fat Tony, fronted as the bosses of the family while Lombardo controlled things from the background.

In 1981, Fat Tony had a stroke and was "pulled down" by Lombardo, Vincent "Chin" Gigante, Manna, and Santora. Lombardo was also in poor health and retired.

Senator Nunn. Could I stop you right there, what do you mean by "pulled down"?

Mr. Cafaro. In other words, he was not the boss any more. He was taken down.

Senator Nunn. It does not mean he was killed, or anything like that, or hurt, or harmed?

Mr. Cafaro. No, no. He was just taken down. He was not a boss any longer.

Senator Nunn. Thank you.

Mr. Cafaro. Gigante became the boss behind the scenes with Santora as the underboss, and Manna as the consigliere. Gigante also allowed Fat Tony to continue to front as the boss, letting the other families believe, as recently as 1984, that Fat Tony still controlled our brugad.

Fat Tony continued to represent the family by sitting on the commission and in meeting representatives of the other families. In fact Fat Tony conferred with Chin on any major matters affecting the family. Chin attended one commission meeting but preferred that Fat Tony go to these meetings.

I remember the day I became a member of the Genovese family. Tony Salerno had told me and Patty Jerome to meet him and Buckaloo one morning. When we arrived, Buckaloo took me to the El Cortile Restaurant on Mulberry Street, where we met with Funzi Tieri, the brugad's underboss, and Fat Tony, who at that time was the consigliere.

I knew what I was there for when I saw a gun, a knife, a pin, alcohol and tissue laying out on the table. Funzi asked me if I wanted to become a member of the family. He said I could accept or not accept, and there would be no hard feelings. But he also said "once you accept you belong to us. We come first. Your family and home come second. We come first, no matter what." And I accepted.

Funzi then showed me the gun and the knife, and says "This is the gun and the knife, you live with the gun and die by the knife."

He told me that Fat Tony had sponsored me, and gave me a piece of paper to let burn in my hand while I took the oath. "If I betray the Cosa Nostra, I shall burn like this paper". He then pricked my trigger finger with the pin and told me, "Now you are amico nostra, you have been born over again. Now you are a man; you belong to us." From that point on, I was amico nostra, a soldier in the Genovese family, the most powerful mob family or "brugad" in New York City, and, for that matter, in the United States.

There were certain rules that all amico nostra lived by: no fooling around with another amico nostra's wife; no "junk"; no dealing with pornography or Government bonds; and never talking about "this thing' to anyone but another amico nostra.

Senator Roth. Would you explain what you mean by "no junk."

Mr. Cafaro. It is narcotics.

Senator Roth. Narcotics. Thank you.

Mr. Cafaro. We were a very disciplined organization. A soldier had to check in at least once a week with his caporegime. A soldier could not make a "score," meaning any illegal business, without the approval of his capo. If he wanted to, a caporegime could demand 10 percent of the profits made by his soldiers on a score. A soldier could not even carry a gun without first getting approval from his capo. Most important, we knew never to ask questions about another amico nostra's business unless it was also our business.

La Cosa Nostra enforces its rules through murder. So we even have rules about who could or could not be murdered, or, as we say on the streets— clipped, whacked or hurt. First of all, killings were mandatory for certain offenses. Messing around with another amico nostra's wife or family; dealing in "junk"; "ratting"; refusing to go on a hit if asked; knowingly killing a cop or other law-enforcement agent. Also, if someone you sponsored "ratted", you would be killed as being responsible for his actions.

No killing or "hit" could take place without the approval of the hierarchy of your family. The first step in getting that approval was to take your "beef to your capo, who in turn gets approval for the hit from the consigliere and the underboss. Ultimately, no hit could go down without the approval of the boss. If the boss okays the hit, the capo assigns it to you to be carried out. You decide who, if anyone, from your own regime, will help you do the job.

If the hit is against a member of another family, your boss will take the beef to the boss of that family. If he agrees, members of that family will carry out the hit. If he disagrees, and the hit takes place anyway, a "war" may result.

As for me, I was never asked to carry out a hit. I never had to kill anyone. This was because Fat Tony always looked out for me.

It was like a father and son relationship. However, I knew that if I was ever asked, I would have to kill or be killed.

What I did for our family was to run the numbers business in West Harlem from about 110th Street to 153rd Street. I had about 72 controllers working under me. We had plenty of willing customers. We paid 6 to 1. The New York lottery only paid 5 to 1. At my peak I was grossing about $80,000 per day with a net of about $65,000 before payouts. I had some bad years, but in a good year I could make as much as $2 million or more. Whatever money I took, I split 50-50 with Fat Tony. Later I expanded my business from numbers into sports betting.

My family made a lot of money from gambling and the numbers rackets. We got our money from gambling but our real power, our real strength came from the unions. With the unions behind us, we could shut down the city, or the country for that matter, if we needed to, to get our way.

Our brugad controlled a number of different unions, some of which I personally dealt with, some of which I knew about from other amico nostras. In some cases we got money from our dealings with the unions, in some cases we got favors such as jobs for friends and relatives, but more importantly, in all cases we got power over every businessman in New York.

With the unions behind us, we could make or break the construction industry, the garment business, the docks, to name but a few.

For example, Bobby Rao—Robert Rao—was a union official with a local of Hotel Workers and Bartenders Union, Hotel, Restaurant Employees, AFL-CIO Production, Service and Sales District Council.

Bobby and his union belonged to our brugad. Every month, Bobby would bring over anywhere from a $1,000 to $2,000 for me to give to Fat Tony, which I would split with Fat Tony. At Christmas, Bobby would bring over $25,000 for me to give to Fat Tony. Fat Tony would tell me how to split the money up—half, or $12,500 to Ben Lombardo who, at the time, was the boss of our family behind Tony; another $6,500 to Tony Provenzano, or

Tony "Pro," a family member who controlled Teamsters Local 560; and the remainder to be split between Fat Tony and myself.

I knew that the money that Bobby Rao delivered was money that was skimmed from union funds, including union dental and medical plans. I knew this because Bobby himself told me so.

Although our brugad probably had the greatest amount of union influence in New York City, the other families also had control of unions in certain areas and industries. As a result, some of the most important industries in New York City, such as the waterfront and shipping industries, construction and concrete industries, the garment center, and the convention center operations, were all subject to mob influence and control.

Another major source of our power and income for our brugad was the mob's control of the concrete industry through what we called the "2 percent club." Fat Tony and Paul Castellano were partners with Nicky Auletta in S&A Concrete. Salerno and Castellano had put up no money, but had provided Auletta with their control and influence of the construction unions. Through S&A Concrete, the Genovese and Gambino families also took over the high-rise construction business of DIG Concrete and Construction.

Castellano also controlled "Biff" Halloran, the owner of Transit Mix and Certified Concrete. Castellano could control Halloran and others like him because Castellano controlled Local 282 of the Teamsters Union. All of the concrete drivers belonged to that Local 282.

For a while, only Halloran was allowed to deliver concrete to construction sites in Manhattan. Fat Tony and Castellano used their influence to insure that contractors bought all of their concrete from Halloran. In return, for every sale arranged by Fat Tony and Castellano, they got back from Halloran $1 per yard of concrete poured.

During the same time, "Junior" Persico, the boss of the Colombo brugad and "Tony Ducks" Corallo, the boss of the Lucchese brugad, raised a "beef about Halloran being the only one allowed to deliver concrete in Manhattan. Both of them had connections with concrete plants and wanted to get a piece of Manhattan. Persico gets $3 to $4 a yard from Ferrara Brothers, Ozone Park, Queens, New York, for concrete sales obtained for them by Junior. Fat Tony and Castellano told them that Halloran was with them, and given the strength of their families, were able to keep Persico and Corallo out of Manhattan.

This worked well until a "beef arose between Castellano and Halloran regarding payment for some damaged trucks. As a result of that dispute, Halloran stopped payments to Fat Tony and Castellano, and other concrete companies were allowed into Manhattan.

To control the award of contracts, Vinnie DiNapoli came up with a plan for the "2 percent Club" consisting of high-rise concrete construction contractors. The Genovese, Gambino, Lucchese and Colombo brugads ran the club. Each family had a "made" guy who knew the construction business as its representative on the club. These individuals ran the club, but any "beefs" were settled by the bosses of the families.

The club members split up all of the jobs over $2 million. S&A Concrete got all the jobs over $5 million. After a while, the smaller contractors who were not members of the club started beefing because there were not enough jobs under $2 million to go around, and eventually, the $2 million rule was raised to $3 million. Anything over $5 million still went to S&A concrete. A club contractor that was given a job had to pay the club 2 per-cent of the contract price. This 2 percent was split among the four brugads.

Senator NUNN. Mr. Cafaro, if I could interrupt you right there, and when you say they control these contracts, and anything over $5 million went to a certain company, anything under $2 million, for a period of time, went to people who were not members of the club, is that right?

Mr. CAFARO. Yes.

Senator NUNN. And then you raised that to $3 million?

Mr. CAFARO. Three million.

Senator NUNN. Now how did they control this? Presumably whoever is awarding the contract wants a low price. Were they doing it through rigged bids?

Mr. CAFARO. Through bid rigging. They would put in a bid of—we say $1.5 million. You would put in your bid for $1.5 million, and me knowing I could get the job, we knew the bids, and I would tell you put in a bid for $1.3 million, and that is how the contractors went along with that.

Senator NUNN. In other words, before the bids were put in, there was an agreement among the members of the club—Mr. CAFARO. You put in a bid for $1.5 million, I put in a bid for $1.3 million, and that is how I got the job.

Senator NUNN. So you knew who was going to be the low bidder before the bids went in?

Mr. CAFARO. Yes, sir.

Senator NUNN. How did you restrict outsiders from bidding?

Mr. CAFARO. Well, there were so many jobs allocated from the Dodge report. They would get the Dodge report and see how many jobs were coming up in a certain amount of time, and they would start to work on the bids from then.

Senator NUNN. Well, you had to make sure nobody that was not a member of the club bid, right?

Mr. CAFARO. Well, you made sure that was not done because of the contractors you had. Most of these contractors got all the work anyway, but you made sure you got so many jobs, I got so many jobs, he got so many jobs, and it was done with the bid.

Senator NUNN. But you are basically saying there was not any competition?

Mr. Cafaro. No, none whatsoever.

Senator Nunn. No real competition?

Mr. Cafaro. No.

Senator Roth. Could I ask one question there, Mr. Chairman?

Does that mean all construction on Manhattan was controlled by these measures?

Mr. Cafaro. I would not say all of it but 75 percent of it.

Senator Roth. Could you estimate what percentage?

Mr. Cafaro. I said 75 percent.

Senator Roth. 75 percent?

Mr. Cafaro. Yes.

Senator Roth. Thank you, Mr. Chairman.

Senator Nunn. Thank you. Go ahead.

Mr. Cafaro. I have reviewed charts of the five New York families which have been shown to me by the Subcommittee staff. I have identified for the Subcommittee staff many of those individuals who I know, either personally or through other amico nostras, including the five current bosses of the New York families: Vincent "Chin" Gigante of the Genovese family; John Gotti of the Gambino family; Victor Amuso of the Lucchese family; Philip Rastelli of the Bonanno family; and Carmine Persico of the Colombo family.

Senator Nunn. How many of those have you met personally?

How many of those individuals? Let's take them one by one, and tell us whether you know them personally, or through others.

Mr. Cafaro. I met—well, Vincente "Chin" Gigante is a boss 1 met.

Senator Nunn. You know him personally?

Mr. Cafaro. Personally. John Gotti, I met him at MCC. Never knew him until I met him at MCC.

Senator Nunn. MCC being?

Mr. Eames. That is the Metropolitan Corrections Center.

Senator Nunn. Right. So you met him personally, too?

Mr. Cafaro. Yes. Victor Amuso, "Little Vic," I met him personally. Philip Rastelli, I don't know him, never met him.

Senator Nunn. You know him by reputation but not personally?

Mr. Cafaro. Not personally. And Carmine Junior, I met him personally.

Senator Nunn. Persico?

Mr. Cafaro. Yes.

Senator Nunn. Thank you.

Mr. Cafaro. As for our own brugad, "Chin" Gigante is clearly recognized on the streets as the boss. To the outside world Gigante is known for his sometimes bizarre and crazy behavior.

In truth, he is a shrewd and experienced family member, who has risen through the ranks from soldier to capo to boss.

Senator Nunn. Could you give us an example of his so-call crazy behavior?

Mr. Cafaro. Well, he walks around with the robe and his pajamas/

Senator Nunn. You mean outside?

Mr. CAFARO. Outside, yes, by the club where he stays. He is always in his robe and his pajamas, and says crazy things. He does crazy things.

Senator NUNN. But it is all a guise, you are saying?

Mr. CAFARO. From what I hear, yes.

Senator NUNN. You are saying he is not crazy?

Mr. CAFARO. I do not think so.

Senator NUNN. Go ahead. Thank you.

Mr. CAFARO. As boss, Gigante ultimately controls any of the family's deals or scores. He directly controls all numbers operations in the area from Sullivan Street up to 14th Street. He runs the St. Anthony Feast, a street festival held annually in Lower Manhattan. When "Tommy Ryan" was killed, Gigante took the book on his shylock business. Since that time that money has gone to Gigante's crew.

I also know that Gigante and John Gotti, as heir to Paul Castellano, and current boss of the Gambino family, both pushed Nick

Auletta for a cut of the profits from the sale of the Bankers and Brokers Building, as a result of promises supposedly made to Fat Tony and Paul Castellano when Auletta first bought the building.

Gotti was seeking the money from Auletta because as the new Gambino boss, he would be entitled to all the business and money that used to go to Castellano.

For example, I remember Gotti asking me if I knew how much money Castellano had been getting kicked back every month from Scoissa Concrete Company. I did not know but I told Gotti he should contact Funzi Mosca, who, as the Gambino representative in the "Concrete Club," would be able to give him the answer. Thank you. That concludes my statement. I will be glad to answer any questions you may have.

Senator NUNN. Thank you very much, Mr. Cafaro. Senator Roth and I have a number of questions. And again, take your time. We are not in any hurry this morning. The first question I have, you have used several terms that may not be clear during your testimony. What do you mean by the term, for instance, of amico nostra?

Mr. CAFARO. Amico nostra is a wiseguy, a made member.

Senator NUNN. I have not heard that term before. What is the difference in that and just being a member of the LCN or a made man? Is that the same thing?

Mr. CAFARO. Well, amico nostra, that is the term I use. Amico nostra. But you could say, friend of ours.

Senator NUNN. Friend of ours?

Mr. CAFARO. When you are making an introduction of a amico nostra to meet another amico nostra.

Senator NUNN. Is that your term uniquely, or do others use that term, too?

Mr. CAFARO. A lot of people do not use those terms. They use "friend of ours."

Senator NUNN. Why do you use amico nostra?

Mr. CAFARO. I am not going to go through that story now. Well, at one time I was drinking at a restaurant in a bar. And two friends of mine walked in, and we were having a few drinks or whatever, talking about everyday things. And I told this amico nostra who was a friend, meet a friend of ours. I do not know if I said friend of ours or friend of mine.

Senator Nunn. You were talking to someone who was a member of the family about someone—Mr. Cafaro. Who wasn't a member of the family.

Senator Nunn. About somebody who was not?

Mr. Cafaro. To this amico nostra, who was a member, I must have said, meet a friend of ours, whatever his name, Jerry or whatever. So he took it upon himself to think that he was amico nostra.

So the next day or a couple of days later, or a week later, they were introducing him as amico nostra, which he was not.

So he come up to see me about a week later, he says, Vince, you told me that so-and-so is a friend. I says, no, I never said he was a friend. But you introduced me. If I introduced you as a friend of ours or a friend, I says, I do not know; what is the problem?

He says, well, everybody is going—I introduced him, and everybody thinks he is a friend of ours. And I say no, he was never straightened out. I did not interpret it that way. And he said, well, he said, I already did it. So I says to him, I says—he says, you got a problem? I says, no, I says I will see Tony, and I will discuss it with Tony. But meanwhile, the kid who was supposed to be straightened out, says, gee, I got straightened out and I didn't even know about it. And that was it.

That is why—some old timer grabbed me, told me, say amico nostra, that's a word that was from Portuguese, the wiseguys over there used to use the word amico nostra, so that the agents or the cops couldn't infiltrate. They would ask you what's the word, and you had to say, amico nostra. And that's where it come from.

So I used to say amico nostra after that.

Senator Nunn. So you quit introducing people as a friend of ours, and started using that term?

Mr. Cafaro. I started using amico nostra.

Senator Nunn. What does the term, brugad, mean?

Mr. Cafaro. That's the family. That's your family.

Senator Nunn. That is the family?

Mr. Cafaro. That all consisted of amico nostras, is the family.

Senator Nunn. Where did that term come from? Is that used commonly by a lot of people? Or is that just your term?

Mr. Cafaro. That is the way I use it. Same fellow I was telling you about, amico nostra, he is dead now.

Senator Nunn. You also refer in your affidavit to beefs and sit-downs. Tell us what a beef is and what a sitdown is?

Mr. Cafaro. A beef is when you can have it within your family or another family with amico nostra; that's a sitdown. You have a dispute about something. It could be about a union; it could be about numbers; it could be anything. That's what a beef means to us.

Senator Nunn. In other words, a beef is a problem, and a sit-down is a negotiation?

Mr. Cafaro. Well, the—it is the same thing. A sitdown, who says a sitdown, who says a beef, it is the same thing.

Senator NUNN. A beef and a sitdown are the same thing?

Mr. CAFARO. Same thing.

Senator NUNN. So a beef is an effort to solve a problem?

Mr. CAFARO. Both are. A beef or a sitdown is the same thing, to solve a problem.

Senator NUNN. Have you taken part in sitdowns?

Mr. CAFARO. Yes.

Senator NUNN. Do sitdowns normally occur between people on the same level? In other words, soldiers, or capos, or bosses? Is there a mixed group?

Mr. CAFARO. Well, usually, if there is a beef soldier to soldier, it is you and the soldier, amico nostras. Or if there is, say, somebody around me that is not amico nostra, he gets into a problem with another fellow around another amico nostra, you let them try and straighten it out.

If they cannot, then we sit down for them. But you go according to rank. If you cannot straighten out the beef, I tell him or he tells me, we are going further. Which means going to your captain.

Senator NUNN. You have explained something about the way you go about requesting permission to murder someone within the family. Were you ever present when this type of approval for a murder was requested?

Mr. CAFARO. Requested by the boss?

Senator NUNN. Requested by anyone. In other words, were you ever present when a member of the family asked the hierarchy for permission to murder someone?

Mr. CAFARO. You have got to go through your captain, if you are a soldier. You go through your captain. And you give him the reason why. I was there one time when this Philly—what is his name?—this Philly Buono had come down, he is amico nostra with us in our regime, and he was looking for an okay with this Nat Masselli.

Senator NUNN. Who was Nat Masselli? Was he a member of the family?

Mr. CAFARO. No. Not that I know of. I do not know him. I just know the name.

Senator NUNN. He was outside the family then?

Mr. CAFARO. Yes, yes. He come down with a piece of paper, about as big as this. And I was standing on the corner on 116th Street with Sammy Santora.

Senator NUNN. In New York City?

Mr. CAFARO. In New York City, yes. And he come down, he pulled this paper out of his pocket, and he showed it to Sammy.

Senator NUNN. Sammy was who?

Mr. CAFARO. He was the underboss in our brugad at the time.

Senator NUNN. Santora?

Mr. CAFARO. Yes. And he showed him the paper. Sammy read it, he said, well, could this hurt you? He says, yeah, I did a few things with this kid. And the kid was supposed to be a rat. So Sammy says, all right, I'll get back to you tomorrow. So I says to Sammy, what are you going to do? He said, I am going to go down and see the skinny guy and the "Chin".

Senator NUNN. Who was the skinny guy?

Mr. CAFARO. That is what I interpret as Bobby Manna.

Senator NUNN. Who was Bobby Manna?

Mr. CAFARO. Bobby Manna is the consigliere in our brugad.

Senator NUNN. Of the family?

Mr. CAFARO. Yes.

Senator NUNN. And who was the "Chin"?

Mr. CAFARO. The boss of the family.

Senator NUNN. And tell us the name of the boss.

Mr. CAFARO. Oh, "Chin" Gigante, Vincent Gigante.

Senator NUNN. So the "Chin" was Gigante?

Mr. CAFARO. Yes.

Senator NUNN. Go ahead.

Mr. CAFARO. And he went down and supposedly seen him that day or that night. And I had seen Sammy the next day or a day later, whatever it was, and

I asked him, I said, how did you do? He says, yeah, I got the okay for Philly. He says, in fact I got to go see Philly and tell him it is okay to do what he wants. And that was the situation.

Senator NUNN. What happened?

Mr. CAFARO. I do not know if it was a week later or two weeks later, whatever, the kid was found killed in his car in the Bronx.

Senator NUNN. The kid being Nat Masselli?

Mr. CAFARO. Nat Masselli, right.

Senator NUNN. The one the request was made on?

Mr. CAFARO. Yes. Yes, Senator.

Senator NUNN. Was anyone ever tried for that murder or hit?

Mr. CAFARO. Yes, they were convicted, this Philly Buono and Sal Odierno.

Senator NUNN. Was anyone else involved in the actual murder?

Mr. CAFARO. Well, not that I know of, Senator.

Senator NUNN. So they were actually arrested, tried and convicted?

Mr. CAFARO. Yes, Senator.

Senator NUNN. Do you know how that murder was carried out?

Mr. CAFARO. No.

Senator NUNN. Was it by gun, or do you know?

Mr. CAFARO. Well, according to what the newspapers say, he was killed in a car.

Senator NUNN. Were you present during conversations regarding the disappearance of Teddy Maritas?

Mr. CAFARO. Well, there was one conversation. I was standing on the corner on 115th Street and First Avenue.

Senator NUNN. That is again in New York City?

Mr. CAFARO. Yes. I was talking to some people. And Vinny DiNapoli asked me—he wanted to ask me something.

Senator NUNN. Who is that?

Mr. CAFARO. Vinny DiNapoli. He is amico nostra with us, with our regime. He says, I am a little worried about this Teddy Maritas.

I say, what do you mean, what? He said, I am a little scared about him. He was standing trial then on some concrete case, something, I do not know what about. I says, so what are you telling me for? Go discuss it with Sammy, Sammy Santora. And that was the extent of it.

Senator NUNN. Do you know whether he did discuss it with Sammy later?

Mr. CAFARO. I do not know, Senator. I never spoke about it anymore.

Senator NUNN. What happened to Maritas?

Mr. CAFARO. Well, according to the newspapers, he was missing.

Senator NUNN. How much later after that conversation?

Mr. CAFARO. I could not tell you offhand.

Senator NUNN. Several months, or within a year?

Mr. CAFARO. Could have been several months, several weeks.

Senator NUNN. Do you know, or do you have any way of knowing, or do you have any belief, about who was responsible for his disappearance?

Mr. CAFARO. I do not know. For him to ask something like that, I would say

Senator NUNN. You would just be guessing, would you not? You do not really know?

Mr. CAFARO. I do not know.

Senator NUNN. Well, let us leave that one off. Was anyone ever convicted in connection with Maritas' disappearance?

Mr. CAFARO. No, Senator.

Senator NUNN. Do you have any knowledge regarding the murder of Tony Bananas? I believe the formal name is Antonio Caponigro.

Mr. CAFARO. Well, when the old man Bruno got killed in Philadelphia.

Senator NUNN. That is Angelo Bruno?

Mr. CAFARO. Yes. And he had got killed, he was the boss of the Philadelphia mob. And there was supposed to have been a power struggle there between this fellow, Chicken, he was the underboss there, and this Tony Bananas.

Senator NUNN. Chicken was Phillip Testa, wasn't it?

Mr. CAFARO. Philly Testa, right. He had come up to New York at one time to see Tony. And who was there was Tony "Ducks", Tom "Mix"

Senator NUNN. Is Tony "Ducks" Corallo?

Mr. CAFARO. He is the boss of the Luchese family, Tony "Ducks"

Corallo. Tom "Mix" Santora was the underboss.

Senator NUNN. Who was Tom "Mix"?

Mr. CAFARO. He was the underboss of the Luchese family.

Senator NUNN. That is his nickname. What is his

Mr. CAFARO. Santoro. And Paul Castellano was there and Fat Tony. And this Chicken went and seen them. So when I seen Tony later on, after they had their meeting in the club, he said that there was a power struggle between Philly Testa and Tony Bananas Caponigro, and that there was a power struggle. And then after that, a couple of hours after that, this Tony Bananas come to discuss it with Tony, and there was present Tony Ducks Corallo of the Luchese mob; Tom Mix Santora, the underboss of the Luchese mob; and Paul Castellano, and Fat Tony.

And whatever they discussed, I do not know. But about a week later this Philly Testa come back. So Tony introduced me to him as the underboss of the Philadelphia mob.

So he says to Tony that he thinks Tony Bananas was guilty of the murder of Angelo Bruno. And that was the extent to that.

Then about a week after that, Tony Bananas come up or 2 weeks after, he wanted to discuss something with Tony, and we were walking. And Tony said, I do not want to get involved. I do not want to hear about it. Go see Chin.

Senator NUNN. Who was he telling that to?

Mr. CAFARO. Tony Bananas. And that was the extent of that part of the conversation. Then about a couple of weeks later, I do not remember the weeks, Tony Bananas had to go to 47th or 48th Street in the diamond center to meet Baldy Dom Cantarino, he is a caporegime in our brugad. And he had to meet Baldy Dom, whatever his name is.

I cannot say the last name, and he had to meet him there between, I do not know, 47th or 48th Street in the diamond exchange.

And then that day or a couple of days later, they were found in the Bronx dead; Tony Bananas.

Senator NUNN. I did not hear that last part?

Mr. CAFARO. I says, Tony Bananas, a couple of days later or next day or two, 3 days later, was found in the Bronx dead.

Senator NUNN. You believe there was a direct connection between those conversations and his murder, then?

Mr. CAFARO. Yes.

Senator NUNN. Do you have any way of knowing who carried out the hit?

Mr. CAFARO. No.

Senator NUNN. So you do not know who carried it out?

Mr. CAFARO. No.

Senator NUNN. I am puzzled by the connection between the Philadelphia family and the New York family. Why was the New York family, your family, concerned about the murder of Bruno in Philadelphia?

Mr. CAFARO. It was not only our family. It was Paul Castellano there, Tony Ducks Corallo was there, and Tom Mix.

Senator NUNN. So there were three families?

Mr. CAFARO. Three families there.

Senator NUNN. Three New York families concerning the murder

Mr. CAFARO. The killing of Angelo Bruno, being that he was a boss of another brugad. And usually it is not done that way, to kill a boss, without discussing it. So there is where the power play must have come in.

Senator NUNN. In other words, Bruno had been killed in Philadelphia

Mr. CAFARO. Yes.

Senator NUNN [continuing]. And he had been killed obviously without a discussion among the other top mob leaders

Mr. CAFARO. Yes, Senator.

Senator NUNN [continuing]. In the country, or at least in New York?

Mr. CAFARO. At least in New York or whatever. It was never discussed.

Senator NUNN. So they felt it was not within the overall protocol or the rules of the mob?

Mr. CAFARO. It wasn't in the rules; no, it wasn't in the rules.

Senator NUNN. To kill the boss without discussing it with other bosses?

Mr. CAFARO. Without discussing any reasoning or whatever.

Senator NUNN. Did they feel that they themselves might be in jeopardy if that protocol broke down, if they didn't enforce it?

Mr. CAFARO. I would say yes. I would say yes.

Senator NUNN. So it was something that offended them pretty seriously?

Mr. CAFARO. Yes, Senator, I would say.

Senator NUNN. Did Tony talk to you about this? Did he go into any detail?

Mr. CAFARO. Well, no, after this killing with Tony Bananas, the following week, he says, I am glad I sent him down to Chin; I did not get involved with this.

Senator NUNN. Why was he glad he did not get involved?

Mr. CAFARO. Well, my interpretation I guess is that because of the killing.

Senator NUNN. So he would prefer not to have been involved.

Mr. CAFARO. That is a family problem within—let them straighten out their own problems.

Senator NUNN. In other words, he would rather for Chin to be the one to make that decision rather than him?

Mr. CAFARO. Either that, or he just did not want to get involved with a family problem from another brugad.

Senator NUNN. Did Fat Tony tell you about the killing? Is that the way you found out about it?

Mr. CAFARO. No, I read it in the papers. It was in the newspapers.

Senator NUNN. And did Fat Tony ever tell you who he thought did the—actually carried out the killing?

Mr. CAFARO. Well, he had said to me, that is how I know about the appointment on 47th or 48th street in the diamond exchange, that it was an appointment made with Baldy Dom down there.

Senator NUNN. Appointment made with?

Mr. CAFARO. With Tony Bananas and Baldy Dom.

Senator NUNN. Baldy Dom?

Mr. CAFARO. Yes, he s a caporegime in our brugad.

Senator NUNN. Did Fat Tony tell you that Baldy Dom's crew actually carried out the killing? Mr. CAFARO. No, he did not tell me they carried out the killing.

My opinion, I would say yes.

Senator NUNN. Your opinion?

Mr. CAFARO. Yes. I misunderstood the question.

Senator NUNN. I believe in your affidavit, let me read that and see if this is correct, you say, reading, that in April 1980—this is page four, for counsel, page four of the affidavit. I am sorry, page 12 and 13 of the affidavit. Let me read this to you and see where it is in error, if in error, or whether it is accurate if it is accurate.

You say, "In April 1980, Tony Bananas' visited Tony Salerno, at the Palma Boys Social Club. After this visit, Tony told me that he had advised "Tony Bananas' to go see "The Chin,' because he did not want to get involved in Philadelphia's problems.

Appendix C

Genovese Membership List in New Jersey Circa 1964

NY 92-2300

Name	Alias	FBI #
LARDIERE, JOHN	Johnny Coke	679989
PECORA, JOSEPH	Joe Peck	1038202
PECORA, THOMAS	Timmy Murphy	110271
PROVENZANO, ANTHONY (Caporegima)	Tony Pro	
BRIGUGLIO, SALVATORE		

BONANNO FAMILY

CARMINE GALANTE (New York)
(Caporegima or Underboss)

Name	Alias	FBI #
ZICARELLI, JOSEPH	Joe Bayonne	1107492

ANTHONY RIELA, FBI #796624C, is considered to be a member of "Causa Nostra" by virtue of his attendance at Apalachin, New York. It has been reported that he has been in business dealings with JOSEPH BONANNO and, therefore, may belong in this "family".

BRUNO FAMILY

NY T-8 has advised that the following persons in the Newark area are under the jurisdiction of ANGELO BRUNO, of Philadelphia.

Name	Alias	FBI #
BATTAGLIA, CARMINE (possibly caporegima)		

-112-

Appendix D

Genovese Family Membership List Circa 1963

NY 92-2300

GENOVESE FAMILY

Set forth below are individuals specifically named by sources as members of the VITO GENOVESE "family" or "vrugad" within the framework of "Causa Nostra".

Name	Alias	FBI Identification #
AGONE, JOSEPH	Joe Curly	233868
ALBANESE, ANTHONY	Tony Katz	
ALBANESE, PHILIP	Phil Katz	
ALBERO, CHARLES	Charley Bullets	59088
ALO, VINCENT	Jimmy Blue Eyes	554810
ALLARDI, ALFONSO		
ALONGI, DOMINICK		4545661
ALTO, JIMMY		
AMAROSA, FRED		
ANGELINO, JIMMY	Jimmy Angelina	68293
ARDITO, JOHN	Buster	1763382
BARBELLA, LOUIS		
BARESE, MIKE (nickname)		
BARRA, MICHAEL	Mickey Morris	
BARRA, GIGIO	Joe	

-72-

NY 92-2300

Name	Alias	FBI Identification #
BATAGLIA, JIMMY	Jimmy Battles	
BELANGI, ROBERT	Bobby Blanche	
BENSOLA, JOSEPH	Joe Pensola	
BIELE, JOHN	Johnny Foto	533787
DOVE, CARMINE		
BRESCIA, LORENZO	Chappie	
BRUNO, JOE (dead)		
CAPABIANCO, EDWARD	Eddie Scar (dead)	
CAPPOCIRO, CHARLEY (dead)		
CARFANO, ANTHONY	Augie Pisano (dead September 25, 1959)	
CARILLO, ANTONIO	Tony the Shiek	333810
CARUSO, OTTILIO FRANK	Frank the Bug	187656
CASERTANO, STEPHEN	Buck Jones (dead)	
CATENA, GERARDO	Jerry	875707
CAVELLA, PAUL		
CELANO, FRANK		
CELANTANO, JULIUS		537427

-73-

NY 92-2300

Name	Alias	FBI Identification
CELEMBRINO, SALVATORE	Little Sally	
CENTORE, LAWRENCE	Larry Black	
CIAFFONE, DOMINICK	Swat Mulligan	
CLEMENTE, MICHELINO	Mike	2675935
COLUMBO, JAKE		1291067
CONSALVO, EDWARD		
CONTALDO, THOMAS	Crazy Tommy	477828
COPPOLA, MICHAEL	Trigger Mike	677976
COPPOLINO, CHARLES	Charley Bananas	
CORELLA, NINO		
COSTELLO, FRANK		936217
CRISCUOLO, AL	Good Looking Al	1529336
CURALLUZZO, ORLANDO	Earl	
CUCOLA, FRANCESCO	Frankie Casino	
DE BELLIS, JOHN	Johnny Dee (dead)	
DE CARLO, ANGELO	Gyp, Ray	
DE CURTIS, EDWARD		
DE CURTIS, GUIDO		
DE FEO, PETER		

-74-

NY 92-2300

Name	Alias	FBI Identification #
DE MARCO, JOSEPH	(deceased)	
DE MARTINO, ANTHONY	Tony the Bum	
DE MARTINO, BENJAMIN	Benny the Bum	1068509
DE MARTINO, THEODORE	Teddy the Bum	1304126
DE MICCIO, TOBIA		
DE NEGRIS, JOE	Joe Ross	
DE QUARTO, DOMINICK	Dom the Sailor	110556B
DEL DUCCA, GENEROSA	Toddo Del (deceased)	
DI BRIZZI, ALEX		787997
DI PIETRO, COSMO	Carlie	315537A
DI SEVERIO, (FNU)	Big Jinx	
DOTO, JOSEPH	Joe Adonis	
EBOLI, PASQUALE	Patsy Ryan	
EBOLI, THOMAS	Tommy Ryan	3061565
EPPOLITO, FREDDY		1824986
EPPOLITO, JIMMY		1218183
EPPOLITO, RALPH	Ralph the Gangster	1432900
ERCOLE, ANIELLO	Mr. T. (deceased)	

-75-

NY 92-2300

Name	Alias	FBI Identification #
ERRA, PASQUALE	Patsy	1593543
FAICCO, ALFRED	Al Butch	227444
FERRARA, RALPH	Whitey	
FERRO, ANTHONY	Buccalo	
FILIPONE, GEORGE		
FLORIO, ANTHONY	Tony Andrews	
FORTUNATO, MATTHEW	Matty Brown	593126
FRASCA, COSMO	Gus	285760
GAGLIANO, JOSEPH	Pip the Blind (dead)	198730
GAGLIODOTTO, CHARLES	Schalutz	590366
GALLUCCIO, FRANK		
GENESE, PASQUALE	Patsy Jerome	
GENOVESE, MICHAEL	Gumba Mike	
GENOVESE, VITO		861267
GERADO, JOSEPH		
GIGANTE, MARIO		
GIGANTE, PASQUALE		323231
GIGANTE, VINCENT	The Chin	5020214

-76-

NY 92-2300

Name	Alias	FBI Identification #
GRECO, THOMAS	Tommy Palmer	
HONEY (nickname)		
IANDOSCO, ANGELO	Jerry the Lug (deceased June 23, 1950)	1261892
LAIETTA, GERARD	Jerry Ryan	571701 (?)
LANZA, HARRY		
LANZA, JOSEPH	Socks	785896
LANZA, JOSEPH		
LANZERI, EDWARD		
LAPI, JOSEPH	Joe Beck	
LEONE, IGGY		
LEONE, PETER	Petey Muggins (dead)	91154
LIVORSI, FRANK	Cheech	792029
LOMBARDI, THOMAS		
LOMBARDO, PHILIP	Ben Turpin, Squint	
LUCANIA, SALVATORE	Charley Lucky, Luciano (deceased)	
LUISI, SALVATORE	Salty	
MAIONE, MICHAEL	Mike Rosie	182756

-77-

NY 92-2300

Name	Alias	FBI Identification #
MANFREDONIA, JOHN	Peanuts	1186770
MARCIONE, PAUL		
MARTINO, TONY	Tony Mimi	
MARTINO, VINCENT	Gene Harlow	
MAURO, VINCENZO	Vinny	760950
MILO, LOUIS	Babe (deceased)	
MILO, SABATO	Bo	
MILO, THOMAS, Sr. (deceased)		108508
MIRANDA, BARNEY		
MIRANDA, MICHELE A.	Mike	91524
MOCCIO, PASQUALE	Patty Mush (deceased)	706840
MOGAVERO, JOSEPH		
MOGAVERO, ROSARIO	Saro	895630
MONACO, FELIX		
MORETTI, WILLIE	Willie Moore (dead)	
MOSIELLO, GERARD	Jerry Moore	3181357
MUSCARELLA, RAYMOND		
MUSTO, THOMAS	Tommy the Priest	

-78-

NY 92-2300

Name	Alias	FBI Identification #
NARDO, DANNY		
NASTI, ANTHONY		
NOBILE, GEORGE	Georgie Hooks	1379511
OFRIA, SEBASTIAN	Buster	702174
PACELLA, LOUIS	Louis Dome	
PAGANO, JOSEPH		4674860
PAGANO, PASQUALE	Big Pat	74687B
PALUMBO, ARTHUR		
PATERRA, JOSEPH	Joe Swede	541984
PELLIGRINO, CARMINE		
PELLIGRINO, PETER		
PELLIGRINO, ROCCO		
PERILLO, ARMANDO	Petey Herman	
PERO, ANGELO		
PEROTTA, ROCCO		
PERRONE, CIRO	Squizel	
PERRONE, JOSEPH	Ju-Ju	
PERRONE, MICHAEL		

-79-

364

NY 92-2300

Name	Alias	FBI Identification #
PERSICO, CARMINE, Jr.	Sonny	113241B
PETILLO, DAVE	Little Davie	
PICARELLI, JAMES	Jimmy Rush	619767
PONDOLFO, SANDINO (dead)		
PRADO, LOUIS		
PRISCO, RUDY	Scarface Rudy	
RANDAZZO, JOSEPH		606995
RAO, JOSEPH (deceased)		33911
RATTENNI, NICHOLAS	Nick Perry	110000
RICCI, ANTHONY	Tony Goebels	
RIZZO, GEORGE	Georgie Lefty	
ROCCOMONTE, ARTHUR		4315158
ROSOTO, ALEXANDER	Al Ross	
RUGGIANO, ANTHONY		
RUSSO, FRANK		
RUSSO, JOHN		
RUSSO, LOUIS	Russolo	
RUSSO, RALPH		
SALERNO, ANGELO	Charley Four Cents	

-80-

NY 92-2300

Name	Alias	FBI Identification #
SALERNO, ANTHONY	Fat Tony	4817958
SALERNO, ANTHONY	Blackie	
SALERNO, FERDINANDO	Cockeyed Freddy	
SALERNO, THOMAS	Bobby Lyons	
SALVO, GIOVANNI BATTISTE	Bart	297699
SANTUCCIO, GIROLOMO	Bobby Doyle	
SAVINO, JOHN	Zacki	
SCARGLATTA, DANIEL	Danny Hogens	
SCHILLACI, JOHN	Al Brown	202010
SCHIPANI, JOSEPH	Joe the Gent	571946
SERPICO, FRANK	Farby	
SIANO, FIORE		109492
SMURRA, GEORGE	Bla-bla	
STASSI, JOSEPH	Joe Rogers	559327
STOPPELLI, JOHN	Johnny the Bug	67649
STRACI, JOSEPH	Joe Stretch	72200
STROLLO	Tony Bender (missing)	4282856 or 8
TERRANOVA, CIRO	Ciro Morell (dead)	
TIERI, FRANK	Funzwah	
TORTORICI, JOSEPH	Joe Stutz	623052

-81-

NY 92-2300

Name	Alias	FBI Identification #
TOURINE, CHARLES	Charley the Blade	
VALACHI, JOSEPH	Joe Cago	544
ZICCARDI, ELI		
ZUMBA, AL		
ZUMBA, FRANCIS	Frank Brooks	933151A
LITTLE ROCKY (nickname)		
PATTY BLACK (nickname)		
BIG MIKE (nickname)	(possibly MIKE PANETTI)	
PETE SICILIAN (nickname)		
JOE SATCHEL (nickname)		
TONY SATCHEL (nickname)		

-82-

Appendix E

The State of New Jersey Commission of Investigation

THE CHANGING FACE OF ORGANIZED
CRIME IN NEW JERSEY 2004

In the battered underworld of traditional organized crime, the New York-based Genovese organization is considered the most formidable element in a field of out-of-shape contenders, having surpassed the once-dominant Gambino LCN group in both strength and numbers over the past decade. State and federal law enforcement authorities estimate the Genovese group's core membership at between 250 and 300, with well over 1,000 criminal associates. While centered in the New York metropolitan region, the Genovese family also maintains a presence in portions of Connecticut, Massachusetts, Florida, California, and Nevada. The family has strong connections with other traditional and non-traditional organized crime groups throughout the United States. The Genovese group is the most active, powerful, and resourceful LCN family in New Jersey, which has played a key role in its evolution and growth. Historically, more high-ranking members of the Genovese family than any other LCN group have called the 106 Garden State their home. It was the first of the five New York-based families to expand its rackets to New Jersey decades ago. Today, there are five main Genovese crews headquartered in New Jersey. Also, at least four New York-based crews have operatives active in New Jersey. Approximately 40 verified rank-and-file soldiers and more than 400 criminal associates are active in New Jersey. The Genovese family has traditionally been a powerhouse in the northern part of the state, particularly in Hudson, Essex, Union, Bergen, and Passaic counties. However, during the past few years, the family has gained strength in Middlesex, Monmouth, and Ocean counties. It runs the largest bookmaking and loan sharking rings in the New York/New Jersey metropolitan area. The family's other major criminal enterprises include extortion and labor racketeering in the construction, demolition, asbestos removal, carting, recycling, trucking, and waterfront industries; theft and kickbacks from pension funds; insurance fraud; narcotics trafficking; infiltration of legitimate businesses; and public corruption. Its influence is particularly strong on the Port Newark/Elizabeth and Hudson County waterfronts. While the organization continues to commit traditional crimes such as murder, extortion, racketeering, loan sharking, and illegal gambling, it has evolved into committing more sophisticated crimes, such as computer fraud, stock/securities fraud, and health-care fraud. Many of these crimes are committed with the assistance of non-traditional organized crime groups, such as those with Russian and Cuban members. Of all the traditional LCN families, the Genovese group has the most contact with non-traditional criminal organizations and the money and power they command. 107 Not only is the Genovese family the strongest LCN group in the nation, but it also is the most unique. Its members and associates are permitted to retain a higher portion of their illegal earnings than those of other LCN families. The Genovese group also is unique among its LCN counterparts in that it has attempted for more than two decades to maintain a "façade" hierarchy designed to disguise the identities of its true leaders and insulate them from scrutiny. Law enforcement experts believe the group adopted this strategy during the late 1970s, in part to minimize the risk of dealing with other crime families that had been penetrated by undercover investigators. In addition, family leaders tend to deeply insulate themselves with layers of highly trusted members. Members of the organization also attempt to avoid law enforcement detection by being so-called "commuter mobsters." This means that members may reside in New York and conduct their illegal activity in New Jersey and vice versa. The resilience, stability, and strength of the Genovese group also can be attributed to its penchant for secrecy and the sophistication of its operations, as well as a lack of cooperation with law enforcement authorities. In recent years, while key members of other LCN groups became government witnesses to the serious detriment of their former comrades, the Genovese family has remained relatively free of turncoats. Since the early 1980s, the "official" boss of the Genovese group continues to be Vincent L. "Chin" Gigante. After years of faking mental illness and incompetence, Gigante was convicted on federal racketeering and murder conspiracy charges in 1997. In early 2003, Gigante gave up his "crazy act" and pled guilty to obstructing justice by feigning mental illness from 1990 to 1997. He received an additional three years on his sentence, and his projected release date is now June of 2010. Prosecutors contended that 108 while incarcerated, Gigante ran the Genovese organization by using his son Andrew V. Gigante as a conduit to relay his father's orders from prison. Law enforcement officials claim that Andrew, although not a "made" member, was a power on the New Jersey waterfront. A federal grand jury indicted Andrew in 2002, along with other key Genovese operatives, for running lucrative extortion rackets on the docks in New Jersey, New York, and Miami. All the defendants, including Andrew, who had no previous criminal record, pled guilty in early 2003. Now in federal prison, Andrew's projected release date is July 2005. Michael J. Generoso served as the organization's "acting" and "official" underboss for several years in the 1990s. Generoso spent 15 months in federal prison in 1997 and 1998 on a plea agreement to avoid a federal racketeering trial. He maintains a residence in Brooklyn. At 86, and due to his advanced age, law enforcement authorities believe that Generoso has become far less active in playing a key leadership role in the organization. Lawrence J. "Larry Fab" Dentico of Seaside Park, N.J., is the "official" consigliere of the group. Dentico has extensive familiarity with family operations. In the 1950s, he served as soldier under the group's namesake boss, the late Vito Genovese. Later, he was a top aide to former consigliere and New Jersey operations chief Louis A. "Bobby" Manna. Once incarcerated for contempt for refusing to testify before the SCI, Manna was sentenced to 80 years in federal prison in 1989 for racketeering and conspiracy to commit murder. Law enforcement officials believe that the top hierarchy of the Genovese family has adopted a less formally structured organization than it had in the past. The family is 109, being managed discretely by a core group of individuals with a high degree of allegiance to Vincent Gigante. Gigante's brother, Mario R. Gigante, a New York-based capo, is currently an acting boss and caretaker of the organization. Mario was released from federal prison in June of 2001 after completing a five-year term for extortion and racketeering in the solid waste hauling industry. Another acting boss is consigliere Dentico. The street boss is John Barbato, a Staten Island resident, and long-time capo in the Genovese organization. Barbato formerly served as chauffeur and bodyguard for former Genovese underboss Venero F. "Benny Eggs" Mangano. Barbato's name appears on the New Jersey Casino Control Commission's Exclusion List. New York-based captain Dominick "Quiet Dom" Cirillo is also believed to play a managing role. The low-keyed Cirillo is a close ally of Vincent Gigante and served as acting boss in the late 1990s and as the street boss for several decades. Cirillo resides in the Bronx but, despite a heart attack in 1998, has been very active in northern New Jersey. Like the actual managing hierarchy, the façade hierarchy is not as formally structured as it once was. From time to time, the Genovese organization will put word out on the street that various individuals are the boss, underboss, or consigliere in order to take the focus of law enforcement away from the individuals who are the actual leaders. At this time, the façade hierarchy is unclear. Some law enforcement officials believe John Barbato is the façade boss. In the past, key captains Liborio S. "Barney" Bellomo, Matthew "Matty the Horse" Ianniello, and Ernest Muscarella have been façade bosses. Bellomo and Muscarella are presently in federal prison on extortion convictions. Bellomo's and Muscarella's projected release dates are February 2005 and December 2007, respectively. Ianniello is a powerful senior member with an extensive background in Genovese family operations. His crew is New York-based, but it has much activity in New Jersey. Another key family leader is Tino R. Fiumara, a high-ranking caporegime and one of New Jersey's most feared mob figures. Fiumara, formerly of Spring Lake, enjoys enhanced status because of his reputation for violence and links to key portions of the organization's racketeering interests in and around the Port of New York and New Jersey – traditionally a major Genovese revenue-producer. Whether Fiumara will actually be able to fulfill his leadership ambitions, however, remains to be seen. He was released from federal prison and placed on probation after serving 15 years of a 25-year racketeering sentence. In 1999, federal authorities ordered Fiumara back to prison for violating the terms of his probation by leaving the New Jersey without permission, associating with known felons, and involvement in a continuing criminal enterprise. During his time on the street, Fiumara served as head of the New Jersey faction of the Genovese organization. In April 2002, the U.S. Attorney's Office for the District of New Jersey obtained an indictment against Fiumara for conspiring to assist fugitive Michael Coppola in Coppola's flight to avoid apprehension and prosecution. While awaiting trial, Fiumara was released from federal prison in June 2002. In March 2003, he pled guilty to conspiring to conceal and failing to report that he had been in contact with Coppola. In November, a federal judge ordered Fiumara back to prison for eight months for concealing Coppola's whereabouts. While Fiumara was imprisoned in the 1980s and 1990s, Coppola supervised Fiumara's crew. Himself a fugitive since 1996, Coppola is wanted for his role as the suspected triggerman in the 1977 murder of John "Johnny Coca-Cola" Lardiere, who, at the time he was shot to death, was on temporary furlough from imprisonment for contempt, having refused to testify before the SCI. The Fiumara/Coppola crew is one of the largest and most resourceful Genovese crews operating in New Jersey, with key influence in the Newark/Elizabeth Seaport. Its area of operation is primarily Union, Essex, and Bergen Counties. Ranking members Michael A. Borelli and Lawrence A. Ricci have been supervising this crew for Coppola and Fiumara. Ricci mainly oversees solid waste removal, trucking, and waterfront industry activities, while Borelli oversees the crew's illegal gambling operations. Borelli also has strong influence in the Teamster's Union, and has been involved in the infiltration of the health-care and construction industries. Angelo M. Prisco, a capo from Yonkers, N.Y., heads a crew with powerful influence in northern New Jersey. Prisco, who was sentenced to a 12-year prison term for arson and conspiracy, was paroled early from state prison in August 2002, allegedly in violation of New Jersey Parole Board protocols. Prisco's name appears on the New Jersey Casino Control Commission's Exclusion List. Prisco now resides in Atlantic County and is believed to have resumed control of his crew. The crew's primary activity takes place in Hudson County, along the Bayonne/Jersey City Waterfront, but it also operates in Monmouth County and Florida. While Prisco was incarcerated, Genovese member Joseph N. LaScala supervised his crew. In March 2002, several members and associates of this crew were charged with shaking down International Longshoremen's Association (ILA) dockworkers at various Hudson County waterfront shipping terminals. In December 2001, another soldier in this crew was convicted on federal charges of embezzling funds from ILA Local 1588 in Bayonne. 112 Another Genovese family crew is based out of Passaic County and commanded by Joseph Gatto, a capo who was released from federal prison in October 2003 after serving 61 months for running a highly lucrative gambling and loan sharking operation. The Gatto crew is most active in Bergen and Passaic Counties. Members of this crew have been involved in racketeering in the solid waste industry, infiltration of the health care industry, illegal video gambling, bookmaking and loan-sharking. A fourth Genovese family crew is based out of Essex County and headed by capo Silvio P. DeVita. His name appears on the Casino Control Commission's Exclusion List. The DeVita crew specializes in construction industry and labor racketeering, the infiltration of legitimate businesses, insurance fraud, gambling, and loan-sharking. Andrew N. Gerardo, who reportedly retired from head of this crew in the early 1990s and moved to Florida, routinely returns to New Jersey to receive a share of the profits and assert his authority when key decisions need to be made. Ludwig A. Bruschi heads a fifth crew. Although he managed to stay under law enforcement's radar for several years, in June of 2003 he was charged with racketeering, leading a criminal enterprise, loan sharking and promoting gambling. Eighteen of his subordinates also were charged in the case. Authorities say that Bruschi oversaw one of the largest illegal gambling and loan-sharking operations in New Jersey, covering portions of Ocean, Monmouth, Middlesex, Hudson, Essex, Passaic and Union counties. The operation is alleged to have booked around $500,000 a week in sports bets and had at least $1 million in illegal loans on the street at any given time, generating hundreds of thousands in interest payment profits. Bruschi is presently out on bail. 113 Although based in New York, a sixth crew, headed by Matthew Ianniello, known as "Matty the Horse," operates in various parts of New Jersey. Ianniello traditionally has led a crew operating in Long Island and Queens, N.Y., but some members of his crew reside and operate in New Jersey and Florida. They are involved in gambling and racketeering in the solid waste and waterfront industries. Some members of Ianniello's crew have close ties to members of the Fiumara/Coppola crew. Law enforcement authorities believe that, due to Ianniello's advanced age, he is semi-retired. Other New York-based Genovese captains who have influence and operatives in New Jersey include Rosario J. Gangi, Alphonso Malangone and Vincent J. DiNapoli. Gangi is presently serving time in federal prison, but his projected release date is August 2008. His crew is based in Brooklyn and Manhattan but is believed to have at least two members active in New Jersey. In the past, Gangi has been involved in a multimillion dollar Wall Street "pump-and-dump" scam, and in shaking down contractors on construction projects in New York and New Jersey. Malangone, a Staten Island resident now serving time in a state prison in New York on a grand larceny conviction, is also believed to have some influence in New Jersey. He can be paroled as early as April 2005, and is listed on the New Jersey Casino Control Commission's Exclusion List. DiNapoli's operations are based in the Bronx, but they extend to Bergen and Passaic counties. His primary criminal activity involves racketeering in the construction industry. Of all the LCN groups, the Genovese criminal organization poses the greatest threat to New Jersey. It has a proven record of resiliency that has enabled it to maintain a grip on lucrative segments of the legitimate economy despite repeated assaults by law 114 enforcement. Elements of this group persist in the solid waste industry, on the waterfront, in organized labor and in public construction. Continued infiltration of the latter poses a particularly stark threat given the fact that New Jersey has embarked upon a program to invest billions of taxpayer dollars in school and transportation construction programs over the next several years. In addition, the organization's influence on the waterfront has the potential to pose an even greater security risk than in the past. By cooperating with elements of various non-traditional criminal organizations in facilitating the movement of cargo, traditional LCN could enable terrorist organizations. Moreover, the Genovese group's diversification beyond traditional LCN activities into sophisticated financial frauds in the health-care field and on Wall Street presents law enforcement with a challenging new frontier.

Appendix F

Press Release

VINCENT GIGANTE, BOSS OF THE GENOVESE FAMILY, PLEADS GUILTY AND ADMITS FAKING MENTAL INCAPACITY TO OBSTRUCT JUSTICE; TWO ACTING BOSSES PLEAD GUILTY TO RACKETEERING; GIGANTE'S SON PLEADS GUILTY TO EXTORTION AND IS BARRED FROM THE WATERFRONT FOR LIFE; GENOVESE FAMILY CAPTAIN, TWO SOLDIERS AND TWO ASSOCIATES ALSO PLEAD GUILTY TO EXTORTION OF WATERFRONT BUSINESSES AND ARE BANNED FROM THE WATERFRONT FOR LIFE

ROSLYNN R. MAUSKOPF, United States Attorney for the Eastern District of New York, **KEVIN P. DONOVAN**, Assistant Director-in-Charge of the New York Office of the Federal Bureau of Investigation, and **RAYMOND W. KELLY**, Commissioner, New York City Police Department, today announced the guilty pleas of VINCENT "Chin" GIGANTE, the boss of the Genovese Family of La Cosa Nostra (the "Genovese family"), to obstructing justice by faking mental illness, LIBORIO "Barney" BELLOMO and ERNEST MUSCARELLA, former acting bosses of the family, to racketeering, ANDREW GIGANTE, the son of VINCENT GIGANTE, to conspiring to extort a large container repair business operating on the piers of New York, New Jersey and Florida, CHARLES TUZZO, a Genovese family captain, to conspiring to extort businesses on the piers in New York, New

Jersey and Florida, PASQUALE FALCETTI and MICHAEL RAGUSA, Genovese family soldiers, to racketeering, and THOMAS CAFARO, a Genovese family associate, to racketeering.

A. VINCENT GIGANTE Pleads Guilty and Admits Using a "Crazy Act" to Avoid Prosecution Genovese Family Boss VINCENT "Chin" GIGANTE today pleaded guilty to obstructing justice by misleading psychiatrists and psychologists evaluating his mental competence with the intention of influencing their testimony in GIGANTE's prior case in this district, United States v. Vincent Gigante, 90 CR 446 and 93 CR 368. GIGANTE's guilty plea carries a stipulated term of incarceration of three years, to be served after he finishes serving the 12-year term of incarceration for which he is presently imprisoned.

Through his public acknowledgment of guilt, GIGANTE's legendary charade has finally and conclusively been put to rest and exposed for the fraud that it is. GIGANTE commenced his act in the mid-1960's, after serving a sentence, along with then-Genovese family boss Vito Genovese and others, for heroin trafficking. In 1969, GIGANTE was indicted in New Jersey Superior Court on charges of corrupting the police force of Old Tappan, New Jersey, by bribing them to provide organized crime with information about ongoing investigations and surveillance. In response, GIGANTE claimed mental incompetence. Medical records reveal that he first began seeking psychiatric treatment at about the time he learned of the New Jersey investigation.

In support of his claim, various psychiatrists opined on behalf of GIGANTE that he was insane, psychotic, mute, schizophrenic, a candidate for electroshock treatment, infantile and primitive. The psychiatric consensus was that GIGANTE's extreme mental disability would never improve and that he was rapidly and progressively deteriorating. In the face of these claims of incapacity, he was found to be insane, and the 1969 indictment was dismissed.

GIGANTE was first indicted in the Eastern District of New York in 1990 in what has become known as the "Windows" case. In that case, based on testimony of mental health experts, GIGANTE again claimed extraordinary and debilitating mental (and physical) incapacity. This resulted in GIGANTE obtaining a severance of his case from his co-defendants including Genovese Family underboss Venero "Benny Eggs" Mangano and others, so that the issue of his alleged mental incapacity could be resolved after the trial.

In April 1993, GIGANTE was again indicted in this district and charged with numerous murders and murder conspiracies, in addition to other crimes, all in his capacity as boss of the Genovese Family.

More competency hearings were held, at which psychiatrists and psychologists again testified that GIGANTE was mentally incompetent. The late Judge Eugene H. Nickerson rejected these claims, and concluded that GIGANTE was a powerful leader of the Genovese Family who had a long history of feigning mental illness designed to prevent him from being successfully prosecuted. Judge Nickerson found GIGANTE both medically and mentally fit to stand trial.

GIGANTE's case was ultimately reassigned to Judge Jack B. Weinstein, who conducted further competency hearings, based on purportedly new findings relating to GIGANE's degenerating mental state. After additional hearings at which mental health experts testified that GIGANTE was mentally incompetent (along with testimony from government witnesses that called this testimony into question), Judge Weinstein reaffirmed Judge Nickerson's conclusion, and found GIGANTE both mentally and physically fit to be tried.

GIGANTE was convicted after trial. He then claimed to be incompetent to be sentenced, and was sent for further evaluation. Additional hearings were conducted, at which a bevy of psychiatrists and psychologists testified on behalf of GIGANTE. These experts represented some of the finest medical schools in this country. The government also presented witnesses, who testified that GIGANTE was feigning mental illness. Over the course of his 30-year crazy act, GIGANTE's psychiatric and psychological witnesses had variously testified that, among other things, GIGANTE was insane, psychotic, demented, and suffered from Alzheimer's disease and schizophrenia. Moreover, over the years, he had been institutionalized for mental health treatment dozens of times, and his family had instituted proceedings to have a legal guardian put in place for him because GIGANTE was purportedly unable to care for his own affairs. Doctors testifying for GIGANTE swore that his condition could never improve and could only get worse.

Judge Weinstein concluded that none of the purportedly new findings undermined the prior findings of competence and that GIGANTE was faking mental illness. GIGANTE was sentenced to a term of incarceration of 12 years and a $1,250,000 fine. The conviction was affirmed on appeal.

GIGANTE's advocates publicly maintained that a tremendous injustice had been visited upon a mentally diseased individual.

By the entry of his guilty plea today six years after his prior conviction, GIGANTE has now acknowledged that the doctors who testified on his behalf were misled, and that the purpose of this fraud was to obstruct justice during GIGANTE's prosecution in the Windows case.

In announcing the guilty plea United States Attorney **MAUSKOPF** stated, "Although mental health experts have literally been fooled by GIGANTE for decades, law enforcement has always recognized GIGANTE for what he is - - the cunning, powerful and feared leader of the Genovese organized crime family. Through his guilty plea, there is no further debate. The strong evidence developed in this case finally forced GIGANTE to expose himself as a fraud and to acknowledge that doctors who testified in his prior case on his behalf were duped. Years ago, he attempted to obstruct justice by presenting false evidence about his mental health in a federal proceeding. We will never tolerate such efforts to tamper with our system of justice, and we were prepared to prove GIGANTE's obstruction at trial. I am proud of the perseverance demonstrated by a long line of prosecutors in this district since 1990 to unmask GIGANTE's elaborate ruse and to bring him to justice."

B. GIGANTE's Son, Two of his Acting Bosses, a Genovese Captain, Two Soldiers and an

Associate Plead Guilty and are Barred from the Waterfront for Life

ANDREW GIGANTE, a Genovese Family associate and the son of boss VINCENT GIGANTE, pleaded guilty today to a conspiring to extort a large container repair and storage company operated by Umberto Guido on the New Jersey, New York and South Florida piers. As part of his plea, ANDREW GIGANTE agreed to forfeit $2,000,000 of his ill-gotten gains from the extortion to the government, and, as part of the settlement of a civil racketeering case that accompanied the criminal prosecution, agreed to be barred for life from any activity on the New York, New Jersey and South Florida piers. The plea agreement calls for GIGANTE to be sentenced to two years in prison.

ERNEST MUSCARELLA, a former acting boss of the Genovese Family, and a former captain of the "uptown" crew of the family formerly headed by Anthony "Fat Tony" Salerno, pleaded guilty to racketeering. As part of his plea, MUSCARELLA admitted that, as part of the racketeering enterprise, he participated in a large securities fraud in which the stock of Orex Gold Mines Corp. was sold under fraudulent pretenses, costing investors of millions of dollars. MUSCARELLA also admitted participation in a Florida gambling operation. The plea agreement calls for MUSCARELLA to be sentenced to five years incarceration. Also as part of his plea, MUSCARELLA settled the civil racketeering case by agreeing to be barred for life from any activity on the New York, New Jersey and South Florida piers, and any involvement with the ILA, as well as from involvement with the International Brotherhood of Teamsters ("Teamster's Union"), International Carpenter's Union ("Carpenter's Union"), Local 32B/J of the Building Services Workers

Union ("Local 32B/J"), the Laborers' International Union of North America ("LIUNA") and the Mason Tenders' District Council of Greater New York ("Mason Tenders").

LIBORIO BELLOMO, the former Genovese Family acting boss, and also a former captain of the "uptown" crew of the Genovese family, pleaded guilty to racketeering, including a conspiracy to extort businesses operating on the piers in New York, New Jersey and Florida, and a conspiracy to gain control of the pension and welfare funds of workers represented by Local 1804-1 of the International Longshoreman's Association (the "ILA"). As part of the extortion of pier businesses, BELLOMO and others schemed to put mafia-controlled officers into the ILA, and then use the union to keep non-mafia controlled businesses off the piers. With control of the ILA, including ILA Local 1804-1, BELLOMO and others then planned to place a Genovese associate as an "investment advisor" to pension and welfare funds, obtain control of the funds and distribute the fees paid by the funds for investment advice throughout the Genovese Family. The plan was disrupted by BELLOMO's incarceration in 1996 in another federal case, in which he was sentenced to ten years incarceration. The plea agreement calls for BELLOMO to be sentenced to four years, to be served after he completes the ten year sentence in his prior case. Also as part of his guilty plea in this case, BELLOMO agreed to be barred for life from any involvement in the waterfront of New York, New Jersey or Florida, and the ILA, as well as from involvement with the Carpenter's Union, Teamster's Union, Local 32B/J, LIUNA and the Mason Tenders.

CHARLES TUZZO, a Genovese Family captain, pleaded guilty to conspiring to extort businesses operating on the piers in New York, New Jersey and Florida. TUZZO, a close associate of BELLOMO, supervised BELLOMO's interests on the piers after BELLOMO went to jail in 1996. The plea agreement calls for TUZZO to be sentence to two and one-half years in prison. Also as part of his guilty plea in this case, TUZZO agreed to be barred for life from any involvement in the waterfront of New York,

New Jersey or Florida, and the ILA, as well as from involvement with the Carpenter's Union, Teamster's Union, Local 32B/J, LIUNA and the Mason Tenders.

PASQUALE FALCETTI, a Genovese soldier in the "uptown crew," pleaded guilty to racketeering, including extorting businesses on the piers, extorting Umberto Guido, the operator of a pier business, and conspiring to control ILA pension and welfare funds on behalf of the Genovese Family. FALCETTI also pleaded guilty to conspiring to bribe a business agent of Local 32B/J, who was an associate of the Genovese Family, on behalf of the owner of an apartment complex of Brooklyn who sought to rid his apartment complex of Local 32B/J labor. The business agent, Ismet Kukic, pleaded guilty on July 10, 2002 in this district to agreeing to be bribed by FALCETTI and others. FALCETTI also pleaded guilty to conspiring to launder through a bank account in the Bahamas over $100,000 stolen from an insurance company, as well as participating in the operation of a gambling business in Florida. The plea agreement calls for FALCETTI to be sentenced to seven years incarceration. Like his captains MUSCARELLA and BELLOMO, as part of his guilty plea in this case, FALCETTI agreed to be barred for life from **any** involvement in the waterfront of New York, New Jersey or Florida, and the ILA, as well as from involvement with the Carpenter's Union, Teamster's Union, Local 32B/J, LIUNA and the Mason Tenders.

MICHAEL RAGUSA, also a soldier in the "uptown" crew of the Genovese Family, pleaded guilty to racketeering, including the conspiracy to extort businesses operating on the piers to gain control of the pension and welfare funds of workers represented by ILA Local 1804-1. The plea agreement calls for RAGUSA to be sentenced to four years, to run consecutive to the ten year sentence imposed in his prior case. Like the other members of his crew in this case, as part of his guilty plea RAGUSA agreed to be barred for life from any involvement in the waterfront of New York, New Jersey or Florida, and the ILA, as well as from involvement with the Carpenter's Union, Teamster's Union, Local 32B/J, LIUNA and the Mason Tenders.

THOMAS CAFARO also pleaded guilty to racketeering. CAFARO was an associate in the "uptown" Genovese Family crew, and was particularly close to BELLOMO. When BELLOMO went to jail in 1996, BELLOMO transferred oversight of CAFARO's crimes with BELLOMO to TUZZO. As part of the racketeering crime to which CAFARO pleaded guilty, CAFARO admitted his involvement in extorting businesses on the piers, conspiring to control ILA pension and welfare funds on behalf of the Genovese Family, conspiring, with MUSCARELLA and others, to defraud investors in regard to the sale of Orex Gold Mining Corp. stock, agreeing to launder through a bank account in the Bahamas over $100,000 stolen from an insurance company, and participating in the operation of a gambling business in Florida. The plea agreement calls for CAFARO to be sentenced to seven years incarceration. CAFARO, like others convicted of illegal activity on the piers in this case, agreed to be barred for life from any involvement in the waterfront of New York, New Jersey or Florida, and the ILA, as well as from involvement with the Carpenter's Union, Teamster's Union, Local 32B/J, LIUNA and the Mason Tenders.

C. The Waterfront Prosecutions

As a result of today's guilty pleas and the recent trial of Peter Gotti, acting boss of the Gambino Family, and Anthony "Sonny" Ciccone, a Gambino Family captain, the leaders of both the Gambino and Genovese Families, three mafia captains, and five soldiers stand convicted for their efforts to control the New York/New Jersey waterfront and to infiltrate the ILA.

United States Attorney **MAUSKOPF** stated, "By convicting the leaders of the Genovese and Gambino Families, law enforcement has taken a firm step towards ridding the New York-New Jersey piers of organized crime influence and all its attendant dangers. We will continue to work towards this goal with criminal prosecutions and all available civil remedies to keep organized crime off the waterfront and out of and the unions."

Assistant FBI Director-in-Charge **DONOVAN** stated, "In the sense that he spent a good portion of his life maintaining the charade, Chin Gigante gave ‹the performance of a lifetime› in trying to convince the courts of his mental incompetence. Unfortunately for Chin, however, the act was panned right from opening night by the agents, cops and prosecutors who maintained throughout the long run that the one-man show was unconvincing. And the courts weren›t swayed, either. Gigante›s plea is the actor finally acknowledging that the critics were right."

Police Commissioner **KELLY** stated, "These individuals would not have finally pled guilty to their lists of crimes were it not for the perseverance of law enforcement. The New York City Police Department, the U.S. Attorney's office, and the FBI have rigorously pursued these criminals for years. Now, thanks to our relentless efforts, we've landed another major blow to organized crime in this city."

The government's criminal case was prosecuted by Assistant United States Attorneys Paul Weinstein, Daniel Dorsky, Paul Schoeman and Joseph Lipton. The government's civil racketeering case was prosecuted by Assistant United States Attorneys Richard K. Hayes, Kathleen A. Nandan and Varuni Nelson.

The Defendants

Name: Liborio Bellomo
DOB: 1/8/57
Address: Incarcerated

Name: Thomas Cafaro
DOB: 12/6/58
Address: 6662 Newport Lake Circle
Boca Raton, Florida

Name: Pasquale Falcetti
DOB: 9/11/58

Address: 3250 Giegrich Place
Bronx, New York

Name: Andrew Gigante
DOB: 9/30/56
Address: 23 17th Street
Norwood, New Jersey

Name: Vincent Gigante
DOB: 3/29/28
Address: Incarcerated

Name: Ernest Muscarella
DOB: 12/7/49
Address: 3247 Glennon Place
Bronx, New York

Name: Michael Ragusa
DOB: 6/22/65
Address: 101 Larrys Lane
Pleasantville, New York

Name: Charles Tuzzo
DOB: 11/22/33
Address: 341-343 E. 75th Street
New York, New York

Appendix G

The Genovese Drug Case

In March 1955, Cantellops attended a meeting at Al's Luncheonette at 34 East 4th Street, New York, with Charles Barcellona, Ralph Polizzano, Carmine Polizzano, Joseph Di Palermo, and Anthony Colonna. Cantellops agreed to transport narcotics to Las Vegas for $1000. At the airport bus, while Barcellona was talking to Cantellops, an unidentified man handed Cantellops a package which he took to Las Vegas. In Las Vegas Carmine Polizzano met him and introduced him to the defendant Fiano to whom he gave the package later that evening. For this delivery of narcotics Cantellops was paid $1000 by Barcellona.

In June, 1955 Cantellops made a trip to Florida to pick up a shipment of narcotics. Carmine Pollizzano gave him a bus ticket and money and he went to Miami where he met Carmine Polizzano and drove to Tampa. When the rendezvous in Tampa was unsuccessful, Cantellops and Carmine Polizzano drove to Key West where outside the La Concha Hotel an unidentified man took a suitcase out of his pushcart and placed it in the back seat of the automobile in which Cantellops was waiting. After driving to Miami Cantellops took the train and delivered the narcotics to Ralph Polizzano at the "plant" at 36 East 4th Street, next to Al's Luncheonette, as Carmine Polizzano watched from across the street. For this trip Joseph Di Palermo and Carmine Polizzano paid Cantellops $600 and later he also received an ounce of heroin as a tip.

Cantellops' third trip in August, 1955, took him to Chicago. Carmine Polizzano instructed him about the trip and gave him a package of narcotics from the trunk of a car parked in front of Al's Luncheonette. Cantellops took a bus to Chicago and the day after his arrival met Carmine Polizzano at a bar on Division Street where he was introduced to a man who picked up the narcotics in the booth where Cantellops had placed them. Cantellops and Carmine Polizzano then drove back to New York and, at Joseph Di Palermo's direction, Carmine Polizzano paid Cantellops. Following the Chicago trip, in August and September, 1955, Cantellops distributed narcotics for Ralph Polizzano.

In October, 1955 Carmine Polizzano asked Cantellops to pick up narcotics in Miami. He told Cantellops that if narcotics were not available in Miami he might have to go to Havana to see certain people. Cantellops went to Miami and at the La Concha Hotel met Charles Di Palermo who introduced him to a man named "Cuba." The three men then drove to the La Concha Hotel in Key West and the next day, upon directions from "Cuba" they picked up a suitcase of narcotics in "Cuba's" hotel room and brought the narcotics to New York by train. Back in New York Cantellops delivered the narcotics to Ralph Polizzano at the basement entrance of Al's Luncheonette upon directions from Carmine Polizzano. For this trip Cantellops was paid $250 by Joseph Di Palermo and $350 by Carmine Polizzano, who also arranged for his assistant, John Russo, to give Cantellops an ounce of heroin as a tip.

In October, 1955, upon Carmine Polizzano's directions, Cantellops explored the policy banks in the Eldridge Street area on Manhattan's lower East Side to find out whether these banks might be used as a front for narcotics distributing plants. After Cantellops had explored the policy banks, Carmine Polizzano invited him to a meeting at Ralph Polizzano's apartment on East 4th Street. This meeting was attended by Ralph and Carmine Polizzano, Joseph Di Palermo, John Russo, John Ormento and Benjamin Levine. The group discussed taking over and operating policy banks as a cover for the distribution of narcotics. Cantellops reported that it would cost between

$100,000 and $150,000 to purchase the banks in the Eldridge Street area. The group reached no final decision as it was stated that the matters would have to be discussed with "The Right Man," who, as Cantellops' testimony later developed, turned out to be appellant Vito Genovese. The meeting also discussed the possibility of importing narcotics through Puerto Rico because of turmoil in Cuba and recent misfortunes respecting two shipments by boat. Cantellops suggested the use of the Island of Vieques, off Puerto Rico, as a distributing point.

During the early part of 1956, at the request of Joseph Di Palermo and Carmine Polizzano, Rosario Colletti delivered narcotics to Cantellops who in turn delivered them to John Gonzalez, alias Guayamita, at Gonzalez's apartment at 793 Ninth Avenue, where they were diluted for resale. In June 1956, Cantellops took over Gonzalez' operations and Joseph Di Palermo and the two Polizzanos arranged for Ralph Polizzano to supply Cantellops with the narcotics necessary to expand this business in the Spanish speaking market. Cantellops called Ralph Polizzano when he needed drugs and he picked them up from Russo at Al's Luncheonette or nearby places. While picking up narcotics at the East 4th Street plant Cantellops saw Ralph Polizzano and Charles Di Palermo diluting narcotics. On two occasions during 1956 when Cantellops was in the East 4th Street neighborhood, he saw Vito Genovese talking to Carmine Polizzano and on one of these occasions when Cantellops approached, he was told by Carmine Polizzano "never to interfere when he was talking to `The Right Man.'" In the summer of 1956 Cantellops, at Ralph Polizzano's request, made other local deliveries of narcotics.

In July, 1956, Cantellops made his fifth out-of-town trip, this time to Cleveland at the behest of Ormento and Carmine Polizzano. Carmine Polizzano introduced Cantellops to appellant Vincent Gigante who drove Cantellops to Lorain, Ohio. At Lorain, Cantellops took the narcotics from behind the spare tire in the automobile trunk and then took them by bus to Cleveland. In Cleveland, he met Charles Di Palermo and he delivered the narcotics to an unidentified woman in a taxicab. After Cantellops returned to New York, Carmine Polizzano arranged for him to meet Ormento and in Mazzie's presence Ormento paid Cantellops for the trip.

In August, 1956, a sale by Colletti to a narcotic agent resulted in the arrest of Colletti and Russo and the latter was replaced by the defendant Salvatore Marino who thereafter handled narcotics deliveries for the Polizzanos, at the Squeeze-Inn Bar, the plant at 36 East 4th Street and Al's Luncheonette at 34 East 4th Street. Thereafter Marino made frequent deliveries of drugs to Cantellops.

In August, 1956, Cantellops made his third trip to Miami to pick up narcotics. Before the Miami trip there were discussions and meetings at which Ormento offered Cantellops $1,500, to pick up narcotics in Mexico. After Cantellops refused to do this, meetings were held with a man called "Mexican," Mazzie and Carmine Galante regarding the details of a trip to pick up drugs. Cantellops still refused to go to Mexico.

The following evening Cantellops went with Ormento, Mazzie, "Mexican" and the appellant Natale Evola to a restaurant on East 86th Street. Here Ormento spoke to Genovese and reported back to Cantellops that "The Right Man" wanted to take a look at Cantellops to see if he was all right.

After this Cantellops went to "Mexican's" hotel room somewhere on West 85th Street and discussed the trip to Mexico with the appellant Salvatore Santora, Evola, Mazzie, Ormento and "Mexican." Cantellops persisted in his refusal to go to Mexico but suggested that he go to Miami instead. As the change in plan involved a delay, Ormento gave Cantellops money to entertain "Mexican" in New York City, which Cantellops did for the next three days. After this Cantellops drove with "Mexican" to Miami. The day after their arrival "Mexican" drove Cantellops to Pompano Beach, secured a suitcase in a motel, and gave it to Cantellops. Cantellops then returned to New York by train and later gave the bag to an unidentified man. For this trip Ormento and Mazzie later paid him $950. After this Cantellops made two deliveries of narcotics to Philadelphia. On the first occasion, Cantellops delivered three or four pounds of narcotics to a lame man, with Mazzie watching the delivery from a distance. For this Ormento paid Cantellops $350 in the presence of Santora and Mazzie and told Cantellops that Santora would have another trip for him.

A few days later Carmine Polizzano arranged for Cantellops to meet with Ormento, Santora and Mazzie at which time Ormento asked him to deliver narcotics to Philadelphia for Santora. Cantellops was driven to Philadelphia and delivered the narcotics according to instructions. For the second Philadelphia trip Santora gave money to Ormento who gave it to Cantellops in the presence of Mazzie and Evola. In addition, Cantellops testified to making a Brooklyn delivery for the same group, for which he was paid by Ormento.

In August, 1956, defendant Contes ordered a large quantity of heroin from Nicholas Lessa and Cantellops delivered this to Contes at the request of Mazzie who paid Cantellops for the delivery. The testimony of Peter Contes tended to confirm these transactions.

A few days later Ormento and Mazzie twice sent narcotics to Daniel and Nicholas Lessa, using Cantellops as the messenger. Mazzie supervised the second delivery and Ormento paid Cantellops for both deliveries.

At the end of August, or early September 1956, Cantellops attended a meeting at Mazzie's home at 2332 Seymour Avenue in the Bronx where plans were made for extending the distribution of narcotics. Earlier in the evening, Cantellops drove to a German restaurant on East 86th Street with Evola, Ormento, Galante and Andimo Pappadio. After Ormento made a telephone call, they all drove to the West Side Highway and met another car. Cantellops and Ormento entered the other car which was driven by appellant Gigante. Ormento introduced Cantellops to Genovese, who was sitting in the back seat, saying to Genovese "This man is doing a good job for us. He is helping us and doing a good job for us." Ormento told Cantellops "This is the Right

Man." Genovese said to Cantellops that they "were going to a meeting where territorial control was to be discussed," that the people at the meeting were counting on Cantellops to help them and that Cantellops could earn some money by doing so. The two automobiles drove to Mazzie's home and everyone entered except Genovese and Gigante who stayed outside. Evola, Mazzie, Ormento, Pappadio, Galante and Cantellops discussed the distribution of narcotics in the Spanish market in the East Bronx by use of policy banks and sealing off the area to eliminate competing narcotics peddlers and policy banks so that they could control the narcotics traffic in this area. Evola and Pappadio thought that the plan would take a month or a month and a half to complete and the others agreed. After twenty or thirty minutes Genovese came in. He wanted to know "what was the decision in the plan, what they had in mind." When he was told about the discussion which had taken place, Genovese said that he needed this information because he wanted to know when to send his men into the area. Later, in the presence of Evola, Ormento, Pappadio and Galante, Cantellops was advised that he would be the contact man for the distribution of narcotics in this area. Cantellops later delivered narcotics in this area at Ormento's request.

In September, 1956, Ormento and Galante sent Cantellops to Puerto Rico for narcotics. In Puerto Rico he contacted someone named Laurensano who instructed him where to find one Perez on the island of Vieques. When Cantellops met Perez he was given a double marine canvas bag containing narcotics. Cantellops advised Laurensano that he was sending the drugs to three fictitious persons in care of General Delivery, Post Office, New York, and Laurensano advised that he would inform Ormento. Cantellops then mailed the heroin in three packages from three separate post offices. When Cantellops returned to New York Carmine Polizzano arranged to have him meet Ormento who said the drugs had arrived and Ormento paid him for the trip.

After this Cantellops met with Joseph Di Palermo, "Cuba" and a man named Montanez, and Montanez advised that there would be no more shipments from Cuba to Miami and Key West for the rest of the year because of unsettled conditions in Cuba. This meeting took place just a few days before Cantellops was arrested in September, 1956, and he remained in prison until February 1957.

According to the testimony of three customs inspectors, Joseph Di Palermo, Jean Capece, and Salvatore Benanti visited Cuba for two days in November, 1956, and returned to New York on November 20. Jean Capece was searched by a customs inspectress who found $9,000 in new one hundred dollar bills hidden in an undergarment. Jean Capece gave three different stories regarding this money.

When Cantellops left prison in February, 1957, he resumed his narcotics dealings with the Polizzanos, the Di Palermos and Ormento. The appellant Alfredo Aviles became a customer and Cantellops and Marino delivered narcotics to him, Cantellops making his deliveries about once or twice a week from the East 4th Street plant. Aviles paid Cantellops who turned the money over to Ralph Polizzano or Marino and received $100 for each delivery. On one occasion, when Joseph Di Palermo was present, Cantellops saw Ralph Polizzano hand to Jean Capece the proceeds of one of these sales to Aviles. Later Aviles bought directly from Ralph Polizzano and Cantellops received commissions on the sales. Aviles in turn resold the drugs which he had purchased from Cantellops and Ralph Polizzano. Marino testified for the government and generally confirmed Cantellops' story about the deliveries and the dealings with Aviles.

Cantellops' fourth and last trip to Miami took place in April, 1957. Joseph Di Palermo and Carmine Polizzano instructed Cantellops to meet Charles Di Palermo in Miami. Carmine Polizzano provided Cantellops with a bus ticket and money, and in Miami, he met Charles Di Palermo and "Cuba" at the La Concha Hotel. The trio then drove to the La Concha Hotel in Key West. In Key West an unidentified man put luggage in the rear seat of their car and Cantellops and Cuba took this back to Miami in the bus. Here they met Charles Di Palermo and, after rearranging the luggage, Cantellops took the drugs back to New York on the train and delivered them to Carmine Polizzano at the plant on East 4th Street. Later Joseph Di Palermo and Carmine Polizzano paid him about $600 for the trip, and he later was given a tip of an ounce of heroin by Marino on Carmine Polizzano's instructions.

At a meeting in May, 1957, in Ralph Polizzano's apartment, there was further talk about sealing up the Eldridge Street territory. Present were Ralph Polizzano, Joseph Di Palermo, Ormento, Cantellops and some friend of Bennie Levine. Cantellops was ordered to start buying up the Spanish policy banks and he attempted to arrange meetings between the owners of these banks and the Polizzanos. Meanwhile Cantellops continued to deliver narcotics for the Polizzanos from the East 4th Street plant until July 1, 1957 when he was arrested.

Appendix II

Bellomo Indictment

United States Attorney Southern District of New York FOR IMMEDIATE RELEASE CONTACT: U.S. ATTORNEY'S OFFICE February 23, 2006 HERBERT HADAD, MEGAN GAFFNEY HEATHER TASKER, BRIDGET KELLY PUBLIC INFORMATION OFFICE (212) 637-2600 U.S. CHARGES ACTING BOSS AND OVER 30 MEMBERS AND ASSOCIATES OF THE GENOVESE ORGANIZED CRIME FAMILY WITH RACKETEERING AND OTHER OFFENSES INCLUDING MURDER, EXTORTION, NARCOTICS TRAFFICKING, AND FIREARMS TRAFFICKING MICHAEL J. GARCIA, the United States Attorney for the Southern District of New York, MARK J. MERSHON, the Assistant Director in Charge of the New York Office of the FBI, JANET DiFIORE, the Westchester County District Attorney, and RAYMOND KELLY, the Commissioner of the New York City Police Department, announced the unsealing in Manhattan federal court earlier today of a 42-count indictment, captioned United States v. Liborio S. Bellomo, et al., S1 06 Cr. 08 (LAK) (the "Indictment"). The Indictment charges 32 defendants, including an Acting Boss and various members and associates of the Genovese Organized Crime Family of La Cosa Nostra, with wide-ranging racketeering crimes and other offenses spanning more than a decade, including murder, violent extortions of various individuals and businesses, labor racketeering, obstruction of justice, narcotics trafficking, money laundering, and firearms trafficking. The Indictment, which targets factions of the Genovese Organized Crime Family based in the Bronx, East Harlem, and Westchester, is the result of a Federal investigation that began in 2003, and a related investigation by state authorities in Westchester County that began in 2005. The Indictment charges LIBORIO S. BELLOMO, a/k/a "Barney Bellomo," JOHN ARDITO, a/k/a "Buster," RALPH BALSAMO, a/k/a "the Undertaker," a/k/a "Skully," SALVATORE LARCA, a/k/a "Sal," GERALD FIORINO, a/k/a "Jerry," VINCENT RUSSO, a/k/a "Vinny," and ALBERT TRANQUILLO, JR., a/k/a "Allie Boy," with racketeering offenses based on their participation in the affairs of the Genovese Organized Crime Family. Specifically, the Indictment alleges that BELLOMO served as Acting Boss of the Genovese Family throughout much of the 1990s and has remained a powerful member of the Family through the present, despite his incarceration following a conviction on extortion charges in this 2 District in 1996. While he was incarcerated in 1998, BELLOMO authorized and sanctioned the murder of Ralph Coppola, a former Genovese Family Soldier and Acting Capo, who had been in BELLOMO's "crew." The murder charge against BELLOMO is punishable by death; however, the Department of Justice has not yet determined whether to seek the death penalty for BELLOMO. Also unsealed today was the guilty plea in July 2005 of long-time Genovese Family associate, and attorney, PETER J. PELUSO. PELUSO pled guilty to participating in numerous crimes committed by the Genovese Family, including racketeering, extortion and obstruction of justice. One of the ways that PELUSO assisted members of the Genovese Family in committing these crimes was by employing his status as an attorney to deliver important messages to and from members of the Family, some of whom were incarcerated. Members and associates of the Genovese Family believed that these communications were less likely to be subject to law enforcement surveillance because of PELUSO's status as an attorney. Among other crimes, PELUSO pleaded guilty to participating in the murder of Coppola. Specifically, PELUSO admitted that he carried the message from the imprisoned BELLOMO to other leaders of the Genovese Family that sanctioned and led to the murder of Coppola. As set forth in the transcript of his guilty plea allocution, PELUSO pled guilty pursuant to a cooperation agreement with the Government. Numerous other made members and trusted associates of the Genovese Family are charged in the Indictment as well. Longtime Capo JOHN ARDITO is charged with racketeering crimes including extortion, obstruction of justice, witness tampering, and money laundering. Genovese Family Soldier RALPH BALSAMO is charged with racketeering offenses, as well obstruction of justice, the operation of an illegal gambling business, narcotics distribution and firearms trafficking. In addition, it is alleged that BALSAMO frequently met with other members and associates of the Genovese Family at the funeral parlor that he operates in the Bronx. Genovese Family Soldier SALVATORE LARCA is charged with obstruction of justice, as well as a labor racketeering scheme with ARDITO and BALSAMO, in which they attempted to corruptly influence certain elected officials of Local 15 of the International Union of Operating Engineers. Also charged with racketeering offenses is GERALD FIORINO, an associate of the Genovese Family and BELLOMO's brother-in-law, who is alleged to have participated in a money laundering scheme with ARDITO, as well as an attempted extortion, together with Soldier LOUIS MOSCATIELLO and associate PASQUALE SPERDUTO, of the owner of a construction company. VINCENT RUSSO, a proposed member of the Genovese Family, is also charged with 3 being part of the racketeering enterprise by participating, together with ARDITO, BALSAMO and LARCA, in a scheme to tamper with a victim of a violent assault at a construction site, whose ear had been partially bitten off in a fight with another Genovese Family Soldier. RUSSO is also charged with participating in an extortion of the owner of a bakery, together with ARDITO and ANGELO AQUILLINO, the President of Local 102 of the Bakery, Confectionary and Tobacco Workers' Union. ALBERT TRANQUILLO, JR., a Genovese Family associate, is charged as part of the racketeering enterprise with carrying out three violent extortions relating to a business that he ran called A&D Carting, also called Transcamp Carting, which maintained contracts to haul trash, dirt and concrete for various entities. Genovese Family Soldier ALBERT "Chinky" FACCHIANO, a member of the Florida faction of the Family, is charged with participating in a scheme, together with BELLOMO and ARDITO, to locate a suspected cooperating witness in order to prevent the witness's testimony at a Federal criminal trial in the summer of 2002. Genovese Family Capo ARTHUR NIGRO, together with Soldier PASQUALE "Scoop" DELUCA, is charged with participating in an extortion of the owner and operator of a piece of commercial rental property. Genovese Family Genovese Acting Capo ANTHONY "Rom" ROMANELLO is charged with the extortion of the owner and operator of a bakery. Finally, the Indictment alleges that BALSAMO oversaw a large-scale cocaine distribution network, which was managed and operated by two associates of the Family, ANDREW SHEA and Michael "Chunk" Londonio, and which employed numerous "runners," also charged in the Indictment, who distributed the cocaine throughout the Bronx and Westchester. Also charged in the narcotics conspiracy are JOHN TOMERO, a primary source of cocaine for this drug conspiracy, and JOSEPH DEROSA, a cocaine customer who then distributed the cocaine, who were arrested on December 6, 2005, pursuant to federal warrants. Also on December 6, 2005, pursuant to an arrest warrant obtained by the Westchester County District Attorney's Office, law enforcement agents attempted to arrest Londonio at his residence in the Bronx. During the execution of this arrest warrant, Londonio fired numerous shots at two New York State Troopers, hitting one in the head and chest (who was saved from serious injuries because he was wearing bullet-proof armor) and hitting and injuring the other Trooper in the leg. The arresting officers then returned fire, and Londonio was killed. In addition, pursuant to a search of Londonio's apartment, numerous firearms, dozens of rounds of ammunition, and a live grenade were found. In this regard, BALSAMO, LARCA, SHEA, and SAMMY LOPEZ are also charged with firearms trafficking with Londonio. 4 Mr. GARCIA praised the efforts of the Federal Bureau of Investigation, the Westchester County District Attorney's Office, and the New York City Police Department, in this investigation. In addition, Mr. GARCIA expressed his appreciation to the Putnam County District Attorney and the Putnam County Sheriff's Offices for their assistance in this investigation. Assistant United States Attorneys

MIRIAM E. ROCAH, JONATHAN KOLODNER, and ERIC J. SNYDER are in charge of the prosecutions. The charges contained in the Indictment are merely accusations, and the defendants are presumed innocent unless and until proven guilty. 06-029 ##

Appendix I

United States v. Bellomo, 944 F. Supp. 1160 (S.d.n.y. 1996)

US District Court for the Southern District of New York - 944 F. Supp. 1160 (S.D.N.Y. 1996)
October 30, 1996

944 F. Supp. 1160 (1996)

UNITED STATES of America,

v.

Liborio BELLOMO, Defendant.

No. 96 Cr. 430(LAK).

United States District Court, S.D. New York.

October 30, 1996.

*1161 *1162 Nelson Boxer, Assistant United States Attorney, Mary Jo White, United States Attorney, New York City, for U.S.

Benjamin Brafman, Brafman, Gilbert & Ross, P.C., New York City, for Defendant.

AMENDED MEMORANDUM OPINION

KAPLAN, District Judge.

Defendant Liborio Bellomo is charged in six counts of a sixty-count indictment that accuses various alleged members and associates of the Genovese organized crime family with participating in a variety of criminal activities. The indictment charges that Bellomo was and is the acting boss of the Genovese family and one of the persons responsible for, among other things, resolving disputes among the five organized crime families in New York City.

Bellomo is charged in both racketeering counts of the indictment and is alleged to have participated in three predicate acts of racketeering murder and/or murder conspiracy, extortion and labor racketeering. He is charged in substantive counts with murder and conspiracy to murder in aid of racketeering, as well as extortion. If convicted of the murder charge, Bellomo faces a mandatory term of life imprisonment. The extortion charge carries a maximum term of twenty years imprisonment.

Bellomo initially consented to the entry of a detention order, pursuant to 18 U.S.C. § 3142(e)-(f), by the Magistrate Judge subject to his right later to seek release pending trial. The matter now is before the Court on Bellomo's (a) application for review, pursuant to 18 U.S.C. § 3145(b), of the detention order, and (b) motion to dismiss the indictment, hold unspecified government officers in contempt and for a gag order, all on the basis that a photograph of Bellomo, obtained by the government six years ago pursuant to a grand jury subpoena, appeared in the press.

Discussion

Bail

The government is entitled to detain Bellomo if it establishes "that no condition or combination of conditions will reasonably assure the appearance of the person as required and the safety of any other person and the community ..." 18 U.S.C. § 3142(e). The factors to be considered in making such a determination include the nature and circumstances of the offense, the weight of the evidence against the defendant, the history and characteristics of the defendant, and the nature and seriousness of the danger to any person or the community that would be posed by the defendant's release. The burden of proof is a preponderance of the evidence, except that a finding adverse to the defendant on the safety to other persons and community branch of the standard must **1163** rest on clear and convincing evidence. *Id.* § 3142(f); *United States v. Martir,* 782 F.2d 1141, 1146 (2d Cir. 1986). The Court, moreover, has broad discretion with respect to the manner in which it obtains information bearing on the relevant factors. *Martir,* 782 F.2d at 1145. It may permit the government to proceed, as it has done here, by proffer rather than presenting live testimony. *See United States v. Ferranti,* 66 F.3d 540, 542 (2d Cir.1995); *Martir,* 782 F.2d at 1145. In considering Bellomo›s application, the Court determines the matter *de novo. United States v. Leon,* 766 F.2d 77, 80 (2d Cir.1985).

The Court finds by clear and convincing evidence that Bellomo is a serious risk of flight, that his release would pose a substantial danger to the community, and that no condition or combination of conditions would assure his appearance or adequately protect the community in the event of his release.

Nature and Seriousness of Offenses

Bellomo faces mandatory life imprisonment if convicted on the murder charge. He faces a maximum sentence of twenty years on each of the extortion charges.[1] Bellomo, who is 39 years old, has great incentive to flee prosecution due to the possibility that he will spend the remainder of his life in prison. The fact that Bellomo is accused of murder and extortion is a factor to be considered in determining whether he is a serious danger to the community.

Weight of the Evidence

While defendant's counsel argues that the government's evidence is meager, the Court finds otherwise. According to the government's proffer, which the Court credits for these purposes, a cooperating witness will describe Bellomo's role in directing, approving and/or sanctioning the murder of Ralph DeSimone, who was killed because it was brought to the attention of Bellomo and others that his behavior suggested that he was an informant.

There is strong evidence as well of Bellomo's participation in the alleged extortion of a company known as Enviro Express and in labor racketeering. The government's proffer indicates that a cooperating witness will testify to the extortion and that the government will offer documents showing monthly "consulting" payments to a company said to have been controlled by Bellomo. The Court is advised also that testimony of cooperating witnesses and court-authorized interceptions of oral communications will show that Bellomo was involved in seeking to retain control of Local 46 of the Mason Tenders District Council of Greater New York, control that would enable the Genovese family to receive unlawful labor payments. The Court credits these representations.

Bellomo argues that the government's case on the murder charge is weak. He relies chiefly on reports of two polygraph examiners, who state in substance that they believe that Bellomo was truthful in denying, under polygraph examination, involvement in the DeSimone murder. The Court is unpersuaded.

The polygraph evidence is properly considered on this application, despite its long established inadmissibility in criminal trials,[2] because the rules of evidence do not apply in detention hearings under the Bail Reform Act. 18 U.S.C. § 3142(f). It is important, however, to be clear as to its relevance.

The issue now before the Court is whether there is a risk that Bellomo will flee the jurisdiction or endanger others before the trial can be held, not whether he is guilty or innocent of the charges in the indictment. The polygraph results therefore are relevant only to the extent they bear on whether Bellomo has an incentive to flee or poses a threat to the community.

*1164 *Questionable Admissibility Makes Polygraph Evidence a Weak Counter to a Strong Government Case*

A major significance in a detention hearing of the strength of the government's case is its bearing on the extent to which the defendant has a motive to flee prosecution if released pending trial. All other things being equal, a defendant facing serious potential penalties in the event of conviction is more likely to disappear if the government's case is strong than if an acquittal appears likely.

As noted, the government in this case has strong evidence of Bellomo's guilt on the murder and murder conspiracy charges. It evidently has an eyewitness who will testify to Bellomo's involvement in ordering or approving the charged murder, evidence that is quite likely to be received in evidence at trial.

Bellomo's polygraph evidence, even if it were persuasive as measured by the standard of polygraph tests generally, would not diminish the strength of the government's case sufficiently to mitigate Bellomo's strong incentive to flee. For one thing, as Bellomo's counsel conceded at argument, polygraph evidence never has been admitted in a federal trial in this Circuit, even in the three years since *Daubert v. Merrell Dow Pharmaceuticals, Inc.,* 509 U.S. 579, 113 S. Ct. 2786, 125 L. Ed. 2d 469 (1993). While the admissibility of polygraph evidence in light of *Daubert* perhaps is an open question, *but see Lech,* 895 F. Supp. at 585-86 (characterizing argument as "tenuous"), Bellomo confronts at least a significant possibility that the evidence will be excluded even if it is offered.[3] Moreover, even if admitted, the polygraph results would not be conclusive, and Bellomo still would face the risk that the jury would accept the government›s evidence rather than that of Bellomo›s polygraphers. The polygraph evidence in the best of circumstances therefore would be of questionable value. It does not overcome the government's proof that Bellomo has powerful reasons to disappear.

Although it fails as a rebuttal to the government's showing that Bellomo is a flight risk, polygraph evidence in theory might be relevant also to the determination of whether Bellomo is a danger to the community. The Court has considered the polygraph evidence, to the extent it believes is appropriate, in regard to this issue as well. However, it does not think the evidence is entitled to much weight.

Weaknesses of the Tests Offered by Bellomo

Bellomo offered results of two polygraph examinations, one conducted by Nat Laurendi and the other conducted by the Arthers. The Court declines to rely on the Laurendi results in view of the government's uncontested proffer that Laurendi failed to recognize obvious signs of deception and failed to follow normal and accepted polygraph procedures.

Nor is the Arther test free of problems. To begin with, the Arther test was administered by Catherine A. Arther, but analyzed and reported upon by Richard O. Arther. Such "blind" polygraph results have been found to be particularly prone to errors. *See* Department of Defense, *The Accuracy and Utility of Polygraph Testing* 59 (1984); Donald A. Dripps, *Police, Plus Perjury, Equals Polygraphy,* 86 J. CRIM L. & CRIMINOLOGY 693, 704-05 (1996). Much more significant, however, is the difficulty raised by the nature of the questions asked in the Arther examination and their relationship to the government's theory of the case.

The validity of polygraph evidence is highly dependent on the questions put to the subject by the examiner. Unless the wording of the questions is unequivocally dispositive of the guilt or innocence of the subject, the subject could be truthful in all responses and still be guilty of the crime in question. In examining polygraph evidence, therefore, courts must examine the questions posed with great care. *See Lech,* 895 F. Supp. at 584 (holding polygraph evidence inadmissible due in part to problems with questions posed). In particular, it is important that the questions focus on the specific ***1165** factual circumstances at issue rather than calling for the subject's belief as to the legal implications of his actions, as the subject's misunderstanding of the legal implications may yield a false result even where the subject's actions warrant a different conclusion. *Id.*

The government's theory in this case is that Bellomo is guilty of murder or conspiracy to murder because he ordered or sanctioned the killing of DeSimone. The indictment, moreover, does not indicate the manner in which Bellomo is alleged to have done so.

The questions posed in the Arther examination were these:

(1) Did you know of any plan to murder Ralph DeSimone?

(2) Did you murder Ralph DeSimone?

(3) Did you see Ralph DeSimone get murdered?

(4) Five minutes before Ralph DeSimone's body was found at LaGuardia Airport, did you already know he was dead?

Questions 2, 3 and 4 are not even arguably responsive to the government's theory. There is no claim here that Bellomo killed DeSimone himself, saw the killing, or learned before the body was found that the killing had been carried out. Question 2, moreover, disregards the alleged act or acts (*e.g.,* ordering or sanctioning the killing) in favor of a conclusory statement concerning legal implications (*i.e.,* whether the subject's conduct constituted the crime of murder). If a subject incorrectly believed that one is guilty of murder only if one directly takes the life of another, the subject could "pass" a polygraph examination on that question even if one had ordered another person to carry out a killing. Further, Bellomo overlooks the fact that his answer to Question 4 was characterized by his own examiner as "irregular and erratic." (Def.Mem.Ex. 1)

Question 1 appears to present a closer issue, but only at first blush. An individual might order or sanction a killing by another while remaining ignorant of the details by which the killing was, or was to be, carried out. If such a person regarded a "plan" to kill another person as the details about the time, place and manner in which the killing was to be accomplished, he or she "truthfully" might deny knowledge of a plan to commit the murder despite the commission of acts warranting the legal conclusion that he or she is guilty of murder. Indeed, Henry II of England did public penance for the murder of St. Thomas à Becket by his minions, who acted without Henry's knowledge in response to his question, "Who will rid me of this meddlesome priest?"

In sum, Bellomo's answers to each of the questions on the Arther polygraph test all might have been "true" in the sense that Bellomo subjectively believed that they were factually accurate, and they still would not necessarily contradict any of the government's proffered evidence. For this reason, among others, the Court finds this polygraph examination of little value.[4]

Defendant's Argument on Probable Accuracy of Tests is Incorrect

Bellomo argues next that his polygraph evidence is especially probative of his innocence because two separate defendants, Bellomo and Generoso, "passed" polygraph tests in which they denied involvement with the murder. Starting with an assumption of a maximum error rate of 30 percent for polygraph tests, the defense argues that the error rate in this case is at most 15 percent because the likelihood of both defendants' deceiving the examiner is half the normal error rate. Defendant's argument is flawed, however, in that the guilt or innocence of each defendant is an entirely separate matter even though the government's theory links them in the commission of the murder. Either defendant could be unrelated to the ***1166** crime, and the other still could be guilty. Each defendant was examined as to an independent event, his own involvement with the alleged murder. Both might not, therefore, be misleading the examiner if both denied involvement with the murder and both passed the test. In such a case, the possibility that Bellomo›s test was flawed still would be up to 30 percent, as the answers given by each defendant are wholly independent of each other.

History and Characteristics of the Defendant

The defendant has submitted voluminous evidence to the effect that he is a good and caring father, a good neighbor, a person with ties to his community, and a patron of charitable causes. He points also to the fact that he has had only one minor criminal conviction in his past. There is no reason to doubt these assertions.

Seriousness of Danger to any Person or the Community

Bellomo argues that his release on bail would pose no danger to the community. He contends that there is "no evidence whatsoever that Mr. Bellomo engaged in any act of violence *after* 1991, nor is there *any* proof that he poses a danger *now*." (Def.Mem. at 51) (emphasis in original). The argument is without merit.

To begin with, Bellomo stands accused of murder and other serious crimes. On the basis of the government's proffer, there is substantial reason to believe that he will be convicted. While the Bail Reform Act clearly does not require that one charged with such crimes be detained, or even that such persons should be detained if the evidence of the charged crime is strong. It would be foolish to suggest that the Court must ignore the crimes charged and the evidence of guilt in making its own independent, case-by-case assessment of danger. Nor is the dangerousness of a defendant determined solely by looking at the acts charged in the indictment. There is no requirement of a nexus between the charged conduct and the basis of a court's conclusion that a defendant is a serious danger to the community. *United States v. Ferranti*, 66 F.3d 540, 542 (2d Cir.1995); *United States v. Rodriguez*, 950 F.2d 85, 88 (2d Cir.1991); *United States v. Quartermaine*, 913 F.2d 910, 917 (11th Cir. 1990); *United States v. Colombo*, 777 F.2d 96, 99-100 (2d Cir.1985). This Court therefore may look beyond the charged conduct to assess the degree of danger that the defendant poses.

The government here asserts and Bellomo has not denied that Bellomo is the acting boss of the Genovese crime family. This is extremely significant. As the Court of Appeals said in *United States v. Colombo,* 777 F.2d at 98, the leader of a criminal enterprise with the ability to order members of that enterprise to engage in criminal actions may be a danger to the community despite the lack of evidence that he directly participated in many, if any, of the charged crimes. *Accord, United States v. Orena,* 986 F.2d 628, 632 (2d Cir.1993).

The evidence at hand persuades this Court by clear and convincing evidence that Bellomo's release would pose a substantial danger to the community. This finding, moreover, is confirmed by although it stands independently of Bellomo's actions in relation to the polygraph examinations.

Polygraph examinations involve measurement of such physical signs as heart rate, blood volume and, in some subjects, galvanic skin responses while subjects respond to questions. The government has proffered evidence that Bellomo instructed Michael Resnick, another inmate in the institution in which Bellomo is incarcerated pending trial, to put aside Resnick's prescribed tablets of lithium so that Bellomo could ingest the tablets in an effort to "beat" the polygraph tests by reducing his reaction to the examiners' questions. Prison records corroborate this information to the extent that they show that Resnick was on a course of approximately 300 mg of lithium daily before Bellomo's first polygraph examination, that he asked before Bellomo's first examination to see the psychiatrist for the purpose of increasing his dosage, and that his dosage thereafter was doubled. Moreover, another entry in the prison medical records shows that Resnick was caught trying to carry medication away from the area in which it was dispensed just one ***1167** week before Bellomo›s first examination. It thus appears that Bellomo sought to improve his prospects on the polygraph examinations by ingesting a drug which he thought would assist in producing the desired results.

Bellomo counters that all of this is a fantasy. He argues that lithium would not assist one in "beating" a polygraph examination because it would affect the subject's responses to both control and other questions equally and then only if substantial quantities were taken over a significant time period. He notes that the government's proffer, even if credited, dates the earliest effort to obtain lithium too close to the first polygraph examination for the lithium to have had any effect. Moreover, he points to the fact that the government's test of samples of his hair failed to confirm ingestion of lithium and was inconsistent with the ingestion of substantial quantities over an extended period.

Bellomo's arguments are beside the point. The Court assumes that lithium would affect polygraph examinations, if at all, only if taken in substantial quantities over an extended period and that Bellomo did not do so. The government's proffer indicates, however, that Bellomo thought that lithium would help him "beat" the examinations and sought a supply for that purpose. And that is what is important. For the Court finds that Bellomo tried to procure and probably took lithium, albeit took it in insufficient quantities to show up in the government's test, in a devious effort to deceive both the examiners and the Court. This attempt, misguided and unsuccessful as it may have been, is evidence of consciousness of guilt and willingness to engage in chicanery to subvert the due course of justice. It therefore is highly probative of defendant's danger to the community.

Adequacy of Release Conditions

The defendant has proposed a bail package consisting of a $2 million, fully secured bond, a personal recognizance bond, and extensive restrictions on his person including electronic monitoring and house arrest. This package, however, is manifestly insufficient.

As in *Colombo* and *Orena,* the nature and extent of the danger that Bellomo presents arises not only from the threat of violent acts on his part, but from his position of leadership in a criminal organization and his ability to plan, order, and supervise criminal activity arising from that position as well. He is a danger at least as much for what he might direct or assist others in doing as for what he might do himself. Keeping him under house arrest would not defuse this danger. Outside of jail, Bellomo might find a number of ways to get orders to his associates. The proposed supervision would be inadequate, and the proposed electronic surveillance could be circumvented. *United States v. Gotti,* 776 F. Supp. 666, 672-73 (E.D.N.Y.1991). The government is not obligated to replicate a jail in Bellomo's home so that he can be released. *Orena,* 986 F.2d 628 at 632; *Gotti,* 776 F. Supp. at 672. Incarceration therefore is the only viable method to ensure that Bellomo is unable to carry out criminal activity that will endanger persons in the community. *See Colombo,* 777 F.2d at 99; *Orena,* 986 F.2d at 632; *Ferranti,* 66 F.3d at 544 (all holding that leaders of criminal groups could not be released because the danger that they presented due to their ability to direct others to engage in criminal activities could not be controlled by bail conditions). Similar considerations warrant this Court›s conclusion that such means could not ensure Bellomo›s appearance at trial.

In consequence, the Court finds, by clear and convincing evidence, that neither the proposed package, nor any other conditions adequately would secure the appearance of the defendant and the safety of the community.

The Grand Jury Secrecy Issues

Bellomo claimed also that the indictment should be dismissed, government officials held in contempt, and a gag order imposed in consequence of an alleged breach by the government of grand jury secrecy.

In or about March 1990, Bellomo was subpoenaed to appear at the offices of the FBI ***1168** and to allow himself to be photographed in connection with a grand jury investigation then pending. He did so. Copies of the photograph appeared in the *New York Daily News* on December 12, 1993 and in August 1996.

The government acknowledges that the photograph was grand jury material the confidentiality of which is protected by FED. R.CRIM.P. 6(e), but contends that its disclosure was inadvertent. It has presented a declaration by an Assistant United States Attorney in the Civil Division of the Southern District of New York stating that the photograph was appended to a witness" affidavit filed in a civil case in February 1993 to confirm the identity of a person identified by the witness only as "Barney." The photo and the declaration to which it was attached were filed with the court and served on Bellomo's counsel in the civil action. The photograph again was attached to a declaration by the same witness in 1994 in another civil action.

The photograph does not indicate on its face that it was obtained pursuant to a grand jury subpoena, and the AUSA has affirmed that she did not know until recently that the photograph was obtained pursuant to such a subpoena. She states that the disclosure of the photo was completely inadvertent. Bellomo's counsel accepted the government's explanation of the photo's release at oral argument.

Dismissal of the indictment for prosecutorial misconduct is an exceedingly rare sanction. It is granted only where "it is impossible to restore a criminal defendant to the position that he would have occupied vis-a-vis the prosecutor" or "when the pattern of misconduct is widespread or continuous." *United States v. Fields*, 592 F.2d 638, 648 (2d Cir.1978). In the Rule 6(e) context, the movant first must establish a *prima facie* case of a violation of Rule 6(e). *United States v. Rioux*, 97 F.3d 648 (2d Cir.1996). In determining whether a *prima facie* case is presented, a court should examine, inter alia, "(1) whether the media reports disclose matters occurring before the grand jury; (2) whether the media report discloses the source as one prohibited under Rule 6(e); and (3) evidence presented by the Government to rebut allegations of a violation of Rule 6(e)." *Id.* Even if a *prima facie* case is established, dismissal should be granted only if a violation substantially influenced the decision to indict or if there is grave doubt regarding the absence of such substantial influence. *Id.*

(citing *Bank of Nova Scotia v. United States,* <u>487 U.S. 250</u>, 256, 108 S. Ct. 2369, 2374, 101 L. Ed. 2d 228 (1988)).

Here there is no evidence that the release of the photo in question influenced the grand jury's decision to indict. Indeed, the first public appearance of the photograph occurred three years before, and the second after, the indictment was returned. Accordingly, there is no basis for dismissing the indictment on the basis of the inadvertent Rule 6(e) violation.

Defendant's motion calls also for the Court to hold the government in contempt for their violation of Rule 6(e), which provides that a knowing violation may be punished by contempt. The Court does not find the government to be in contempt in view of the sworn explanation, which all parties accept, that the releases of the photo were accidental. While the government should not be lauded for such mistakes, they are not a basis for holding the government in contempt.

The Court sees no need to impose a gag order at this stage. It assumes that all parties and counsel will comply with S.D.N.Y.CRIM.R. 7 and that counsel will discharge their obligations under the Code of Professional Responsibility.

Conclusion

For the foregoing reasons, Bellomo's motion to dismiss the indictment and for other relief is denied in all respects. Bellomo is committed to the custody of the Attorney General for confinement in a corrections facility separate, to the extent practicable, from persons awaiting or serving sentences or being held in custody pending appeal. He shall be afforded reasonable opportunity for private consultation with counsel. The person in charge of the corrections facility in which Bellomo is confined shall deliver him ***1169** to a United States marshal for the purpose of appearances in connection with court proceedings.

SO ORDERED.

Appendix J

United States v. Bellomo, 954 F. Supp. 630 (S.D.N.Y. 1997)

U.S. District Court for the Southern District of New York - 954 F. Supp. 630 (S.D.N.Y. 1997)

January 17, 1997

954 F. Supp. 630 (1997)

UNITED STATES of America,

v.

Liborio BELLOMO, et al., Defendants.

Nos. 96 CR 430(LAK), S1 96 CR 430(LAK).

United States District Court, S.D. New York.

January 17, 1997.

*631 *632 *633 *634 *635 Nelson Boxer, Maria Barton, Assistant United States Attorneys, Mary Jo White, United States Attorney, Jack Litman, Litman, Asche, Gioella & Bassin, Michael Ross, LaRossa, Mitchel & Ross, New York City, for Defendant Liborio Bellomo.

David Breitbart, Alan S. Futerfas, New York City, for Defendant Michael Generoso.

Jeffrey Hoffman, Hoffman & Pollack, New York City, for Defendant James Ida.

Alan Polak, New York City, for Defendant Nicholas Frustaci.

Mark Herman, Herman & Beinin, New York City, for Defendant John Schenone.

Joel Winograd, Winograd & Winograd, New York City, for Defendant Anthony Pisapia.

Lisa Scolari, New York City, for Defendant Thomas Barrett.

Gerald LaBush, New York City, for Defendant James Pisacano.

Paul Brenner, for Defendant Joseph Pisacano.

Diarmuid White, New York City, for Defendant Vincent Romano.

Phyllis Mingione, New York City, for Defendant Colombo Saggese.

Michael Washor, New York City, for Defendant Louis Zacchia.

Kenneth Wirfel, New York City, for Defendant Leonard Cerami.

Ralph Fresolone, Hauppauge, NY, for Defendant Michael Autuori.

Howard Jacobs, for Defendant Louis Ruggiero, Sr.

Harold Borg, Kew Gardens, NY, for Defendant Albert Setford.

David Wikstrom, for Defendant Vincent Batista.

OPINION

KAPLAN, District Judge.

The original indictment in this case contains sixty counts against a total of 19 defendants. The superseding indictment charges ten of those defendants with much the same offenses. This opinion disposes of the defendants' pretrial motions with respect to both indictments to the extent those motions were not resolved previously.[1] The matters remaining for decision include motions to (1) suppress wiretap evidence from a cellular telephone; (2) dismiss a racketeering act on the ground that it does not state an offense; (3) dismiss a racketeering act on double jeopardy or collateral estoppel grounds; (4) sever the trials of various defendants; (5) dismiss the forfeiture allegations in the indictment as to certain defendants; and (6) vacate the pretrial restraint of certain defendants' substitute assets.

Facts

The core of the indictments are charges under the Racketeer Influenced and Corrupt Organizations Act, 18 U.S.C. § 1961 *et seq.* ("RICO"). The enterprise is the alleged Genovese organized crime family, said to be one of the five "families" that reportedly dominate organized crime in the New York area. Twelve of the defendants,[2] including all ten named on the superseding indictment, are said to be members or associates of the family. They are charged in counts one and two with conspiring to conduct and conducting the affairs of the enterprise through a pattern of racketeering activity including murder, conspiracy to murder, solicitation to *636 murder, extortion, attempted labor racketeering, operation of illegal bookmaking and gambling businesses, loansharking, money laundering, mail and wire fraud, obstruction of justice, and interstate transportation of stolen property. 18 U.S.C. §§ 1962(c), 1962(d). Other counts of the indictments charge these defendants with a wide variety of substantive offenses, all or most of which are alleged as RICO predicate acts in the first two.

The seven other defendants are not charged with violation of RICO. Louis Ruggiero, Sr. is charged in counts nine and ten with murder and conspiracy to murder, although the murder and murder conspiracy are charged as RICO predicate acts against certain other defendants. In counts sixteen through twenty-one, Albert Setford, Colombo Saggese, Joseph Pisacano, James Pisacano, Vincent Batista, and Vincent Romano, in addition to a number of the RICO defendants, are charged with conducting illegal bookmaking businesses and/or transmitting wagering information via wire.

Discussion

Defendants' Motions to Suppress Communications Intercepted Over Ida's Cellular Phone

In an order dated November 3, 1994, Honorable Milton Pollack authorized, for thirty days, the interception of communications on a cellular phone registered to a company named IPPI and used by James Ida. Judge Pollack subsequently renewed this order for another thirty days on December 7, 1994. James Ida, Liborio Bellomo and Michael Generoso move to suppress the conversations intercepted under these orders on a variety of grounds.

Ida's Motion

Alleged Lack of Probable Cause Initial Application

Ida seeks to suppress first on the ground that there was no probable cause for the issuance of the initial order.

As an initial matter, the Court notes that Judge Pollack's determination that probable cause existed for the interceptions is entitled to substantial deference. *See United States v. Wagner,* 989 F.2d 69, 72 (2d Cir. 1993) ("[a] reviewing court must accord substantial deference to the finding of an issuing judicial officer that probable cause exists."). Therefore, if this Court determines that Judge Pollack had a substantial basis for his finding of probable cause, Ida›s argument must be rejected. Furthermore, any doubt about the existence of probable cause will be resolved against the challenge to Judge Pollack›s determination. *See Illinois v. Gates,* 462 U.S. 213, 237 n. 10, 103 S. Ct. 2317, 2331 n. 10, 76 L. Ed. 2d 527 (1983).

Probable cause is not an especially demanding standard in this context. "'Only the probability, and not the prima facie showing, of criminal activity is the standard of probable cause.'" *Id.* at 235, 103 S. Ct. at 2330 (quoting *Spinelli v. United States,* 393 U.S. 410, 419, 89 S. Ct. 584, 590-91, 21 L. Ed. 2d 637 (1969)). In assessing the proof presented by the government on the issue of probable cause, the court must "make a practical, common-sense decision whether, given all the circumstances set forth in the affidavit before [it], including the `veracity' and `basis of knowledge' of persons supplying hearsay information, there is a fair probability that contraband or evidence of a crime will be found in a particular place." *Id.* In other words, the government›s affidavit in support of probable cause "must be read as a whole, and construed in a realistic and common sense manner, so that its purpose is not frustrated." *United States v. Ruggiero,* 824 F. Supp. 379, 398 (S.D.N.Y.1993), *aff'd,* 44 F.3d 1102 (2d Cir.1995) (citing *United States v. Harris,* 403 U.S. 573, 577-79, 91 S. Ct. 2075, 2078-80, 29 L. Ed. 2d 723 (1971)).

Ida attempts to pick apart the government's presentation to Judge Pollack. However, his argument ignores the admonition of cases like *Ruggiero* and *Gates* that a court must look at the government›s support for probable cause as a whole. The affidavit taken as a whole clearly provided an ample basis for Judge Pollack›s finding.

The government's initial application to Judge Pollack was based upon a detailed affidavit of FBI Agent Campi. The proof of probable cause was substantial. Reliable informants ***637** stated that Ida was a high ranking member, the "consigliere," of the Genovese crime family. These sources, two of whom were identified by name and their previous reliability detailed, told the FBI that Ida held regular Monday night meetings to discuss illegal activities. The informants stated also that Ida held conversations while taking walks out-of-doors (so called "walk-and-talks") so that his conversations could not easily be recorded. Observation by law enforcement agents confirmed the existence of the walk-and-talks. Moreover, some law enforcement agents related having overheard portions of conversations during walk-and-talks that seemed criminal in nature.

The government's affidavit established that Ida was using the cellular phone to contact members and associates of the Genovese crime family. Although the phone was registered in the name of IPPI, toll records and pen registers showed that the majority of calls from the phone were to organized crime figures, none of whom was associated with IPPI, and to Ida's family, not to commercial establishments. Furthermore, an intercepted conversation from another source showed that Ida was using the cellular phone to set up the Monday meetings of his criminal crew.

The affidavit demonstrated substantial basis for belief that this crew was involved in numerous criminal activities including illegal gambling, loansharking, and robbery. Electronic surveillance had revealed conversations dealing with the cellular telephone targets concerning these illegal activities, and sources informed that the crew was engaged in such activity. This evidence, taken as a whole, constituted a strong showing that Ida had used, and would continue to use, the cellular phone to discuss the various criminal activities specified in the government's application.

In addition, the affidavit adduced evidence suggesting that Ida used the phone to communicate about alleged money laundering. It gave reason to believe that Ida had income beyond his means and that he apparently used other persons' names to hide his assets. Specific incidents of Ida's apparent use of others' names in purchasing expensive items were shown, some involving James Hickey, a principal in IPPI. Furthermore, information possibly linking Hickey to previous Genovese money laundering schemes was presented. While Ida argues that IPPI was a legitimate business, the FBI's showing of Ida's suspiciously large net worth and his penchant for making large purchases in other people's names, coupled with Hickey's alleged complicity in hiding assets for Ida as well as others, established probable cause to believe that money laundering would be discussed over the cellular phone.

Alleged Lack of Probable Cause First Renewal

Ida challenges also the first renewal order authorizing the continued interception of conversations over the cellular phone. He takes issue with the evidence that the government produced to support the renewal, claiming that it all had an innocent explanation. The government counters that although the conversations, if taken alone, might be explained away, they demonstrated probable cause when looked at in context and with the aid of an expert's interpretation of their meaning.

In addition to incorporating all of the information contained in the initial application, the affidavit executed by Agent Campi in support of the renewal referenced a number of intercepted conversations that were said to illustrate Ida's participation in the affairs of the crime family and his position of control over many of its members. Conversations in which Ida told certain crime family members to attend specific meetings suggested that Ida ran the Monday night meetings and that criminal activity was discussed in them. In addition, there were a number of intercepted communications which showed that certain Genovese family members reported to Ida intermittently.

Other, coded conversations were said to show Ida communicating with Bellomo to set up meetings in undisclosed places to discuss, among other things, the alleged head of the Genovese crime family, Vincent "The Chin" Gigante. Several recorded conversations showed Ida discussing business affairs with Hickey in a way that suggested that the two were working out the details of money laundering operations. Finally, a number of conversations *638 were said to show Ida discussing possible labor racketeering activities with an unidentified male.

While the intercepted conversations, considered separately, may not be dispositive of guilt on the particular issues that is not the relevant standard.

The evidence presented in support of the renewal application was sufficient to support Judge Pollack's finding of probable cause as to the cellular phone and the allegedly criminal conversations sought to be intercepted, and so Ida's motion is denied.[3]

Good Faith Exception

Even if probable cause was lacking, the intercepted communications still would escape suppression. Under *United States v. Leon,* 468 U.S. 897, 104 S. Ct. 3405, 82 L. Ed. 2d 677 (1984), evidence gathered pursuant to a warrant which later is found not to have been based on probable cause need not be suppressed if the officers enforcing the warrant relied in good faith on its validity. Although *Leon* does not directly address electronic surveillance, numerous courts have extended its holding to such evidence. *See United States v. Moore,* 41 F.3d 370, 376 (8th Cir.1994), *cert. denied,* ___ U.S. ___, 115 S. Ct. 1985, 131 L. Ed. 2d 872 (1995); *United States v. Malekzadeh,* 855 F.2d 1492, 1497 (11th Cir.1988), *cert. denied,* 489 U.S. 1024, 109 S. Ct. 1149, 103 L. Ed. 2d 209 (1989); *United States v. Ambrosio,* 898 F. Supp. 177, 187 (S.D.N.Y.1995); *United States v. Milan-Colon,* 1992 WL 236218, at *22, *24 (S.D.N.Y. 1992); *United States v. Gambino,* 741 F. Supp. 412, 414-15 (S.D.N.Y.1990); *but see United States v. McGuinness,* 764 F. Supp. 888, 897 n. 2 (S.D.N.Y.1991). This Court sees no principled basis for distinguishing electronic surveillance from other searches and seizures in this respect and therefore agrees that *Leon* applies in these circumstances.

Under *Leon,* evidence obtained pursuant to a warrant which later is found to have been issued without probable cause will be suppressed only if: (1) the issuing judge abandoned his detached, neutral role; (2) the agent was dishonest or reckless in preparing the supporting affidavit for the wiretap order; or (3) the agents› reliance on the warrant was not reasonable. *See Leon,* 468 U.S. at 922-25, 104 S. Ct. at 3420-22.

Ida does not rely on the first *Leon* prong. Rather, he maintains that since probable cause for the warrants so obviously was lacking, the government was reckless in preparing affidavits which maintained that there was probable cause. He makes no allegation that the government included false facts in the affidavit either intentionally or recklessly.

The government's reliance on an order based on the extensive and persuasive showing of probable cause laid out in Agent Campi's affidavits and accepted by Judge Pollack cannot be characterized as unreasonable, even if a court later were to determine that probable cause was lacking. Ida has not demonstrated any lack of good faith on the part of the government. This Court therefore finds that even if probable cause was lacking in the initial and renewal applications presented to Judge Pollack, the good faith exception in *Leon* would compel this Court to deny suppression of the evidence.

Alternative Means of Investigation

Ida claims also that the government failed to demonstrate the inadequacy of alternative investigative means for obtaining the information sought through the wiretap and that its application therefore was insufficient.

As a predicate to approving a wire-tap application, a judge must determine that "normal investigative procedures have been tried and have failed or reasonably appear to be unlikely to succeed or to be too dangerous." 18 U.S.C. § 2518(3) (c). This is far from an insurmountable hurdle. The government must demonstrate only that normal investigative techniques would prove difficult. ***639** It need not show that any other option would be doomed to failure. As the Second Circuit has explained:

"the purpose of the statutory requirements is not to preclude resort to electronic surveillance until after all other possible means of investigation have been exhausted by investigative agents; rather, they only require that the agents inform the authorizing judicial officer of the nature and progress of the investigation and of the difficulties inherent in the use of normal law enforcement methods." *United States v. Torres,* 901 F.2d 205, 231 (2d Cir.), *cert. denied,* 498 U.S. 906, 111 S. Ct. 273, 112 L. Ed. 2d 229 (1990).

"A reasoned explanation, grounded in the facts of the case, and which 'squares with common sense, is all that is required.'" *United States v. Ianniello,* 621 F. Supp. 1455, 1465 (S.D.N.Y.), *aff'd* 808 F.2d 184 (2d Cir. 1985) (quoting *United States v. Shipp,* 578 F. Supp. 980, 989 (S.D.N.Y.1984) (Weinfeld, J.), *aff'd sub nom. United States v. Wilkinson,* 754 F.2d 1427 (2d Cir.), *cert. denied,* 472 U.S. 1019, 105 S. Ct. 3482, 87 L. Ed. 2d 617 (1985)). Additionally, like the issuing judge's determination of probable cause, a determination that the government has made this showing is entitled to substantial deference from a reviewing court. *See id.*

Ida claims that the government's affidavits failed to make this showing because the government had alternative methods with which to observe the Monday night meetings. He contends that the government's claims that it had used all available means of investigation were mere boilerplate that was not sufficient to satisfy the requirements of the statute.

Ida's argument incorrectly assumes that observation of the meetings was the purpose of the wiretap. The wiretap, however, was sought and authorized in order to allow law enforcement officers to intercept conversations regarding certain criminal activity that it believed would take place over Ida's cellular phone. A probable cause showing was made to justify such interceptions. The alternative methods that Ida proposes for surveilling the Monday night meetings would not have aided the government's attempts to hear telephone conversations discussing illegal conduct. The wiretap application was necessary so that this investigative aim could be achieved, and no other technique would have served the same purpose.

Ida's attack on the government's affidavit is equally unavailing. The affidavit describes with specificity a number of other possible techniques that the government might have employed in its efforts and why those techniques probably would not have been effective. It may have been similar in this respect to affidavits presented in support of other applications in this case, but that similarity did not render its language ineffective. Many of the reasons presented by Agent Campi for the authorization of the wiretap are of particular relevance to the Genovese crime family and similar organizations, such as their consciousness of surveillance and the fear of informants to testify. It should come as no surprise that the facts supporting the conclusion that the alternative methods would be unavailing were similar from application to application.

For the reasons explained above, Ida's various arguments for suppression of the evidence intercepted from his cellular phone lack merit. His motion therefore is denied in all respects.

Bellomo and Generoso Motions to Suppress

Defendants Bellomo and Generoso also move for suppression of conversations intercepted from the Ida Cellular phone, arguing that the initial application and its various renewals lacked probable cause.

Standing

As a threshold mater, Bellomo lacks standing to make this motion as to the initial wiretap application. This Court held, in *United States v. Montoya-Eschevarria,* 892 F. Supp. 104, 106 (S.D.N.Y.1995), and in its December 27, 1996 Order in regard to other suppression motions by Ida and Generoso, that a defendant who was not a named target or interceptee of a wiretap must submit proof by affidavit that he or she was overheard on the wiretap in order to establish standing to seek suppression of such evidence. Bellomo does not admit that he was intercepted on Ida's cellular phone. He was neither a target ***640** nor a named interceptee in the initial application. The disputed allegations of the government, or the claim by his attorney that Bellomo often spoke with Ida on the phone, do not establish a sufficient interest in the interceptions for Bellomo to have standing. He must establish that his voice was intercepted. Absent a sworn statement by Bellomo or someone with personal knowledge averring that Bellomo's voice was intercepted on the cellular phone, he lacks standing to seek suppression of the evidence that the wiretap on that phone produced. Bellomo's motion to suppress the fruits of the initial order therefore is denied.

Probable Cause

Bellomo and Generoso argue that they are entitled to suppression of the intercepts involving the Ida cellular phone because the government, although it named them as targets in most of the applications, in fact lacked probable cause to believe that they had committed or were about to commit any offense. [4] The government does not now contend that it demonstrated probable cause with respect to Bellomo or Generoso. Rather, its position is that the Fourth Amendment and the statute require, in the relevant respect, only that there be probable cause with respect to its belief that at least one of the individuals named in the order has committed or is about to commit an offense. [5] As there was probable cause to believe that Ida had committed or was about to commit an offense, the government argues, any lack of probable cause as to Bellomo, Generoso or anyone else named in the application is immaterial.

A logical starting point is the statute, Title III of the Omnibus Crime Control and Safe Streets Act of 1968, 18 U.S.C. §§ 2510-20. In brief summary, Title III requires that an application for authority to intercept electronic communications contain, among other things, "the identity of the person, if known, committing the offense and whose communications are to be intercepted ..." 18 U.S.C. § 2518(b) (iv). A judge may authorize interception upon a determination, insofar as is relevant here, that "there is probable cause for belief that an individual is committing, has committed or is about to commit" a relevant offense. *Id.* § 2518(3) (a). The authorizing order shall specify, among other things, "the identity of the person, if known, whose communications are to be intercepted ..." *Id.* § 2518(4) (a). Within 90 days after the application is made, the judge shall cause a notice to be given to "the persons named in the order or the application, and such other parties to intercepted communications as the judge may determine ..." *Id.* § 2518(8) (d). An "aggrieved person" may move to suppress an communication intercepted pursuant to Title III on the grounds, among others, that the communication was unlawfully intercepted or the order of authorization was insufficient on its face. *Id.* § 2518(10).

The statutory scheme thus makes clear, as the Supreme Court confirmed in *United States v. Kahn,* 415 U.S. 143, 94 S. Ct. 977, 39 L. Ed. 2d 225 (1974), that the government's obligation to name persons in Title III applications is limited to those who, it has probable cause to believe, committed or are about to commit an offense. The government need not seek to discover and name all those who may be overheard.

The next question that logically occurs is as to the consequence, if any, of the government's failure to name in an application a person as to whom probable cause exists. The Court answered that question in *United States v. Donovan,* 429 U.S. 413, 97 S. Ct. 658, 50 L. Ed. 2d 652 (1977). Reasoning that the naming requirement of Section 2518(1) (b) (iv) does not play "a central, or even functional role in guarding against unwarranted use of wiretapping or electronic surveillance," the Court held that suppression is not required in such circumstances. *Id.* at 437-40, 97 S. Ct. at 673-74 (quoting ***641** *United States v. Chavez,* 416 U.S. 562, 578, 94 S. Ct. 1849, 1857, 40 L. Ed. 2d 380 (1974) (internal quotation marks omitted)). While *Donovan* is not dispositive here because this case is its converse, its conclusion with respect to the significance of the naming requirement does tend to suggest that the mistaken naming of a person in an application does not warrant suppression. This is confirmed by the cases that have dealt with the issue.

In *United States v. Shipp,* 578 F. Supp. 980 (S.D.N.Y.1984), Judge Weinfeld rejected substantially the same argument made by Bellomo and Generoso here. Stitmon, one of the movants, sought suppression on the ground that there was no probable cause to believe that he was involved with the suspected criminal activity of another target of the interceptions. *Id.* at 984, 986. But Judge Weinfeld denied the motion on the ground that it misstated the requirements of probable cause. He pointed out that "[t]here is no requirement that probable cause be established with respect to every defendant ultimately indicted" and that the probable cause requirement in the wiretap context is "satisfied by identification of the telephone line to be tapped and the particular conversations to be seized." *Id.* at 986-87 & n. 18.

Other cases are to the same effect. In *United States v. Martin,* 599 F.2d 880 (9th Cir.1979), the Ninth Circuit affirmed the denial of a motion to suppress that was based on the contention that a Title III applicant must establish probable cause as to every probable interceptee, holding that neither the Fourth Amendment nor Title III imposes any such requirement. *Id.* at 884-85. Several other judges of this Court have reached the same conclusion. *United States v. Ambrosio,* 898 F. Supp. 177, 183-85 (S.D.N.Y. 1995); *United States v. Milan-Colon,* No. S2, S3 91 Cr. 685(SWK), 1992 WL 236218, at *16 (S.D.N.Y. Sept. 8, 1992); *United States v. McGuinness,* 764 F. Supp. at 899-900.

This is an entirely sensible result. The Supreme Court already has held in *Donovan* that the failure to name in a Title III application a person as to whom the government has probable cause does not require suppression. As the shelves of reported cases dealing with the issue in a myriad of factual contexts demonstrates, the question whether probable cause exists in particular circumstances often is an exceedingly close judgment as to which reasonable minds may differ. By requiring suppression if the government mistakenly characterizes as probable cause its showing as to a particular interceptee, the courts would provide an incentive for the government to call all the close cases against naming the individual, as it thereby would ensure admissibility by the omissions, at least if the omissions were reasonable. This would disserve the interests the statute was designed to serve because the effect of the omission would be that the intercepted whose name was omitted would not be entitled, as a matter of right, to the notice contemplated by Section 2518(8) (d). *See Martin,* 599 F.2d at 885; *Ambrosio,* 898 F. Supp. at 184.

Accordingly, the motions of Bellomo and Generoso to suppress the product of the Ida cellular telephone intercepts on the ground that the government lacked probable cause to believe that they had engaged or were about to engage in criminal activity are denied.

Bellomo's Request for a Franks Hearing

Bellomo asks also that the Court grant a hearing under *Franks v. Delaware,* 438 U.S. 154, 171-72, 98 S. Ct. 2674, 2684-85, 57 L. Ed. 2d 667 (1978), to determine whether Bellomo was misidentified as one of the persons intercepted over Ida's cellular phone. To warrant a *Franks* hearing, a defendant must make a "substantial preliminary showing" that the misidentification arises from the identifying agents "deliberate falsehood or ... reckless disregard for the truth." *Id.*

Bellomo has offered an affidavit by one of his attorneys who, after an "in-depth firsthand examination of the tapes on which Bellomo's voice purportedly appears," claims that the government's identification of Bellomo is incorrect. (Bellomo Reply Mem. 11-12) Bellomo argues that since his lawyer swears that Bellomo was misidentified, and since his misidentification allegedly was critical to a determination of probable cause, he is entitled to a hearing to determine whether the identifying agent was reckless.

*642 The opinion of Bellomo›s attorney that the voice on the tape is not Bellomo›s, even if correct, is not enough to raise an issue of fact as to whether the agent deliberately or recklessly identified Bellomo. Absent some other evidence, there is no reason to believe that any error, if error there was, was anything but a mistake insufficient to raise a *Frank's* problem.

Ida's Motion to Dismiss Racketeering Act 7(a)

Racketeering Act 7(a) in the RICO counts alleges that defendant James Ida and others committed extortion by:

"obtaining property, that is, the right of a labor organization's members to free speech and democratic participation in union affairs ... and to loyal and responsible representation by the members' union officers ... from and with the consent of officers and employees of [said union] which consent would have been and was induced by the wrongful use of actual and threatened force, violence, and fear...."

in violation of the Hobbs Act.[6] Ida seeks to have Racketeering Act 7(a) dismissed on the ground that the union members› rights are not "property" within the meaning of Section 1951(b) (2) and so his alleged actions do not state a violation of the statute.

Ida's argument is flatly contrary to the established law in this Court. Every judge in this district to consider the matter has found that union members' rights to free speech and democratic participation in union affairs are property for the purposes of the Hobbs Act. *See United States v. Local 1804-1,* 812 F. Supp. 1303, 1335 (S.D.N.Y. 1993), *aff'd in part,* 52 F.3d 1173 (2d Cir. 1995), *cert. denied,* ___ U.S. ___, 116 S. Ct. 934, 133 L. Ed. 2d 861 (1996); *United States v. District Council of New York City,* 778 F. Supp. 738, 754 (S.D.N.Y.1991); *United States v. International Brotherhood of Teamsters,* 765 F. Supp. 1206 (S.D.N.Y.1991), *appeal dismissed,* 1991 WL 346072 (2d Cir. 1991), *cert. denied,* 502 U.S. 1075, 112 S. Ct. 975, 117 L. Ed. 2d 139 (1992); *Rodonich v. Local 95,* 627 F. Supp. 176, 178-79 (S.D.N.Y. 1985). So too have the Third and Sixth Circuits. *See United States v. Debs,* 949 F.2d 199, 201-02 (6th Cir.1991); *United States v. Local 560,* 780 F.2d 267, 281-82 (3d Cir.1985).

Ida presents no directly contrary authority. Rather, he contends that language in *Town of West Hartford v. Operation Rescue,* 915 F.2d 92 (2d Cir.1990), in which the Court of Appeals said that "the term 'property› cannot plausibly be construed to encompass altered official conduct" for Hobbs Act purposes, *id.* at 102, requires the conclusion he advocates. (Ida Reply Mem. 11) He contends too that this result is required by *McNally v. United States,* 483 U.S. 350, 107 S. Ct. 2875, 97 L. Ed. 2d 292 (1987).

The plaintiffs in *Town of West Hartford* contended, *inter alia,* that the defendants, in violation of the Hobbs Act, "extorted" a softer municipal reaction to their protest activities by the threat, among others, that an unaltered municipal policy would require added police expenditures by the town and restrict its ability to provide police protection for other citizens. 915 F.2d at 95-96, 102. The comment relied upon by Ida came in the court›s rejection of that claim. The court went on to say that "virtually any conduct that elicits a governmental response will require activity by ... salaried government employees" and that "[i]t is simply not tenable to translate the activation of such a response into a Hobbs Act obtention of `property.'" *Id.* at 102.

The Circuit's holding in *Town of West Hartford* was a response to an argument, the ***643** logical implication of which would have transformed into a violation of the Hobbs Act almost any conduct which required a governmental body to consider that a response other than that which actually occurred might be more expensive. The Court explicitly adverted to the First Amendment difficulties that such a view might raise. *Id.* at 102. The decision therefore turned on the special difficulties of applying the Hobbs Act in the public context. It cannot be applied uncritically outside that context, as indeed is suggested by the fact that the Court reiterated its prior holding that "`property› under the Act `includes, in a broad sense, any valuable right considered as a source or element of wealth ...'" *Id.* at 101 (quoting *United States v. Tropiano,* 418 F.2d 1069, 1075-76 (2d Cir.1969), *cert. denied,* 397 U.S. 1021, 90 S. Ct. 1258, 1262, 25 L. Ed. 2d 530 (1970)).

This case presents a fundamentally different situation. Unions are not governmental bodies. Their members' rights to participate effectively in their affairs have direct economic value because the advancement of the members' economic interests through collective action is the *raison d'etre* of unions. The history of labor corruption in this country is an eloquent testament to the proposition that the suppression of union democracy often has been closely linked with the sacrifice of the interests of the rank and file to the enrichment of union leaders and those who have corrupted them. Thus, unlike the interest in unaltered official conduct that was put forward in *West Hartford,* the interests at stake in this case, although intangible, are very similar to the intangible economic rights held to be property in cases cited by the *West Hartford* panel. They are, to quote *Tropiano,* "valuable right[s] considered as a source ... of wealth ..." 418 F.2d at 1075-76.

Ida next argues that the Supreme Court's decision in *McNally* which held that the term "property" as used in the mail fraud statute, 18 U.S.C. § 1341, does not include "the intangible right of the citizenry to good government," 483 U.S. at 356, 107 S. Ct. at 2879[7]requires the conclusion that Racketeering Act 7(a) does not state an offense. The argument assumes, of course, that the term "property" as used in the mail fraud statute has the same meaning as in the Hobbs Act, a debatable proposition in view of the different histories of the two statutes. *See Debs,* 949 F.2d at 201 n. 2; *cf. McNally,* 483 U.S. at 356-58, 107 S. Ct. at 2879-81. Even granting that assumption, however, the result that Ida advocates does not necessarily follow for substantially the reasons already discussed the link between tangible economic benefits and the free exercise of union members' rights is considerable stronger than that between such readily recognizable "property" and the honest services of public officials.

In all the circumstances, this Court sees no reason to depart from the considered and established interpretation which courts universally have given to the term "property" in the Hobbs Act. Racketeering Act 7(a) therefore is legally sufficient. Ida's motion is denied.

Schenone's Motion to Dismiss Racketeering Act 32 or for Other Relief

Double Jeopardy

Count one of the indictments alleges a conspiracy to conduct the affairs of the alleged enterprise through a pattern of racketeering activity in violation of 18 U.S.C. § 1962(d). Count two alleges that specified defendants actually conducted the affairs of the alleged enterprise through a pattern of racketeering in violation of 18 U.S.C. § 1962(c). Racketeering Act 32, which is incorporated in counts one and two in the original indictment (Racketeering Act 35 of counts one and two of the superseding indictment), alleges that:

"It was a part of the pattern of racketeering activity that from on or about November 1, 1994, through in or about April 1995, in the Southern district of New York and elsewhere, James Ida ..., and John Schenone ..., and others known and unknown, unlawfully, willfully, and knowingly did ***644** transport in interstate and foreign commerce a good, namely, a Caterpillar 950B Front End Loader, having a value in excess of $5,000, knowing the same to have been stolen and converted, in violation of Title 18, United States Code, Sections 2314, and 2."

Defendant John Schenone seeks dismissal of this racketeering act, claiming that its inclusion in these indictments would subject him to double jeopardy or is precluded by collateral estoppel. Alternatively, he seeks the unsealing of the grand jury minutes.

The operative facts may be stated briefly. In May 1995, Schenone was arrested and charged in the Eastern District of New York with conspiring to transport stolen property during the period beginning in October 1994 and continuing until May 11, 1995. (*See* Schenone Mem.Ex. A) Insofar as is relevant here, the overt act with which he was charged involved the theft of a front end loader on December 15, 1994. Schenone pleaded guilty on July 14, 1995.[8] He was sentenced after the court received a presentence report in which the Probation Office stated the view that the offense was unrelated to organized crime activities of the Colombo family, which then were the subject of a separate investigation.

The RICO conspiracy with which Schenone is charged in this case allegedly commenced in 1980 and continued to the date of the present indictments, June 1996 in the case of the original indictment and December 1996 in the case of the superseder. The racketeering act in these indictments to which Schenone objects involved the same front end loader that was a subject of the Eastern District case. The last predicate act with which Schenone is charged in this case is said to have occurred in March 1995. (*See* Gov.Mem. 146)

Schenone contends that the indictment, in order to pass double jeopardy muster, must "allege `some type of post-plea unlawful conduct' on the part of the defendant or `post-plea accumulation of evidence' which establishes a second predicate offense or participation in a criminal enterprise." (Schenone Mem. 4) (Quoting *United States v. Persico,* 620 F. Supp. 836, 844 (S.D.N.Y.1985) (*"Persico I"*)) He argues that he is entitled to dismissal of this racketeering act because the indictments in this case do not allege any predicate act by, or the accumulation by the government of pertinent evidence against, him after the date of his guilty plea in the Eastern District of New York.

It is helpful in dealing with Schenone's argument to begin with the language in *Persico I* upon which Schenone relies. The indictment in that case charged four of the defendants with substantive violations of, and conspiracy to violate, RICO. Eight of the alleged racketeering acts involved a bribery scheme. All of the moving defendants previously had been convicted of one offense or another relating to that scheme. The question presented was whether a defendant previously convicted of an offense later could be charged in a RICO indictment with a predicate offense consisting of the previously convicted conduct. The district court applied the analysis laid out in *Garrett v. United States,* 471 U.S. 773, 105 S. Ct. 2407, 85 L. Ed. 2d 764 (1985), where the Court held that a prior felony conviction could be relied upon by the government, consistent with the Double Jeopardy Clause, to support a subsequent continuing criminal enterprise indictment. The district court concluded first that Congress regarded RICO violations as crimes separate from the predicate offenses and intended separate punishment. 620 F. Supp. at 840-44. And it held that the reliance on prior convicted conduct for predicate offenses in the RICO indictment did not violate the Double Jeopardy Clause because the predicate acts are not lesser included offenses. *Id.* at 844-46. In the course of this analysis, the district court made the observation to which Schenone points:

"Although one or more prior convictions or racketeering acts, obtained pursuant to a plea agreement, are unquestionably valid to support a RICO charge, there must also exist an allegation of either (1) some type ***645** of post-plea unlawful conduct, [*Garrett,* 471 U.S. at 799, 105 S. Ct. at 2422], or (2) a post-plea accumulation of evidence sufficient to establish either a second predicate offense or participation in a criminal enterprise, *see Brown,* 432 U.S. at 169 n. 7, 97 S. Ct. at 2227 n. 7; *cf. Oyler v. Boles,* 368 U.S. 448, 452 n. 6, 82 S. Ct. 501, 505 n. 6, 7 L. Ed. 2d 446 (1962). This test would not, as the Supreme Court cautioned against [in] *Garrett,* leave prosecutors with the untenable choice of having to `choose between prosecuting the [racketeer] on the offense of of which it could prove him guilty or releasing him with the idea that he would continue his [racketeering] activities so that the Government might catch him [again] and then be able to prosecute him on the [RICO] offense.' [471 U.S. at 785-87] 105 S. Ct. at 2415. At the same time, this standard would preclude an ambitious federal prosecutor from scraping together a defendant's two prior pleas to predicate acts and charging him, although he had done nothing other than that for which he had pleaded guilty and was sentenced, under the RICO statute. In so doing, it allows courts to preserve the finality of judgments in criminal prosecutions and protect the defendant from prosecutorial overreaching without needlessly hampering federal prosecutors in their enforcement of federal criminal laws." *Id.* at 844.

The district court proceeded to note, in denying the motions to dismiss, that each of the moving defendants was charged in the RICO indictment before it with "a variety of separate post-plea racketeering acts." *Id.* at 845.

The Second Circuit affirmed *Persico I* on an interlocutory appeal, holding that it had applied *Garrett* correctly. *United States v. Persico,* 774 F.2d 30 (2d Cir.1985) (*"Persico II"*). It specifically noted, however, that:

"We need not and do not decide whether, as Judge Keenan believed, 620 F. Supp. at 840, subsequent RICO charges can survive double jeopardy objections only if the subsequent indictment alleges conduct that post-dates the plea to the prior charges or if evidence, accumulated subsequent to that plea, establishes either a second predicate offense or participation in a criminal enterprise." *Id.* at 32.

The defendants were convicted. On the subsequent appeal, the Second Circuit expressed "serious doubt as to whether evidence of post-plea involvement is necessary to defeat a double jeopardy challenge to RICO convictions based on predicate acts that were the subject of prior guilty pleas." *United States v. Persico,* 832 F.2d 705, 711 (2d Cir.1987) (*"Persico III"*). It was not, however, required to decide the issue in view of the presence of such post-plea involvement in that case. *Id.* at 711-12. Nor has it been compelled to do so in subsequent cases, as each case potentially raising the issue has revealed such post-conviction activity. *United States v. Giovanelli,* 945 F.2d 479, 492 (2d Cir.1991); *United States v. Coonan,* 938 F.2d 1553, 1563 (2d Cir.1991), *cert. denied,* 503 U.S. 941, 112 S. Ct. 1486, 117 L. Ed. 2d 628 (1992); *United States v. Gambino,* 920 F.2d 1108, 1112-12 (2d Cir.1990), *cert. denied,* 502 U.S. 810, 112 S. Ct. 54, 116 L. Ed. 2d 31 (1991); *United States v. Scarpa,* 913 F.2d 993, 1013-14 & n. 8 (2d Cir.1990).

In considering whether the Double Jeopardy Clause bars a subsequent RICO indictment to the extent it alleges prior convicted conduct as a predicate act, it is useful to bear in mind that the *Persico* cases together stand for the proposition that RICO offenses are crimes separate and distinct from the predicate acts of racketeering. As the district court wrote in *Persico I*, "[t] he language, structure and legislative history of RICO ... make Congress› intent ... unmistakably clear." 620 F. Supp. at 841. *Accord, Persico II,* 774 F.2d at 32. This is critical in analysis of the double jeopardy issue.

The Supreme Court wrote in *North Carolina v. Pearce,* 395 U.S. 711, 717, 89 S. Ct. 2072, 2076-77, 23 L. Ed. 2d 656 (1969), and reiterated in *Garrett,* 471 U.S. at 777, 105 S. Ct. at 2410-11, that the Double Jeopardy Clause protects against "a second prosecution for the same offense" after either an acquittal or a conviction and prevents multiple punishment "for the same offense." *Accord, Persico III,* 832 F.2d at 710; *Persico I,* 620 F. Supp. at 839. As a RICO violation is an offense separate and apart from the ***646** predicate acts, it cannot be said that prosecution on RICO charges based on a predicate act which resulted in a prior substantive conviction is a second prosecution, or that a RICO conviction results in multiple punishment, "for the same offense" as the predicate act. That is true irrespective of whether the RICO prosecution, although relying on conduct that resulted in a prior conviction, alleges additional post-conviction conduct. Any different view would be inconsistent with the premise that the RICO offense is an offense distinct from the underlying predicate acts.

To be sure, the language in *Persico I* upon which Schenone relies reflects an additional consideration, concern with prosecutorial overreaching. The government, *Persico I* suggests, ought not to have two bites at the apple, at least if it is or should have been fully aware of the evidence that would be required for the second prosecution at the time of the first. This is a concern that has been adverted to elsewhere in double jeopardy jurisprudence. *E.g., Garrett,* 471 U.S. at 795-96, 105 S. Ct. at 2419-20 (O›Connor, J., concurring); *Ohio v. Johnson,* 467 U.S. 493, 498-99, 104 S. Ct. 2536, 2540-41, 81 L. Ed. 2d 425 (1984); *United States v. DiFrancesco,* 449 U.S. 117, 128, 136, 101 S. Ct. 426, 432-33, 437, 66 L. Ed. 2d 328 (1980). And certainly there is reason to question whether the government should be permitted to subject a defendant to successive trials "affording the prosecution another opportunity to supply evidence which it failed to muster in the first proceeding." *Burks v. United States,* 437 U.S. 1, 11, 98 S. Ct. 2141, 2147, 57 L. Ed. 2d 1 (1978). But this Court doubts that this concern properly may be grounded in the Double Jeopardy Clause in view of a change in the law since *Persico* and, if it may, whether post-plea unlawful conduct is the only means of addressing that concern.

If one accepts, as we must, that (1) the Double Jeopardy Clause does not forbid successive prosecutions for different offenses, and (2) RICO violations are offenses different from the predicate acts they comprehend, there could be only two bases for precluding a RICO prosecution, even in the circumstances postulated by *Persico I* a subsequent RICO violation alleged to consist entirely of two predicate acts, each of which had resulted in a prior conviction on a substantive charge. The first would be that each prior conviction barred subsequent prosecution for another offense involving the same *conduct*. The other would be a notion that the Double Jeopardy Clause requires the government to join in a single indictment all charges then known to it. Neither, this Court concludes, is a tenable proposition, at least as applied in the circumstances of this case.

The first of these possible bases was rejected by the Supreme Court in *United States v. Dixon,* 509 U.S. 688, 113 S. Ct. 2849, 125 L. Ed. 2d 556 (1993), after the conclusion of the *Persico* litigation. *Dixon* expressly overruled *Grady v. Corbin,* 495 U.S. 508, 110 S. Ct. 2084, 109 L. Ed. 2d 548 (1990), and held that the Double Jeopardy Clause does not preclude successive prosecutions for different offenses even where conduct constituting an offense for which the defendant already has been convicted is an essential element of the second alleged crime. Hence, the fact that Schenone already has been convicted of an offense involving the transport of the stolen front loader does not alone preclude a RICO charge which also rests in part on the transport of the front end loader.

This Court is not aware of anything in the Double Jeopardy Clause, and the defendant has cited nothing, that suggests a requirement that the government join all criminal conduct of which it is aware in one indictment save the lesser included offense doctrine, which holds that the government ordinarily may not try a defendant for a more serious offense after it has convicted him of a lesser included offense. *Brown v. Ohio,* 432 U.S. at 168-69, 97 S. Ct. at 2226-27. As *Garrett* suggested, however, "'lesser included offense› principles of double jeopardy" cannot readily be transposed to "multilayered" conduct such as that at issue here. 471 U.S. at 789, 105 S. Ct. at 2417; *accord, Persico III,* 832 F.2d at 711. If they can be transposed at all, moreover, the transposition must be sensitive to the legitimate interests of law enforcement as well as the concerns of prospective defendants.

*647 Any requirement of joinder must rest on the notion that the Double Jeopardy Clause prohibits the government, with all its resources, from subjecting a defendant to successive trials if the prosecutions, although involving technically different offenses, are sufficiently similar. While *Dixon* precludes the conclusion that any RICO prosecution even a RICO prosecution based exclusively on two predicate acts, each of which had been the subject of a prior convictions the "same offense" as the predicate acts, it perhaps is arguable that the Double Jeopardy Clause is sufficiently broad to protect against successive prosecutions where the defendant allegedly has done little or nothing wrong beyond whatever was the focus of the earlier prosecutions. That indeed seems to have been the principal concern in *Persico I,* where Judge Keenan explained that the standard there proposed "would preclude a federal prosecutor from scraping together a defendant›s two prior pleas to predicate acts and charging him, *although he had done nothing other than that for which he had pleaded guilty and was sentenced,* under the RICO statute." 620 F. Supp. at 844 (emphasis added).

Assuming *arguendo* that the Double Jeopardy Clause embodies such protection, although that is doubtful after *Dixon,* the standard employed must be responsive to the underlying concern. Post-plea criminal conduct or post-plea accumulation of evidence of a second predicate offense could serve the function of depriving the government of two bites at the apple in what otherwise in substance would be the same case. But so too could other circumstances distinguishing a subsequent RICO prosecution from prior prosecutions of predicate acts. Here, for example, Schenone is charged with racketeering acts including participation in a murder conspiracy, solicitation to commit another murder, loansharking, mail and wire fraud in connection with the San Gennaro street festival, and obstruction of justice as well as the unlawful transportation of the stolen front end loader. To suggest that Schenone now is being prosecuted although he is not alleged to have done anything unlawful other than that for which he pleaded guilty previously would be ridiculous. That would be true irrespective of whether any of the predicate acts with which he is charged in this case pre- or post-dates the end of the prior prosecution. There simply is not the degree of congruence between the prior prosecution and this one to justify a serious concern with similar successive prosecutions.

This view is buttressed by the serious issues for law enforcement that would be created were Schenone's argument accepted. If a law enforcement agency conducting complex, lengthy investigations of organized crime were to learn of unlawful conduct by a low or middle ranking figure before the investigation had borne the fruit ultimately hoped for, it would be put to a hard choice in determining whether to prosecute. Prompt prosecution on non-RICO charges would entail the risk that the government would not learn of another predicate act, post-conviction, that would enable it to charge the defendant with the RICO offense that otherwise would be chargeable if the investigation reached a successful conclusion. If the government, on the other hand, were to defer prosecution in order to preserve the RICO option in the event the investigation were successful, however, it would be risking the possibility that the passage of time ultimately would prevent prosecution of the defendant at all should the broader investigation fail. As the Supreme Court indicated in *Garrett,* the Double Jeopardy Clause is not intended to "force the Government›s hand in this manner." 471 U.S. at 789-90, 105 S. Ct. at 2416-17.

Accordingly, the Court holds that Schenone's double jeopardy challenge to the front end loader racketeering act is without merit. Given *Dixon,* the Double Jeopardy Clause does not preclude a RICO prosecution even where all the predicate acts have been the subject of prior prosecutions. If it does limit RICO prosecutions based on predicate acts which have been the subject of prior prosecutions, which this Court doubts, it does so only where the RICO charge overlaps the prior prosecution to an extent far greater than is true here, a point on which the existence of post-prosecution misconduct is relevant but on which it is not dispositive.

*648 Nor need the Court rest at this point with respect to the RICO conspiracy charged in count one. The conspiracy count alleges that Schenone conspired to violate RICO from in or about 1980 until the date of the indictment, June 1996 in the case of the original indictment and December 1996 in the case of the superseder. The essence of the offense of conspiracy is an unlawful agreement, and a conspirator's adherence to a conspiracy continues for its entire duration absent withdrawal. *E.g. United States v. Gotti*, 644 F. Supp. 370 (E.D.N.Y.1986). In consequence, the conspiracy count in these indictments alleges post-plea participation in the RICO conspiracy and thus satisfies the standard articulated in *Persico I*.[9]

For the reasons explained above, this Court finds that the inclusion of the front end loader racketeering act does not violate the Double Jeopardy Clause. Schenone's motion to dismiss the act on double jeopardy grounds is denied.

Collateral Estoppel

Schenone claims also that the inclusion of this racketeering act in the indictments violates principles of collateral estoppel in view of the presentence report in the Eastern District case where, he says, the Probation Office said that the front end loader conspiracy was not related to organized crime. This argument has no merit for several reasons, most notably the fact that Schenone's plea agreement specifically provided that his guilty plea might be used in a future RICO prosecution. What the Probation Department thought of the issue of Schenone's organized crime connections is of no moment.

Grand Jury Minutes

Schenone seeks disclosure of the grand jury minutes under FED.R.CRIM.P. 6(e) (3) (C) (ii), which authorizes a court to disclose grand jury minutes "upon a showing that grounds may exist for a motion to dismiss the indictment because of matters occurring before the grand jury." He contends that disclosure is warranted because the Eastern District presentence report with respect to the previous front loader conviction "shows that predicate act 32 has no place in the instant indictment; [and] that the Government was in possession of facts showing that the offense was not in furtherance and or the employment of racketeering activity." (Schenone Reply Mem. 3) The argument is frivolous because the presentence report says no such thing. It states only that the front loader incident was independent of "a separate organized crime investigation pertaining to [Schenone's] association with known *Columbo* family ... members ..." (Schenone Mem.Ex. B, ¶ 33) (emphasis added) Nothing suggests that the incident was unconnected to the Genovese family.

Schenone has failed to show particularized need for the disclosure of the grand jury minutes. His motion therefore is denied. *See United States v. Moten,* 582 F.2d 654, 662 (2d Cir.1978).

Severance

A number of the defendants have moved under FED.R.CRIM.P. 14 and FED.R.CRIM.P. 8 for severance of their trials.

In considering motions for severance, it is important to bear in mind that "[t]here is a preference in the federal system for joint trials of defendants who are indicted together." *Zafiro v. United States,* 506 U.S. 534, 537-38, 113 S. Ct. 933, 936-37, 122 L. Ed. 2d 317 (1993). However, *United States* ***649** *v. Casamento,* 887 F.2d 1141, 1151-52 (2d Cir.1989), *cert. denied,* 495 U.S. 958, 110 S. Ct. 2564, 109 L. Ed. 2d 746 (1990), altered this preference in multi-defendant trials where the presentation of the prosecution›s case is likely to require more than four months. In such cases, "the judge should oblige the prosecutor to present a reasoned basis to support a conclusion that a joint trial of all the defendants is more consistent with the fair administration of justice than" a division of the case into two or more trials. *Id.,* at 1152. Additionally, "the judge should oblige the prosecutor to make an especially compelling justification for a trial of more than ten defendants." *Id.*

On July 17, 1996, the Court then confronted with 19 defendants and a preliminary estimate that the government's case would last four to six months informed the parties that it would follow the procedures set out in *Casamento* for the determination of severance in multi-defendant RICO trials. It ordered the government to (a) provide the Court with a good faith estimate of the time anticipated to present the governments case; and (b) justification of the need for a trial exceeding four months, and especially a joint trial of more than ten defendants. On October 11, 1996, the government replied that it could not justify a single trial of all the defendants in this case [10] and proposed a severance into two trials, one with ten defendants, and the other with nine. The proposed first trial for which the government's case was estimated to take four months would include defendants Bellomo, Generoso, Ida, Frustaci, Cestaro,[11] Schenone, Pisapia, Zacchia, Cerami, and Ruggiero (the "Principal RICO Defendants"), all of whom would be included in this proposed trial because they are charged with involvement in the same, broad, ongoing criminal enterprise. The proposed second trial would join Barrett, Coiro,[12] and Autuori (the "Secondary RICO Defendants"), all of whom also are named on the RICO counts, together with Saggese, Pisacano, James Pisacano, Setford, Batista, and Romano (the "Gambling Defendants"). The Gambling Defendants are not named on any RICO charges.

Defendants Saggese, Romano, Cestaro, Pisapia, Zacchia, James Pisacano and Joseph Pisacano seek severance beyond that proposed by the government. [13] With the exception of the Pisacanos, all of the moving defendants argue essentially that joining their trials to those of defendants charged with more serious crimes would result in prejudicial spillover and deprive them of their rights to a fair trial. The Pisacanos argue that they are joined improperly in violation of FED.R.CRIM.P. 8(b).

A defendant seeking severance under Rule 14 has the "'extremely difficult burden'" of proving not merely that he would be prejudiced by a joint trial, but that the prejudice would be so great as to deprive him of his right to a fair trial. *Casamento,* 887 F.2d at 1149 (quoting *United States v. Carpentier,* 689 F.2d 21, 27 (2d Cir.1982)); *accord, United States v. Rosa,* 11 F.3d 315, 341 (2d Cir.1993), *cert. denied,* 511 U.S. 1042, 114 S. Ct. 1565, 128 L. Ed. 2d 211 (1994); *United States v. Friedman,* 854 F.2d 535, 563 (2d Cir.1988), *cert. denied,* 490 U.S. 1004,

109 S. Ct. 1637, 104 L. Ed. 2d 153 (1989). Many courts have recognized also that the prejudice to the defendant must be weighed against the benefit to courts and jurors that accrue from joint trials. *See Casamento,* 887 F.2d at 1151 (citing cases); *United States v. Lanza,* 790 F.2d 1015, 1019 (2d Cir.), *cert. denied,* 479 U.S. 861, 107 S. Ct. 211, 93 L. Ed. 2d 141 (1986).

*650 The motions by defendants Pisapia and Zacchia do not show that sufficient prejudice would result from a joint trial to justify severing them from trial with the other Principal RICO Defendants. They argue basically that because they are not named in the most serious charges in the indictment, they would be prejudiced by the presentation of the evidence that tends to establish the more serious crimes. However, "[a] RICO charge allows the government to introduce evidence of criminal activities in which a defendant did not participate to prove the enterprise element." *United States v. Tellier,* 83 F.3d 578, 582 (2d Cir.), *cert. denied,* ___ U.S. ___, 117 S. Ct. 373, 136 L. Ed. 2d 262 (1996). In addition, courts have held that the inclusion in a joint trial of evidence of more serious acts by other members of a criminal organization does not deny another member of that organization a fair trial. *See Rosa,* 11 F.3d at 342. Thus, even if the case against Pisapia and Zacchia were severed, much of the evidence that these defendants object to would be admitted in order to establish the enterprise element of the RICO charge. While counsel argues that this evidence perhaps could be stipulated, in an effort to minimize its damaging effect, there still is little doubt that the government would have the right to put much of the same evidence before the jury in a severed case that it might offer in a joint trial. Thus, even assuming that these defendants would be prejudiced by a joint trial, which the Court does not accept, it is not clear that a separate trial would insulate them from the prejudice they claim they would suffer.

Zacchia and Pisapia may be correct in arguing that the evidence of alleged murders involving other defendants would not be admissible at a separate trial and that such evidence, if admitted without explanation, might prejudice the jury against all defendants in a joint trial. However, numerous courts have held in similar situations that a jury instruction could counteract any possible prejudice to the defendants. The Court will instruct the jury to consider the guilt of each defendant individually and only with regard to the evidence admitted as to that defendant. This instruction will be sufficient to counteract any spillover prejudice from the charges against the other defendants. *See United States v. Hernandez*, 85 F.3d 1023, 1029-30 (2d Cir.1996); *United States v. Zackson*, 6 F.3d 911, 922 (2d Cir.1993); *United States v. Lasanta*, 978 F.2d 1300, 1307 (2nd Cir.1992) ("the district court countered any possible spillover with specific instructions to the jury ... that the jury should consider the evidence separately as to each defendant."); *Casamento*, 887 F.2d at 1153 (instructions to afford each defendant separate consideration leads to finding of no unfair prejudice) (citing *United States v. Carson*, 702 F.2d 351, 367 (2d Cir.1983)); *United States v. Potamitis*, 739 F.2d 784, 790 (2d Cir.), *cert. denied*, 469 U.S. 918, 105 S. Ct. 297, 83 L. Ed. 2d 232 (1984); *United States v. Gallego*, 913 F. Supp. 209, 218 (S.D.N.Y.1996).

In addition to finding no sufficiently serious risk of prejudice from a joint trial, the Court notes that judicial resources will be saved by avoiding another long trial on the RICO enterprise in question in this case. Furthermore, Zacchia and Pisapia are charged with many crimes in common with the RICO defendants, and there is a presumption that these charges should be tried together. The inclusion of Zacchia and Pisapia in the trial with the other Principal RICO Defendants is proper, and their motions for severance are denied.

The motions by defendants Saggese, Romano, and the Pisacanos are markedly different from those of Zacchia and Pisapia. Absent severance, these defendants would face a lengthy trial that would include evidence of a RICO enterprise in which none of them is charged with participating. This evidence might prejudice these defendants significantly because the trial would include a great deal of evidence about an organized crime enterprise and its operations which would not be presented at a separate trial and which is not alleged to have been a part of their criminal activity. Thus, there is clear potential for spillover prejudice in this case. Nor, as the government's proposal nearly concedes, is there any reason to subject these defendants to a lengthy RICO trial, much of which will have nothing to do with them. The Gambling Defendants therefore **651** will be tried separately from the Principal RICO Defendants.

The next question is whether Autuori and Barrett, who are named on the RICO counts, should be tried with the Gambling Defendants, as the government proposes. Doing so would be unfair to the six Gambling Defendants. The Gambling Defendants are alleged to have committed only a small number of violations of the gambling laws, yet the government proposes to have them go through a trial in which a large criminal enterprise will be alleged. This state of affairs would be unnecessarily prejudicial to the Gambling Defendants, and this prejudice suggests that they should not be tried with Autuori and Barrett.

In addition to the unfairness of presenting the RICO evidence at the Gambling Defendants' trial, severance of Autuori and Barrett from the Gambling Defendants is warranted because this Court concludes that judicial economy thus would be served. There simply is no good reason to force the judge in the gambling case to conduct a trial involving various RICO allegations, many of which will be presented in the trial of the Principal RICO Defendants. For all these reasons, the Court directs that the Gambling Defendants be tried separately from Autuori and Barrett.[14]

This leaves the question of how Autuori and Barrett should be tried. The Court has the power, under FED.R.CRIM.P. 13, to order that "two or more indictments ... be tried together" as long as all of the charges against all of the defendants could have been brought in one indictment. Here, the original indictment joined all of the charges against Autuori and Barrett with those against the Principal RICO Defendants, a joinder which neither Autuori nor Barrett claimed was impermissible under Rule 8. A joint trial of the superseding indictment against the Principal RICO Defendants and the original indictment against Autuori and Barrett would serve the interests of judicial economy, as both cases involve the same RICO allegations. A separate trial of Autuori and Barrett alone would be a significant waste of judicial resources. Additionally, Autuori and Barrett would suffer no serious prejudice from a joint trial with the Principal RICO Defendants for the reasons explained in regard to the motions by Zacchia and Pisapia.[15]

Such a joint trial would not raise a *Casamento* problem. With the plea of Cestaro, a joint trial of the Primary and Secondary RICO Defendants now would have only eleven defendants, even assuming no further pleas. Moreover, the Court is convinced that the presentation of the government›s case in such a trial is likely to take less than four months. While the government estimated four months for its case in the trial of the ten Principal RICO Defendants, the estimate assumed that Cestaro would go to trial. He was a major figure in the case. He was charged with seventeen RICO predicate acts (including nine of which no other defendants are accused) and over thirty substantive offenses (including more than a dozen of which no other defendants are accused). His plea took a substantial part of the case out of the trial, thus rendering the four month estimate excessive. Although Barrett, and to a lesser extent, Autuori are charged with some predicate acts unique to them, the incremental trial time added by their inclusion is quite likely to be significantly less than the time saved by Cestaro›s plea. Hence, a trial which includes Autuori and Barrett but not Cestaro is quite likely to be shorter than the government›s estimate before Cestaro›s plea. As the case now stands, the joint trial of Autuori and Barrett should not result in a trial in which the government›s case would exceed the four month guideline set up in *Casamento,* and the Court conceives of no reason why such a joinder should not be ordered.

*652 The government has elected, on the record, to proceed to trial on the superseding indictment, which charges the Principal RICO Defendants. All severance motions with regard to the supersede are denied. As respects the defendants remaining on the original indictment, the trial of defendants Saggese, Joseph Pisacano, James Pisacano, Setford, Batista and Romano is severed from that of Autuori and Barrett. Autuori and Barrett, the remaining defendants on the original indictment, will be tried together with the defendants on the superseding indictment under FED.R.CRIM.P. 13.

The Forfeiture Allegations

Generoso moves to dismiss the forfeiture allegations. Schenone joins in the motion. They contend, first, that the forfeiture allegations fail "to provide notice of the government's claim." (Generoso Mem. 4) Second, they argue that they are improper because they do not allege that any of their property "was derived, directly or indirectly, from the racketeering activity alleged or that any such property is subject to forfeiture." (Generoso Mem. 4) Neither of these arguments has merit.

As Generoso's silence on the point in response to the government's brief seems to recognize, the government quite adequately has put Generoso on notice that his property is subject to forfeiture. The indictment states that Generoso and Schenone have property which constitutes proceeds from racketeering activity and that the government will seek its forfeiture. The indictment further states that the government will seek substitute assets, if necessary, in the amount subject to forfeiture. Generoso has, or shortly will have, a bill of particulars outlining exactly what property is subject to forfeiture.[16] (Gov.Forfeiture Mem. 8-9)

The notice that Generoso and Schenone received was sufficient. As the Court of Appeals reasoned in *United States v. Grammatikos,* 633 F.2d 1013, 1024 (2d Cir.1980):

"Though pleaded in barebones statutory language, the indictment advised appellant that the government would seek forfeiture of virtually all of his property. Furthermore, the bill of particulars identified each item of property deemed susceptible to seizure and enabled appellant to marshal evidence in defense of them. Plainly he was not prejudiced because those properties were specified in a bill of particulars rather than in the indictment itself." 633 F.2d at 1024.

Generoso argues next that the forfeiture allegations fail because they do not allege that Generoso derived any proceeds from the racketeering activity alleged against him. In essence, Generoso claims that the forfeiture allegations cannot apply to him because the indictment specifies certain predicate acts that allegedly resulted in forfeitable property, and Generoso is not charged in any of those predicate acts. He argues that:

"[t]he indictment stakes out a position that the proceeds forfeitable amount to $18,386,000 and that they derive from specific, identified racketeering acts not charged against Mr. Generoso. These other racketeering acts add up to the total forfeitable proceeds of $18,386,000. Thus, it is clear that the indictment deliberately and necessarily excludes the racketeering acts charged against Mr. Generoso from those that produced forfeitable proceeds." (Generoso Mem. 3)

Generoso makes a number of errors in his argument.[17] To begin with, the indictment does not stake out the position that the forfeitable property amounts to $18,386,000. Rather, it states in paragraph 140 that the "Cash Proceeds" of the alleged racketeering enterprise amount to that sum, and in paragraph 139 specifically notes that the forfeitable assets are "not limited to" those listed in **653** paragraph 140. Therefore, his argument that the proceeds sought are limited to those related to the specified racketeering acts is incorrect.[18]

Additionally, Generoso argues that "since [he] is not alleged to have engaged in any racketeering activity that resulted in forfeitable proceeds ... none of his assets is subject to forfeiture." (Generoso Mem. 3) Generoso overlooks paragraph 139, where it is alleged that:

"Through the aforesaid pattern of racketeering activity ... Michael Generoso ... [and the other RICO defendants] have property constituting, and derived from, proceeds which they obtained, directly and indirectly, from racketeering activity in violation of [18 U.S.C. § 1962], thereby making such property, or the amount of cash equivalent thereto, forfeitable to the United States of America."

Paragraph 139 quite adequately alleges that Generoso has forfeitable proceeds. The fact that the specified racketeering counts that gave rise to some of the forfeitable property do not immediately concern Generoso is beside the point. Forfeiture is not sought because of the commission of the predicate acts, it is sought because of the violation of the RICO statute. This count clearly alleges that Generoso has forfeitable assets as a result of a RICO violation.

The motions by Generoso and Schenone to dismiss the forfeiture allegations in the complaint are denied.

Substitute Assets

Generoso and Schenone next argue that the restraint of substitute assets allowed by the post-indictment restraining order issued by Judge Mukasey in this case is improper, and they ask the Court to vacate the order as it pertains to their assets.

In an order dated September 16, 1996, this Court rejected precisely the same argument by defendants Thomas Cestaro and Anthony Pisapia. It there stated that it regarded the issue as foreclosed by *United States v. Regan*, 858 F.2d 115 (2d Cir.1988). Generoso and Schenone acknowledge this, but argue that the Court should reconsider its prior decision based upon *United States v. Gigante*, 948 F. Supp. 279 (S.D.N.Y.1996), which came to a different conclusion.

The *Gigante* court read *Regan* as containing no suggestion that the statute permits "forcible pre-trial restraint of substitute assets over the asset-holder's objection." *Id.* at 281. With great respect, this Court is not persuaded. The *Regan* panel viewed a forcible pretrial restraint on all of the assets of Princeton/Newport which included far more than (a) the interests in Princeton/

Newport of the indicted defendants, and (b) any traceable proceeds of their alleged racketeering activity as within the district court's power, although it went on to express a preference for less extreme measures. 858 F.2d at 120-21. It is true that the restraint was imposed to preserve the value of the defendants' interests in Princeton/Newport, which may well have proved forfeitable, rather than on the theory that Princeton/Newport's entire assets were substitute assets. Nevertheless, if, as Generoso and Schenone argue, the statute simply does not permit pretrial restraint of any assets other than those which themselves are forfeitable pursuant to 18 U.S.C. § 1963(a), the basis for the panel's view of the district court's power is not readily apparent. [19] Moreover, the panel took pains to say that substitute assets should be restrained at least in some circumstances, *id.* at 121, a statement difficult to square with the view that the pretrial restraint of substitute assets is unauthorized.

The Court acknowledges that defendants' arguments, if one were writing on a clean slate, would have force and, indeed, that *Regan* did not address the point at issue here in a parallel factual context. Nevertheless, the logic of *Regan,* in this Court's view, cannot be reconciled with defendants' position. Accordingly, this Court believes defendants' argument is better addressed to the Court of ***654** Appeals, particularly where an erroneous grant of the motion at this level might result in the irremediable dissipation of assets that later may prove forfeitable to the government. The motion therefore is denied.

Government's Motion for an Anonymous Jury

The government moves the Court for an anonymous jury. Specifically, it asks the Court to order that:

"(1) the potential jurors on the voir dire panel, and the jurors and alternates selected, not reveal their names, addresses, or places of employment; (2) during trial, the jurors be kept together during recesses and taken to or provided lunch as a group each day by the United States Marshals Service;

and (3) at the end of each trial day the jurors be transported together by the United States Marshals Service from the Courthouse to an undisclosed central location, from which they can leave for their respective communities." (Gov.Jury Mem. 1)

While the government points out that many courts in this district have granted such requests, empaneling an anonymous jury nevertheless is a measure that should be taken only with care. Because the Court is satisfied that the special circumstances of this case demonstrate the necessity for such action, and also because it is convinced that any prejudice to the defense can be dealt with through *voir dire* and a proper instruction to the jury, the governmentʹs motion is granted.[20]

In the Second Circuit, an anonymous jury:

"May be warranted when the jury needs protection, as when the government has demonstrated a defendant's ʹwillingness ... to tamper with the judicial process." *United States v. Thai,* 29 F.3d 785 (2d Cir.1994) (quoting *United States v. Vario,* 943 F.2d 236, 239 (2d Cir.1991), *cert. denied,* [502 U.S. 1036] 112 S. Ct. 882 [116 L. Ed. 2d 786] (1992)).

The *Thai* case makes clear also that extensive pretrial publicity in cases involving allegations of violent conduct may justify empaneling an anonymous jury. *See Thai,* 29 F.3d at 801; *United States v. Paccione,* 949 F.2d 1183, 1192 (2d Cir.1991), *cert. denied,* 505 U.S. 1220, 112 S. Ct. 3029, 120 L. Ed. 2d 900 (1992).

In *United States v. Aulicino,* 44 F.3d 1102, 1116 (2d Cir.1995), the Second Circuit discussed three factors that a district court should examine when considering a motion for an anonymous jury. The court should look to whether: (1) the charges against the defendants are serious; (2) there is a substantial potential threat of corruption to the judicial process; and, (3) considerable media coverage of the trial is anticipated. These factors all weigh strongly in favor of the government's request. *See United States v. Aulicino,* 44 F.3d 1102, 1116 (2d Cir.1995); *Thai,* 29 F.3d at 801.

Seriousness of Charges

The defendants in this case are charged with a plethora of very serious crimes, including murder, conspiracy to murder and extortion. A number of the crimes charged deal with violence or threats of violence to achieve the aims of the charged criminal enterprise, including murder to eliminate suspected co-operators with law enforcement and extortion of money and business opportunities. A number of the defendants face murder charges, conviction on which could carry mandatory life sentences. In addition, all of the defendants face terms of up to 20 years if convicted under the RICO statute in addition to significant penalties for conviction on the numerous alleged substantive violations. As a practical matter, many of the defendants, if convicted, could spend the rest of their lives in prison.

The government's proof of some of the most serious charges appears to be substantial. The government has proffered that at least one witness will testify that defendants Bellomo and Generoso ordered the killing of Ralph Desimone. The government also has recorded evidence showing that defendant **655** Schenone solicited the murder of Richard Sprague.

Given the seriousness of the charges and the exposure of the defendants to long periods of incarceration, there are significant incentives to attempt to subvert the trial process by threats or violence. Moreover, a jury, unless shielded, well could fear malevolent action by defendants accused of these crimes.

Threat to Judicial Process

The government has substantial evidence that suggests a threat to the judicial process in this case. A number of instances of obstruction of justice are alleged, including the intimidation of prospective witnesses through threats of violence and the murder of suspected co-operators. Schenone is alleged to have threatened a prospective grand jury witness and displayed a gun in order to keep him from disclosing the truth about criminal activities at the Feast of San Gennaro. Cerami is alleged to have instructed a witness to give false information to a law enforcement officer to conceal the criminal activities being engaged in with respect to the San Gennaro feast. Zacchia is alleged to have instructed another grand jury witness to lie in an attempt to cover up schemes at the feast. Ida allegedly conspired to murder and aided and abetted the murder of Antonio DiLorenzo because he was suspected of co-operating with law enforcement. Bellomo, Generoso, Ida and Ruggiero allegedly conspired to murder and aided and abetted the murder of Ralph Desimone because they suspected that he was co-operating with law enforcement. Finally, it is alleged that Schenone solicited the murder of Richard Sprague because Schenone felt that Sprague was aiding the authorities.

This information is doubly significant. First, it suggests the existence of a real threat to the trial. Second, it raises a substantial risk that the jurors, absent anonymity, will fear reprisal. Hence, the second of the *Aulicino* factors is satisfied.

Publicity

Judging from the amount of publicity that this case has received to date, the Court is confident in holding that the publicity that the trial is likely to receive militates in favor of granting an anonymous jury. Numerous press reports have appeared with regard to pretrial matters.[21] Given the amount of press coverage that organized crime traditionally has received, the profile of the trial is likely to become higher. Indeed, this case appears to have entered cyberspace, as substantial coverage has appeared on a website dedicated to organized crime. In short, this case has received, and likely will continue to receive, substantial coverage in the media.

The defense asserts that granting anonymity would limit their ability to use their peremptory challenges effectively. They argue that:

"a person's name, place of residence, and occupation are three of the major indices used in selecting jurors. In a name, counsel can usually detect nationality, and sometimes, religious preference. A person's residence is also important. Many neighborhoods have specific characteristics that influence the outlook of the people who live there. A juror's leadership qualities are more often than not learned through the specific type of work that he or she does." (Def.Jury Mem 3)

But defendants overstate their case. The proposed order would not limit inquiry into the occupations of the jurors, only information about their specific places of employment. The defense therefore will have access to the information it seeks on this issue. This Court doubts that a defendant has any legitimate use for knowledge of jurors' religions and nationalities in light of *Batson v. Kentucky*, 476 U.S. 79, 106 S. Ct. 1712, 90 L. Ed. 2d 69 (1986), and its progeny. Finally, the motion by the government seeks only to preclude the disclosure of jurors' "addresses." The Court intends to inquire as to the county in which each prospective juror resides. Moreover, the defense will have ample opportunity to suggest areas of inquiry **656** for *voir dire.* Thus, the defense should have no problem in assessing the possible bias of prospective jurors.

Finally, the Court will present a neutral explanation to the jury for their anonymous status that will seek to preclude any negative inferences against the defendants. Such an instruction will adequately protect the defendants from prejudice. *See United States v. Thai,* 29 F.3d 785, 801 (2d Cir.1994); *United States v. Paccione,* 949 F.2d 1183, 1193 (2d Cir.1991), *cert. denied,* 505 U.S. 1220, 112 S. Ct. 3029, 120 L. Ed. 2d 900 (1992); *United States v. Tutino,* 883 F.2d 1125, 1133 (2d Cir.1989), *cert. denied,* 493 U.S. 1081, 1082, 110 S. Ct. 1139, 107 L. Ed. 2d 1044 (1990).

The government's motion for an anonymous jury is granted.

Conclusion

All of the defendants' pretrial motions, to the extent not previously resolved, are denied except that the severance motions by defendants Saggese, Romano,

James Pisacano and Joseph Pisacano are granted to the extent described above. The trial of defendants Saggese, Romano, James Pisacano, Joseph Pisacano, Setford, and Batista on the original indictment is severed and assigned to Honorable Robert J. Ward with his consent. The trials of the remaining defendants on the original and superseding indictments in this case are joined under FED.R.CRIM.P. 13. Trial will commence in the ceremonial courtroom on February 3, 1997 at 9:30 a.m., as previously scheduled. An anonymous jury will be empaneled.

SO ORDERED.

NOTES

[1] In view of the similarity between the original and the superseding indictments with respect to the ten defendants common to both, the parties agreed that the pretrial motions of those defendants with respect to the original indictment would be deemed applicable to the superseding indictment. (Tr., Dec. 9, 1996, at 63) The common defendants were afforded an additional opportunity to make pretrial motions with respect to new issues raised by the superseding indictment. Only defendant Louis Zacchia did so.

[2] Liborio Bellomo, Michael Generoso, James Ida, Nicholas Frustaci, Thomas Cestaro, Thomas Barrett, John Schenone, Anthony Pisapia, Louis Zacchia, Anthony Coiro, Michael Autuori and Leonard Cerami.

[3] This conclusion is not disturbed because many of the conversations were in vague and coded language. A court is justified in relying on an expert's opinion as to evidence in a wiretap application, and Agent Campi provided credible interpretations of the content of these conversations. It would defeat the purpose of the wiretap statute to allow criminals to avoid detection simply by using nicknames and code to disguise their activities.

[4] Bellomo was named as a target in all the renewal applications and therefore has standing with respect to the subsequent interceptions.

[5] The government acknowledges of course that there must be probable cause also to believe that particular communications concerning the offense will be intercepted. *See* 18 U.S.C. § 2518(3) (b). Bellomo and Generoso do not question the adequacy of that aspect of the requisite probable cause showing.

[6] The statute provides in relevant part:

"(a) Whoever in any way or degree obstructs, delays, or affects commerce or the movement of any article or commodity in commerce, by robbery or extortion or attempts or conspires so to do, or commits or threatens physical violence in furtherance of a plan or purpose to do anything in violation of this section shall be fined under this title or imprisoned not more than twenty years, or both.

"(b) As used in this section

* * * * * *

"(2) The term ʻextortion' means the obtaining of property from another, with his consent, induced by wrongful use of actual or threatened force, violence, or fear, or under color of official right." 18 U.S.C. § 1951.

[7] Much of *McNally* of course effectively was overruled by the enactment of 18 U.S.C. § 1346. This amendment does not necessarily dispose of defendantʋs argument because it applied only to the statutes immediately affected by *McNally,* 18 U.S.C. §§ 1341 and 1343.

[8] Schenone's plea agreement specifically provided that "[t]his agreement does not bar the use of such conduct as a predicate act ... in a subsequent prosecution including, but not limited to, a prosecution pursuant to the RICO statute." (Gov.Mem. 141)

[9] This is not true of the substantive RICO count. The statute makes it unlawful for covered persons "to conduct or participate, directly or indirectly,

in the conduct of such enterprises' affairs *through a pattern of racketeering activity."* 18 U.S.C. § 1962(c) (emphasis supplied). "Racketeering activity" is a defined term that refers to predicate crimes. *Id.* § 1961(1). In consequence, the gravamen of the offense is the participation in the affairs of the enterprise through the commission of a pattern of predicate crimes. If the government's reliance on the front end loader predicate act may be squared with the Double Jeopardy Clause only if Schenone is charged with a predicate act that post-dates the front end loader prosecution, its reliance is barred. The last predicate act of which Schenone is accused in this case allegedly occurred in March 1995, approximately four months before his guilty plea in the Eastern District case. The allegation that Schenone participated in unspecified activity relating to the alleged enterprise after the date of the plea is immaterial because post-plea activity that does not amount to predicate acts is not punishable on the substantive RICO count.

[10] One is left to wonder why the government indicted as it did.

[11] Defendant Cestaro pleaded guilty on January 15, 1997. Thus, the proposed ten defendant trial actually would have only nine defendants.

[12] Defendant Coiro has pleaded guilty to two counts in the indictment. Thus, as a practical matter, the proposed nine defendant severed trial actually would have eight defendants. (*See* Gov. Mem. 150-51)

[13] Defendants Ida and Autuori have objected to a joint trial of the entire nineteen defendant indictment, but make no further objection to a severance along the lines proposed by the government, of which they have been on notice for some time. (Ida Mem. 65-67; Autuori Mem. 1-2)

[14] Since the Court has granted the Pisacanos' motions for severance under Rule 14, it need not consider their argument under Rule 8(b), which sought similar relief. The Court sees no need for a further severance on any of the grounds advanced by the Pisacanos.

[15] Autuori's motion to be severed from the nineteen defendant trial, to the extent that it objects to being tried with the other RICO defendants, is denied for the reasons expressed in the denial of the similar motions made by Zacchia and Pisapia.

[16] The Court expresses no view as to whether the forfeiture allegations afforded sufficient notice in the absence of the particulars provided by the government.

[17] This argument has little application to Schenone, who is alleged to have committed numerous predicate acts that are specified in the indictment as having garnered forfeitable assets. However, to the extent that he would advance this argument, the Court's discussion applies to him as well.

[18] Identical provisions appear in the superseding indictment at paragraphs 146-48.

[19] Indeed, the *Regan* panel specifically declined to rest its decision on common law principles, concluding that the order sought was not in the nature of an injunction, and rested on the RICO statute itself. 858 F.2d at 120.

[20] This decision applies only to the trial of the superseding indictment and Barrett and Autuori, and not to the severed trial of the Gambling Defendants. The propriety of an anonymous jury in that case, if sought by the government, will be determined by the judge presiding.

[21] In a pretrial submission, the defense bemoaned the press coverage that a released grand jury photo of defendant Bellomo had received and referred to numerous articles discussing his alleged place in the Genovese crime family.

Made in the USA
Las Vegas, NV
19 July 2023

74999639R00262